Higher Education:
A Part-time Perspective

Higher Education: A Part-time Perspective

Malcolm Tight

The Society for Research into Higher Education
& Open University Press

Published by SRHE and
Open University Press
Celtic Court
22 Ballmoor
Buckingham MK18 1XW

and

1900 Frost Road, Suite 101
Bristol, PA 19007, USA

First Published 1991

British Library Cataloguing in Publication Data

Tight, Malcolm
    Higher education: a part-time perspective.
    1. Great Britain. Higher education institutions. Part-time courses
    I. Title
    378.41

    ISBN 0 335 09611 5
    ISBN 0 335 09610 7 pbk

Library of Congress Cataloging-in-Publication Data

Tight, Malcolm
    Higher education: a part-time perspective / by Malcolm Tight.
        p.   cm.
    Includes bibliographical references and index.
    ISBN 0-335-09611-5 – ISBN 0-335-09610-7 (pbk.)
    1. Education, Higher – Great Britain – Evaluation. 2. Students, Part-time – Great
Britain. 3. College students – Great Britain. 4. Universities and colleges – Great
Britain – Statistics. I. Title.
    LA637.T53   1990
    378.41 – dc20

                                                            90-38141 CIP

Typeset by Rowland Phototypesetting Limited,
Bury St Edmunds, Suffolk
Printed in Great Britain by St Edmundsbury Press Limited,
Bury St Edmunds, Suffolk

To Joy, with all my love

And with thanks to Sheila, for all her help

Contents

List of Tables and Figures

List of Abbreviations

ACACE	Advisory Council for Adult and Continuing Education
BTEC	Business and Technician Education Council
CAT	College of Advanced Technology
CNAA	Council for National Academic Awards
CRAC	Careers Research and Advisory Council
CVCP	Committee of Vice-Chancellors and Principals
DES	Department of Education and Science
DMS	Diploma in Management Studies
ECCTIS	Educational Counselling and Credit Transfer Information Service
FTE	Full-time equivalent
HMI	Her Majesty's Inspectorate
HNC/D	Higher National Certificate/Diploma
NAB	National Advisory Body
OECD	Organization for Economic Co-operation and Development
PCFC	Polytechnics and Colleges Funding Council
SCOTVEC	Scottish Vocational Education Council
UCACE	Universities Council for Adult and Continuing Education
UFC	Universities Funding Council
UGC	University Grants Committee
UNESCO	United Nations Educational, Scientific and Cultural Organization
USR	Universities Statistical Record
WEA	Workers' Educational Association

1

Definition and Scope

This book has two related aims: to provide a comprehensive analysis of part-time higher education; and to examine higher education from a part-time perspective. In this introductory chapter, I will consider the meaning of part-time higher education, illustrate its scope and look at its relation to higher education as a whole. I will then briefly summarize the structure of the book, and indicate why I believe an analysis of this kind is both important and timely.

Definition

Clearly part-time higher education can be defined in a number of ways – in terms of its relationship to full-time higher education, or more directly and functionally; from the top down or the bottom up. It makes sense to begin by considering briefly what is meant by 'higher education' itself.

In the United Kingdom, higher education is usually thought of as something that is undertaken by qualified school-leavers in universities or in other institutions upholding similar standards. Such an undertaking requires preparation and is legitimated by the award of a degree from a recognized authority. But this is not the only valid conception of higher education. A good deal of educational activity at higher level takes place outside formal educational institutions, often under the direct control of the learner or learners concerned. Higher education in this wider sense can be thought of as serious and sustained learning engaged in by adults; although we still require a comparator such as undergraduate study in order to define the learning as being at 'higher' level.

What, then, is part-time higher education? The simplest definition is that part-time higher education includes all higher education that is not full-time. In the United Kingdom, full-time higher education – and we are unusual in this country in making such a clear distinction (see Chapter 4) – consists of nothing more nor less than those higher education courses provided by universities, polytechnics and colleges which are funded as full-time courses and for which eligible home students are entitled to have their fees paid and to receive a mandatory grant award.

For statistical purposes, the Universities Statistical Record (USR) has adopted the following definition:

> Full-time students are those following a course of study or research lasting an academic year or longer, to which they are expected to devote the whole of their time . . . Except where otherwise stated, the figures of 'full-time students' include students on sandwich courses irrespective of whether they are at university or undergoing a period of industrial training . . . Part-time students are registered students who are either: (i) undertaking a course lasting an academic year or longer which they attend part-time only, or (ii) postgraduates undertaking a course which lasts for one term or more but for less than an academic year, irrespective of whether they attend full or part-time.
>
> (USR 1986, p. 56)

It should be stressed that these distinctions are primarily about funding, and only secondarily to do with the actual time which students devote to their studies or take to achieve a given level or qualification. In these terms, therefore, part-time higher education comprises all higher education which is not funded as full-time provision or for which students are not eligible for mandatory support.

From the point of view of prospective students, such a definition may not seem that relevant. For the part-time student, part-time higher education is something which can be engaged in alongside their pursuit of another major role or roles in their everyday lives. Part-time students are typically employed; they may have a young family or other dependants to support and care for; they may be heavily committed to social or community activities. From their perspective, we may define part-time higher education as higher education undertaken by people who are unable or unwilling – for whatever reason or combination of reasons – to enrol as full-time students. For most practical purposes, it can reasonably be assumed that this definition is complementary to those used for funding and statistical purposes.

Scope

Part-time higher education should not be thought of as a single or homogeneous entity. On the contrary, it comprises a very varied field of activity. Some of this variety is indicated and summarized in schematic form in Figure 1. The figure is intended to be suggestive rather than definitive, and could be amended or added to in different ways. It suggests that variation within the field of part-time higher education occurs more or less continuously along a series of dimensions. There are multiple and competing models of provision and practice in existence. All six of the dimensions portrayed apply to the full range of provision: from sub-degree level, through degrees and postgraduate courses, to research; and from short courses, through courses lasting for three years and longer, to continuing education with no definite end in view.

Evening only ↔ Day and evening ↔ Day release
Distance ↔ Mixed provision ↔ Face-to-face
Part-time only ↔ Mixed mode ↔ Full-time option
Modular credit ↔ Intermediate award ↔ Degree only
Open entry ↔ Special entry ↔ Restricted entry
Independent study ↔ Structured options ↔ Fixed curriculum

Figure 1   The diversity of part-time higher education

Taking the first of the dimensions indicated, part-time higher education courses are currently offered at different times of the day in order to suit the varied needs and availability of intending students. Daytime, day release, block release, day and evening, afternoon and evening, evening only, evening and weekend, weekend only and vacation patterns of attendance can all be found. Those offering provision demonstrate a sensitivity of response to varied patterns of demand and availability that is not found in full-time higher education, which tends to assume a captive market and expect standard daytime attendance.

The development of distance education can be interpreted in a similar way, freeing students from the need to attend an institution at all, and enabling them to pursue their studies wherever – at home, at work, in transit – and whenever they have the free time and inclination. Such arrangements suit the house-bound, those who live outside urban areas and those who work long or irregular hours. Distance education is almost by definition part-time, and is certainly funded and structured on that basis. In practice, however, it is unusual to find pure forms of either distance or face-to-face provision. Much of the former, as in the case of the Open University, either requires or makes available a certain amount of face-to-face contact between students and staff; while most courses based on lectures, seminars and laboratory work assume that students will spend time in unsupervised study outside classes. Truly mixed forms of distance and face-to-face provision have been slow to develop in this country (Tight 1987a).

By comparison, arrangements which enable students to alternate periods of part-time and full-time study are more common. Where possible, part-time students may be encouraged to arrange periods of concentrated full-time study prior to their final examinations. In a somewhat similar way, full-time students who perform unsatisfactorily in their end-of-year examinations may be able to repeat these after spending a year in revision, registered as 'part-time'. Mixed-mode study formalizes these kinds of arrangements and extends them to allow individual students to adopt a variety of study modes which can be changed from year to year. It is most commonly found where provision is organized on a modular basis, enabling students to build up individual courses, with appropriate guidance, from the range of possibilities available (Watson *et al.* 1989). Successful students can be credited for completing modules or groups of modules rather than entire courses, and may be able to transfer this credit to continue their studies at another institution (Educational Counselling and Credit Transfer Information Service 1989a).

Of course, not all part-time higher education is undertaken for credit, especially outside formal education institutions. After all, short courses, whether they are taken for vocational or non-vocational reasons, come within the definition of part-time study. Even here, though, the gradual acceptance and extension of schemes for the accreditation of experiential learning (Evans 1988) provides an opportunity for such learning to count towards an eventual qualification if desired.

Part-time higher education also demonstrates a greater flexibility in practice than full-time provision regarding entry requirements and the curriculum studied. In an increasing number of cases, mature students (which is what most part-time students are) are accepted by institutions through special entry schemes (Tight 1987b). These schemes vary a great deal, but normally require students without standard entry qualifications to demonstrate evidence of their ability by, for example, sitting an entry test, submitting a portfolio, completing a preparatory course or undertaking a probationary period of study.

Providers of part-time higher education, recognizing the greater experience and maturity of their students, have relaxed their control over the teaching/learning process in a number of ways. Those which offer modular schemes of study generally permit their students a considerable degree of freedom in how they put together programmes from the modules available, though in some cases their choice may be structured in terms of prerequisites and preferred study routes. Independent study schemes, such as those offered by East London Polytechnic and Lancaster University (Percy *et al.* 1980), have progressed a good deal further down this route by passing the responsibility for devising the curriculum of study and its method of assessment almost entirely to the student. The external degree system of the University of London, to take another and perhaps less well known example, offers a rather more restricted form of freedom by setting the curriculum (i.e. the examination), but leaving it up to the students to prepare themselves for it as they see fit (Tight 1987c).

Approach

Part-time higher education is, then, a varied but distinctive field. It is important because it represents an adaptation (or, rather, a series of adaptations) of higher education to the differing circumstances of those who are unable or unwilling to study full-time. This diverse group of people comprises the great majority of the population.

This book seeks to provide a guide to the past, present and future of part-time higher education in the United Kingdom. It describes the institutions and students involved, and the context in which they operate. But this is not *just* a book about part-time higher education. In looking at higher education from a part-time perspective, my intention is to try and enlarge our understanding of the field as a whole. We need to enlarge our understanding if we are to expand and develop higher education so as to better serve the needs of more people in the future.

The remainder of the book is in three parts. The first part (Chapters 2, 3 and 4) provides an overview of the history and current position of part-time higher education in the United Kingdom, and compares the position here with that found in other developed countries. The second part (Chapters 5 and 6) examines the characteristics of provision in more detail, and looks at the students or clients involved. The final part (Chapters 7, 8 and 9) considers the context of this provision, arguing the case for part-time higher education in terms of its value by comparison with full-time higher education. Alternative models of higher education are explored, and the prospects for the future development of part-time forms of provision are examined.

2

History

Introduction

The aim of this chapter is to provide a useful, if necessarily brief, history of the development of part-time higher education in the United Kingdom over the last century and a half. This presentation will help to provide the context for the analysis of present patterns of provision and practice in the remainder of the book. The account which follows does not pretend to be a comprehensive one, though it does draw on research undertaken, together with Bob Bell, for a related book (Bell and Tight, forthcoming).

Two caveats need to be stated right at the beginning of the chapter. First, our understanding of higher education, its aims, content and practice, has changed significantly over time. In the middle of the nineteenth century, for example, higher education institutions might be in competition with schools for students; while the curricula they offered would frequently now be covered in secondary or further education (Bell 1973).

Second, without the time or resources to undertake an extensive survey of primary sources of information, such as they are, this chapter relies mainly on readily available sources: national statistics, institutional histories and other published material. National statistics have been collected for the universities since the 1890s, though they have some limitations. However, the further education statistics only separately identify higher level students from 1954 onwards.

There are few general works on the history of British higher education, and these rarely deal with part-time provision (but see Elliott 1989). The great majority of published material takes the form of histories of individual institutions, the bulk of them relating to universities. Though some of these are useful and well researched, most are not very helpful for the present purpose. Much attention is usually devoted to buildings, heraldry, financial problems, student societies and the eccentricities of professors; with relatively little given to what was being taught, to whom and how, and the wider social context of this activity. Frequently, in fact, the official statistics tell a rather different story from the institutional histories, which sometimes seem concerned to disown anything in the past – such as part-time provision – which diverges from currently accepted practice.

This historical review begins in the nineteenth century, when the developments which led to our modern higher education system were getting under way.

The nineteenth century

In England, at the beginning of the nineteenth century, formal higher education outside the Inns of Court and the medical schools was essentially confined to the universities of Oxford and Cambridge. These medieval foundations stressed the virtues of residence, and their students were mainly drawn either from the social elite or from those seeking employment in the church. An alternative and more democratic tradition flourished in Scotland. Here, after the Reformation, the universities in the main cities of Glasgow, Edinburgh and Aberdeen did not concern themselves with residence, to which there were religious objections; and they encouraged local attendance, which was often on a part-time basis. It was this tradition, rather than that of Oxbridge, which was taken up by the civic universities and university colleges founded in England during the nineteenth century, first in London and then in other major urban centres.

The universities in Victorian Scotland were different from the institutions which we know by that name today. Students might enter at the age of 12 and professors' incomes came mainly from student fees. Few restrictions were placed on entry and a very entrepreneurial attitude was adopted to recruitment. Those taking a degree would follow a broad general course of study, with much emphasis placed on philosophy (Davie 1961), but most opted not to graduate and many took only particular classes.

> many students were only able to give part-time attendance. In 1876 George Ramsay, professor of Humanities at Glasgow, administered a questionnaire to his junior class. This met twice a day, at 8 and 11 a.m. Of the 283 students who replied, 97 came only to the 8 o'clock class, and then went on to their work, mostly as 'clerks in law offices' (56) or teachers (30). A further 44 came to the 11 o'clock class, but also had full-time jobs. Of the remaining 142 students, 74 were free in the winter but had to work in the summer . . . That left only 60 students who had no other cares, a figure which also applied to Ramsay's senior class . . . This was even more true of classes which were not part of the arts curriculum. At Edinburgh, for example, the professor of Engineering gave his class at 9 a.m., and many of his students went on to a full day's work as draughtsmen or assistant engineers, while the professor of Political Economy had forty-eight students who mostly worked in offices or banks, and he held the class at 5 p.m. to accommodate them.
>
> (Anderson 1983, pp. 76–7)

Similar patterns of attendance, together with the accompanying commercial approach necessary for survival, were to be found in the newly created institutions that came to make up the University of London. University College offered evening classes in a variety of subjects from its foundation in 1826, including law, medicine, architecture and chemistry (Bellot 1929, pp. 51, 54, 168, 266, 283). King's College went further, setting up in 1855 an Evening Class Department which became one of the most successful parts of the college. Student numbers peaked at 674 in 1867, but held up well and the department remained in operation until the First World War (Hearnshaw 1929, pp. 252–8, 306–12, 454). In other London institutions associated with the University, notably Birkbeck College and the polytechnics (Webb 1904; Burns 1924), the main emphasis of provision was always on part-time day and evening classes.

The federal university system which was established in London in 1836 gave a major impetus to part-time higher education: in London, throughout the British Isles and overseas in the Empire and beyond. With the university in the role of an examining body, associated colleges and institutions carried out the teaching:

> The nineteenth-century University of London was, in modern terms, an amalgam of an Open University and a Council for National Academic Awards. It had neither the technology of the one, nor the system of inspection of the other, but its functions were perceived as a sort of cross between the two.
>
> (Harte 1986, p. 25)

At first, other institutions, from schools to medical colleges, were recognized by the University for the purposes of submitting students for its examinations. This practice gradually fell into disuse after the 1858 charter opened up the non-medical examinations to all comers (though only men at first), regardless of how and when they studied – full-time or part-time, in an educational institution, by correspondence, or by private study. A distinction was made between internal students, those studying at the London colleges most closely associated with the University, and external students. Subsequently, the external degree was to provide the means by which aspirant universities in England and the Empire could establish themselves.

Unfortunately, it is not possible to determine from London University's own records how many of its thousands of students, both internal and external, prepared for their examinations on a part-time basis. In 1895, for example, there were 6219 entries for all the examinations, of whom 2987 passed, 479 gaining Bachelor's degrees (ibid, p. 139). However, the evidence from the institutions which prepared students for the external degree indicates that the numbers studying part-time were considerable.

External forms of higher education were also offered by other institutions. Non-resident study for degrees became possible at Trinity College Dublin in the late eighteenth century, and by 1852 half of their undergraduates were non-resident, some of them living in England (McDowell and Webb 1982, pp. 113–17, 326–7). The federal University of Ireland adopted the London pattern in 1880 (Moody and Beckett 1959). External students were recruited later in the nineteenth century by the universities of Durham (in music – Whiting 1932) and St Andrews (the LLA qualification for women – Cant 1946). As with London, it is probable that the majority of these students were studying part-time.

Part-time courses were a major, if not the major, part of the activities of all of the university colleges established in provincial English cities during the latter half of the nineteenth century (Lawson 1975; Rothblatt 1983). In these institutions force of financial necessity, if not municipal pride, dictated an emphasis on local students and their needs and aspirations. Such students could rarely afford to support themselves to study full-time, and few other sources of financial aid were then available. In some cities, the university colleges established close links with local technical and evening institutes, many of which subsequently developed into colleges of technology or polytechnics (Dent 1949; Argles 1964).

All of the university colleges prepared students for the London external degree, though this was the apex rather than the mainstay of their work:

They were not university students in any modern sense: young people studying full-time by day for three years for a degree qualification. Rather they were a motley mixture of young ladies attending afternoon lectures on Renaissance Art, foremen from the steelworks or laboratory assistants from the dyeworks taking night classes in chemistry, possibly for a City and Guilds examination, schoolboys getting up some science before taking an Oxford or Cambridge scholarship, intending school-teachers in training, and the hard core of the dedicated studying for a London external degree.

(Sanderson 1972, pp. 95–7)

Whether they were 'university students in any modern sense' or not, part-time students loom large in the early histories of the university colleges. At Owens College in Manchester (from which Manchester University evolved), founded in 1851:

Almost from the beginning . . . there had been evening students and these had increased in twenty years from about 100 to over 500 . . . It was ten years before there were as many as 100 day students and another eight years before there were 200. And even of the day students, the majority did not take a 'regular course', that is a systematic course of three years of which the natural goal was then the London Degree. In the [eighteen] sixties there were never as many as 50 full-time students and in one session there were only 19.

(Fiddes 1937, p. 51)

At Yorkshire College in Leeds (later Leeds University) in 1879–80 there were 113 'registered', 28 medical, 140 occasional and 143 evening students (Gosden and Taylor 1975, p. 43). In its first year of operation, 1881, University College Nottingham recorded 381 day students, 623 evening students and 346 on government science classes. Though the numbers of day students rose slowly to reach 460 in the 1890s, evening students increased more rapidly to reach over

1500 (Wood 1953, p. 29). Other examples could be quoted from Birmingham (Vincent and Hinton 1947, p. 67), Bristol (Cottle and Sherborne 1959, p. 13), Southampton (Patterson 1962, p. 99) and elsewhere.

Two other developments of importance to part-time higher education took place in the last quarter of the nineteenth century. The first of these was the growth of correspondence education, which was dependent upon contemporary technological innovations in printing and communication, and on the establishment of a cheap and reliable postal service (Elliott 1973, 1978). It was also greatly stimulated by the growth of a meritocracy based on national systems of examination. The external degrees offered by London University can be seen as one aspect of this development. Much more significant in terms of the numbers involved, however, were the examinations of professional bodies and the civil service, and those for teachers. Correspondence colleges were established to offer tuition to those studying in their spare time in all of these areas. Some university colleges were involved as well (e.g. Hearnshaw 1929, p. 370).

The second development was the growth of the university extension movement. Largely based on the universities of Cambridge, London, Manchester and Oxford, this movement brought university lecturers and lecture courses to towns and cities in many parts of the country. Through its work, many thousands of people who were unable to attend university were exposed to higher education on a part-time basis. Though a good deal of the provision made was at a fairly low level, a proportion of participants followed courses over a period of years to gain certificates or diplomas, and, in a few cases, subsequently enrolled on university courses. Such developments might even have led to the creation of a national system of part-time higher education not too dissimilar to the present Open University:

> By 1884 the leaders of University Extension were prepared to offer an almost unspeakable alternative. Access to degrees must be made the apex of an enlarged and systematised version of their own scheme, the peripatetic lecture courses and associated paraphernalia of teaching and private study. The English people could be induced to sacrifice time and money to strenuous self-improvement if the universities would only recognise their efforts by throwing open, without regard to age, circumstances or class, the ultimate distinction. Our visionaries asked in fact for a part-time, nonresident teaching university operating a system of academic credits.
>
> (Marriott 1981, p. 15)

In the event, these aspirations proved to be rather too ambitious, and the energies of those involved in the extension movement were channelled into developing university extra-mural studies and the tutorial class system. Yet, even if there was nothing approaching a national system of part-time higher education at the end of the nineteenth century, part-time higher education was the norm. Outside Oxbridge – whose students could hardly be described as 'full-time' in the modern sense of the term – part-time students outnumbered full-timers in most higher education institutions; and their ranks were swelled by the increasing numbers taking extension or correspondence courses, or pursuing private study for external awards.

The first half of the twentieth century

While it would be wrong to suggest that the end of the nineteenth century represented a critical turning point in the history of higher education, a series of changes was taking place about then which would together have a profound effect on subsequent developments.

In 1889, grant aid was made available by the government, subject to certain conditions, to support the work of universities and university colleges (the Scottish universities had been subsidized by the state since the Reformation). The amounts dispensed steadily rose, and in 1919 the University Grants Committee (UGC) was set up to oversee the dispersal of these funds. Financial support for students also became more available through the establishment of scholarships and exhibitions of various kinds.

The provision of secondary education was greatly expanded after the passing of the 1902 Education Act, thereby providing higher education institutions with more and better prepared candidates. The resulting expansion in the demand for secondary teachers also enlarged the market for higher education's services (Dent 1977). The university curriculum also changed, notably through the development of science degrees and postgraduate work, and became more standardized.

The general effect of these changes was to focus the work of the universities in a narrower and more elitist way. They were able to steadily dispense with, marginalize, or drop altogether the now non-standard aspects of their provision which had developed over the years. Matriculation became the business of the schools, with the universities introducing entrance requirements of increasing rigour. As their full-time provision slowly expanded, part-time higher education was taken over by the polytechnics, technical institutes and evening schools. At the same time, the nascent further education sector was itself expanding and reorganizing; notably through the development of national schemes of examination, such as the national certificates that were introduced in the 1920s.

The increasing emphasis placed in the universities and university colleges on full-time study is illustrated by Table 1, which reproduces the official statistical returns for selected institutions and years. It should be noted that these returns exclude certain categories of part-time student: notably those enrolled by extra-mural departments and those taking external degrees by correspondence or private study.

Perhaps the most significant change . . . is the decline of part-time teaching in these institutions. At their outset several of these colleges proliferated evening and day-release courses, most aimed at young workers in local industries. When this function was taken on by technical colleges, and as industry increasingly demanded training through full-time courses, the pattern changed, with only those colleges which had derived originally from a strong local university extension tradition, such as Nottingham, resisting the trend until at least the First World War. The figures suggest, too, that the contraction of part-time work coincided not with the granting of full university status but with the First World War, after which no institution resumed its earlier character completely.

(Lowe 1983, pp. 45–7)

Table 1   Numbers of full-time (FT) and part-time (PT) students at selected universities and university colleges, 1908–48.

Institution	Mode	1908	1919	1928	1938	1948
Birmingham	FT	756	1,754	1,362	1,433	3,250
	PT	228	183	195	191	206
Bristol	FT	442	932	778	1,005	2,238
	PT	413	41	46	135	517
Leeds	FT	657	1,358	1,385	1,757	3,209
	PT	508	733	208	408	461
Liverpool	FT	997	2,190	1,560	2,055	3,314
	PT	147	415	449	446	428
London	FT	2,768	8,034	9,141	13,191	16,884
	PT	2,113	6,969	7,293	6,286	8,203
Manchester	FT	1,167	1,742	2,023	2,108	4,305
	PT	618	472	399	345	753
Newcastle	FT	407	1,185	985	1,297	3,210
	PT	999	506	332	596	374
Nottingham	FT	377	830	499	582	2,048
	PT	1,986	161	833	351	150
Reading	FT	345	489	615	584	976
	PT	888	13	16	26	22
Sheffield	FT	255	850	690	767	1,908
	PT	1,634	1,183	97	352	229
Southampton	FT	210	323	296	268	892
	PT	498	633	348	117	60
Wales	FT	1,317	2,473	2,664	2,779	5,149
	PT	195	162	204	369	275
Edinburgh	FT	n.a.	4,182	3,616	3,205	5,640
	PT	n.a.	308	650	511	1,060
Glasgow	FT	n.a.	3,808	4,949	4,175	5,889
	PT	n.a.	44	421	342	889
Total	FT	9,698	37,081	44,309	50,002	83,690
	PT	10,227	15,234	14,239	13,418	18,180

The source of these statistics, and of those quoted elsewhere in the text, is the annual *Reports from Universities and University Colleges in Receipt of Grant*. It should be noted that their reliability is not absolute, that definitions have changed somewhat over the years and that returns for some years are missing (hence the inclusion of figures for 1919 rather than 1918). The number of institutions in receipt of grant has also changed. In 1908/9, there were only 17, whereas in 1919/20 it rose to 49 and remained at about that level subsequently. Thus the totals quoted refer to different populations. See also Lowe (1983), who includes a similar table.

Table 1 both reveals and conceals a number of interesting trends. It shows that, allowing for periods of war and depression, the number of full-time students in universities and university colleges increased substantially during the first half of the twentieth century, whilst the number of part-time students fluctuated and rose only slightly over the period as a whole. During the forty years illustrated, there is a move away from a position where there were roughly equal numbers of full-time and part-time students in the university system, to one where full-timers far outnumber part-timers.

What the table does not show is that full-time and part-time students differed in kind, and that their nature changed over the period. In 1928, for example, 78% of all full-time university students were registered on first-degree courses, with 16% studying for diplomas and 5% pursuing advanced level study (i.e. postgraduate courses or research). By comparison, only 11% of part-time students are shown as studying for first degrees, with 21% taking diploma courses and another 11% pursuing advanced level study. The balance of 57% are classified as 'occasional' students: in other words, they were taking non-degree courses, were following only part of a course, or were not registered for a qualification. Over the period in question, the relative importance of diploma students declined for both full-time and part-time provision, while advanced level study expanded, accounting for 8% of full-time and 24% of part-time student numbers by 1948.

The general rise in full-time university student numbers is reflected in the growth of each of the fourteen institutions listed in Table 1, but the pattern of part-time registrations is more variable. At the beginning of the century, many universities and university colleges were still expanding their part-time provision at first-degree level. A five-year evening BA degree course was launched by Liverpool in 1905, aimed at teachers in their early twenties and above, and a similar course was started by Sheffield in 1907 (*University Review* 1905, p. 222; 1907, p. 312). At Manchester, evening teaching was undertaken in the Faculty of Commerce from its creation in 1903, but rejected in arts (except for the first year of the degree), sciences and technology (Fiddes 1937, p. 154; Charlton 1951, p. 112). Queen's College in Belfast also introduced an evening degree in commerce in 1915, in co-operation with the local technical institute, followed by part-time degrees in applied science and technology in 1920 (Moody and Beckett 1959, pp. 462–3, 472).

Subsequently, there was a gradual fall-off in part-time registrations at some institutions, such as Leeds, Nottingham, Sheffield and Southampton. At Leeds, the growth in the part-time provision made by other local institutions led to the University concentrating its evening teaching after 1906 in particular subjects: mechanical and electrical engineering, leather manufacture, mining, textiles and dyeing (Gosden and Taylor 1975, p. 263). At Nottingham, the principal did not conceal his delight at being able to discontinue, despite local demand, two-year day training courses for teachers in the 1930s, replacing them with more academic four-year courses (Wood 1953, p. 112).

The case of Reading – the first modern British university to aim to provide residential accommodation for the majority of its students – illustrates, however, that a selective use of statistics can be misleading. Though the figures in Table 1 indicate that part-time registration at Reading virtually ceased after the First World War, there were in fact several hundred evening students each year up until the Second World War taking 'courses not of a university standard' (Holt 1977, pp. 24, 44).

In other institutions the number of part-time students remained fairly constant throughout the period, though it represented a decreasing proportion of the total: for example, Birmingham, Bristol, Liverpool, Manchester, Newcastle (see Bettenson 1971, p. 45) and Wales. The trend at Edinburgh and Glasgow was very different, however, with both recording substantial increases in the number of part-time students registered between 1919 and 1948.

London University is another exception to the general pattern, retaining a large number of part-time students throughout the period. Indeed, after the First World War, London accounted for roughly half of all the part-time university registrations in the country. Once again, though, the overall London statistics conceal more complex changes. East London (subsequently Queen Mary) College dropped its evening provision and concentrated on full-time students on gaining university recognition in 1907 (Godwin 1939, p. 80). King's College similarly dropped its civil service classes and lower level work after 1911, under pressure from the University (Hearnshaw 1929, p. 422). It still had 1030 part-time students in 1928, 145 of them registered for first degrees; though these figures fell to 259 and 126 by 1948. University College recorded even higher numbers of part-time students during this period – 1386 in 1928, 781 in 1948 – though only a handful were studying for degrees.

The decline in part-time teaching in some London colleges, and its relative absence in others such as Imperial College and the medical schools, was compensated for by the accession to the University of the School of Economics in 1900 and of Birkbeck College in 1920. These two colleges registered 1720 and 1018 part-time students respectively in 1928, and 1215 and 1434 in 1948. Though only about one-quarter of those at the School of Economics were studying for a degree, the proportion at Birkbeck was three-quarters. After it became a School of the University (its economics teaching had been transferred to the School of Economics in 1909), Birkbeck concentrated on the provision of part-time degree courses in the evening for those employed during the daytime (Burns 1924, pp. 136, 160).

The external side of the University's work accounted for many more part-time students. In 1938 there were 10,839 external registrations, one-third of whom were estimated to have been studying at London institutions, one-third at provincial university colleges and technical colleges and one-third privately (some of them following correspondence courses), with about one-tenth of the total resident overseas (Harte 1986, pp. 238, 241).

The provision of part-time extra-mural courses of study by universities and university colleges increased markedly after the First World War (Burrows 1976; Marriott 1984). In the 1903–4 session, for example, 1640 candidates completed their courses and passed the associated examinations organized by the London extension movement; Oxford had 1204 successful candidates and

Cambridge 951 (Roberts 1906). The university returns for 1928 show a total of 20,093 students registered on extra-mural classes in Great Britain. The largest single provider was Nottingham University College, with 2537 students; substantial numbers were also registered at Cambridge, Edinburgh, Leeds, Liverpool, London and Oxford. By 1948, the total enrolment had more than quadrupled to 91,156, and London had emerged as the leading provider, with 13,667 registrations, followed by Birmingham with 8,564.

The expansion of further and technical education was even more dramatic:

> The ten-fold growth in the numbers attending university and teacher training college [between 1861 and 1931] was far outweighed by the growth of part-time technical education. Thus, while ... a dramatic transformation came over English society with some kind of post-school education becoming a real possibility for many young people, it must be remembered that most of this took place in the low prestige, part-time 'compensatory' institutions whose development allowed the universities to remain above the hurly-burly of this change.
>
> (Lowe 1983, p. 50)

Lowe quotes statistics showing that the number of students in receipt of technical education in classes recognized by the government in England rose from 285,444 in 1901 to 767,121 in 1911 and 1,776,568 in 1921 (in England and Wales), falling back to 1,020,991 in 1931 (ibid, p. 49).

While the great majority of these students were not studying at higher level, a proportion were, and their numbers were also increasing rapidly. Following the establishment of the national certificate system in 1921, 168 higher national certificates (HNCs – a sub-degree level qualification) were awarded in 1923, 749 in 1931, 1331 in 1939 and 5042 in 1950. By 1949 technical colleges were providing university degree courses for 11,295 part-time day students, with 8772 studying full-time (Foden 1951; Ministry of Education 1951).

The London polytechnics became involved in higher education very early in their history:

> In spite of the prevailing view that ... the polytechnics should provide trade classes and elementary instruction, there was a strong pressure from the large student body in London for more advanced studies in both day and evening, including university work. By 1904, six polytechnics were providing complete degree courses, fifty of their teachers were recognised [i.e. by the University of London] teachers, instructing 500 undergraduates. By 1908–9, this had increased to 100 recognised teachers, and 836 matriculated students, four-fifths of whom were evening students ... This growth of an 'evening class university' met the growing demand by the lower middle-classes and working classes for an advanced university education which had not previously been accessible to them.
>
> (Cotgrove 1958, pp. 64–5)

In 1912, the South West London Polytechnic (later Chelsea College) had 124 students registered for London internal degrees, 55 of them studying during the evening, and a further 24 registered for external degrees. By 1950, the number of internal students had increased to nearly 900 (Silver and Teague 1977, pp. 26, 50). Woolwich Polytechnic registered 40 internal degree students in 1921, 83 in 1931 and 316 in 1938 (Locke 1978, p. 29). In its 1945–6 annual report, the Northampton Polytechnic (later City University) recorded 65 honours degree successes in Engineering, 35 of them by part-time study, together with 24 pass degrees (17 part-time) and 55 HNCs (Laws 1946, pp. 19–20). Not all the polytechnics followed this route, however: Borough (later South Bank) Polytechnic resisted offering courses for London degrees throughout much of this period (Evans 1969).

By the early 1950s, 44 technical colleges were recognized by the University of London for preparing students for its B.Sc. degree in Engineering (Cotgrove 1958, p. 45). Acton Technical College (later Brunel University) was one of these. Opening in 1928, it concentrated on advanced level work after 1931 and in 1934 reported 5 B.Sc. degree successes, a further 7 passes at intermediate level, 4 matriculations and 31 HNCs (Faherty 1976, p. 26). London was not the only university offering such recognition. Sunderland Technical College, founded in 1901, switched its affiliation to Durham University in 1930 (Whiting 1932, p. 308). Glasgow Royal Technical College (later Strathclyde University) was associated with Glasgow University. By 1948, it had, according to the university returns, 5043 registered students on higher level courses, of whom 3735 were studying part-time, 81 of them for degrees.

From the 1950s to the 1980s

The period since the end of the Second World War has been characterized by continued growth and regular bouts of restructuring in British higher education (Lowe 1988). New institutions have been created, others have amalgamated, and the mechanisms for their validation and control have changed. Entry standards have risen as courses have become yet more standardized and demanding. The government has become increasingly involved in higher education policy, beginning with a sheaf of White Papers during the immediate aftermath of the war and culminating in three policy statements in the 1960s which largely set the scene up until the mid-1980s (the most recent policy developments are discussed in Chapter 9). The overall effect of these developments was (again) to place greater emphasis on full-time provision, while decreasing the relative importance and availability of part-time higher education.

The first of the three 1960s policy statements, the report of the Anderson Committee on student financing (Ministry of Education, Scottish Education Department 1960; Carswell 1988) was probably the most significant, though it is frequently overlooked. Its main recommendation, which was accepted by the government, was that mandatory maintenance grants should be made available to all full-time first degree students who had two A levels or their equivalent, to enable them to study at any institution in the country. This replaced the existing arrangements whereby local education authorities in England and Wales differed widely in their policies on grant allocation; although by then the majority of full-time students did receive some support. In the case of part-time students, however, financial support remained entirely discretionary.

The second statement, the Robbins Report (Committee on Higher Education 1963), is often thought of as both a blueprint for future development and a rigorous reaffirmation of liberal education values. In reality it was neither of these things, but more like a progress report on changes which were already well under way – a report conditioned by a prejudice for the contemporary university model. Part-time higher education was actually outside the official remit of the Robbins Committee, although it did get brief consideration, mainly as a temporary safety valve to be used during the expansion of the system. Unlike the report of the Anderson Committee, however, many of the Robbins recommendations were not acted upon by the government. Universities in the big cities were not expanded to the extent envisaged, teacher training was not brought within the university system and fewer new universities were established than recommended.

Instead, the Labour governments of the 1960s, in the third main policy development referred to, set the seal on a binary system of higher education. The local authority or public sector of provision was substantially strengthened and expanded to provide an alternative higher education route separate from the university sector. Thirty polytechnics were established in England, Wales and Northern Ireland (but not in Scotland, where the central institutions were left untouched) to serve as the apex of this sector (Robinson 1968; Pratt and Burgess 1974). The polytechnics, in contrast to the universities, were meant to be more local in their orientation, to develop links with industry and the community, and to maintain a strong part-time tradition (or, in other words, to do what the civic universities did in the nineteenth century).

Table 2 indicates the trends in student numbers in the period following the Second World War. So far as the universities are concerned, the table shows a general continuation of the trends noted in the first half of the century. While the number of full-time university students nearly quadrupled over the thirty years between 1954 and 1984, the number of part-time enrolments more than doubled, and much of the latter expansion was in the last part of the period. In 1954, 17% of all university students were recorded as studying part-time; by 1984, this proportion had fallen to 12%. As university colleges became universities in their own right, freed of their link with the London external degree, they quickly shed part-time courses. The new universities that were set up from scratch after the Second World War focused almost exclusively on full-time provision right from the start (UGC 1964a).

Postgraduate provision continued to expand, and accounted for an increasing proportion of part-time university students. In 1954, 31% of all part-timers were registered as postgraduates: by 1984 the proportion was 78%, though the increase was partly due to a change in the way in which occasional students were recorded in the statistics. First degree courses became overwhelmingly full-time. The only university institution which retained significant numbers of

Table 2   Higher education students by mode, level and sector, 1954–84.

Sector	Mode	1954	1964	1974	1984
University	FT first degree	64,778	109,058	205,491	249,410
	FT other	16,927	29,653	52,192	55,598
	Total full-time	81,705	138,711	257,683	305,008
	PT first degree	1,576	1,376	1,666	5,479
	PT other	14,570	16,711	23,710	35,273
	Total part-time	16,146	18,077	25,376	40,752
Further education	FT first degree	2,700	21,450	54,278	137,664
	FT other	6,960	32,000	153,960	100,449
	Total full-time	9,660	53,450	208,238	238,113
	PT first degree	4,790	2,730	4,894	15,895
	PT other	22,320	101,970	111,137	156,018
	Total part-time	27,110	104,700	116,031	171,913

Source: Reports from Universities and University Colleges in Receipt of Grant and Statistics of Education: Further Education. Care should be taken in interpretation as the university statistics refer to the United Kingdom whilst those for further education only cover England and Wales, and, in 1984, just England. The 1974 and 1984 further education statistics also include teacher training establishments, which were previously excluded. A number of institutions moved from the further education sector to the university sector after 1964. Open University students are not included in these figures.

part-time first degree students throughout this period was Birkbeck College. In 1964, for example, it accounted for two-thirds of all the university students in the country taking part-time first degrees. Goldsmiths' College, which began to recruit part-time first degree students in the mid-1960s (Scales 1981), did not appear in the university statistics at that time: it was classified by the University of London as an 'institution having recognized teachers' and only subsequently became a School of the University.

These trends, and the consequences of institutional transfers from the further education sector to the university sector, are illustrated by the brief history of the Colleges of Advanced Technology (CATs). Following the 1956 White Paper on Technical Education (Ministry of Education 1956), ten CATs were designated to serve as centres of excellence in the further education sector. As intended, they concentrated on advanced level provision – that is, on higher education rather than further education – but they also steadily shed both part-time and non-degree level work, which had not been intended. Between 1956 and 1964, the proportion of advanced level students in the CATs who were studying part-time fell from 69% to 30% (Burgess and Pratt 1970, pp. 52, 187; Venables 1978). Following the report of the Robbins Committee in 1963, the CATs were redesignated as universities and then quickly dropped the bulk of their remaining part-time provision.

The university statistics quoted in Table 2, like those in Table 1, exclude part-time students in a number of areas: those enrolled on extra-mural courses, those registered for external degrees with the University of London (except where they were enrolled at other universities), and those studying with the Open University.

The numbers enrolled on university extra-mural courses in Great Britain nearly trebled between 1954 and 1984, rising from 98,446 to 272,039. The largest single provider in 1984 was Manchester University with 23,023 enrolments; 38 universities and university colleges made some provision of this kind. There was a growth during this period in the number of extra-mural courses leading to examination and certification, notably in London (Duke and Marriott 1973), though these remained a minority of the total provision. The statistical returns for 1984 (Universities Statistical Record 1986, table 21) also give figures for the numbers enrolled on short courses organized by other university departments, a type of provision which has been of increasing significance in recent years. There were 83,524 students registered on short postgraduate medical or dental courses, nearly half of them in London, and a further 125,765 enrolments on post-experience courses in other subjects.

When the remaining English university colleges were freed from their tutelage to the London external degree in the 1950s, and the Council for National Academic Awards (CNAA) was established in 1964 to validate degree courses in the public sector, it was argued by some that the external degree system had outlived its usefulness (see Duke 1967). The creation of the Open University in 1969 seemed only to confirm this point of view. Yet the University of London registered more external than internal students throughout the period between 1941 and 1957, and the number of external students peaked at 34,198 registrations as late as 1971 (Harte 1986; Tight 1987c). Nevertheless, a gradual run-down of the external system began, with the successive abandonment of the degree syllabuses in engineering, science and general arts; and, in 1977, the ending of all registrations of students from overseas (this was reversed in 1982) and from public educational institutions in the United Kingdom. By the mid-1980s, the great majority of the 25,000 or so students who remained were studying either law or economics.

The expansion of the Open University has been one of the most significant developments in part-time higher education in recent years, and has tended to draw attention away from the continued existence of the external degree system. The Open University stressed the importance of a high-quality multi-media teaching system right from the start (Perry 1976). Its courses were produced by teams of academics and specialists, and they applied distance learning techniques through print packages and broadcast television and radio. Students were recruited throughout the United Kingdom, with no previous educational qualifications required, and they were supported in their spare-time studies by a network of local tutors. By 1984, the Open University had 76,295 undergraduate, postgraduate and associate students, as well as an increasing number using its short courses, making it the largest university in the country (Open University 1989, table 1).

The trends in study patterns shown for the further education sector in Table 2 differ markedly from those in the university sector. The rare of growth of advanced further education far exceeded that in the universities during this period, starting from a much lower base level (Cantor and Roberts 1969). In 1954, part-time students dominated the sector, accounting for 74% of all those studying at an advanced level. Full-time student enrolments only surpassed part-time numbers in the latter part of the period (the actual date depends upon whether the, predominantly full-time, teacher training statistics are included), partly because of the transfer of the CATs out of the sector in the mid-1960s. By 1984, the advanced further education sector was challenging the university sector in terms of size, with part-time students still accounting for 42% of its enrolments.

The split in part-time enrolments in the advanced further education sector between daytime and evening study changed over the period. Daytime study made up 54% of all part-time enrolments in 1958, rising to 75% in 1984. As in the university sector, a relatively small proportion of part-time enrolments were on first degree courses: 18% in 1954, falling to 9% in 1984. The mainstay of part-time provision in the advanced further education sector was, and remains, courses leading to higher national certificates or diplomas and to the qualifications of the various professional bodies.

There have also been changes in the subject balance of part-time advanced further education. In the early part of the period, the technical colleges were significant providers of part-time degrees in science and technology:

> In 1957, 37 per cent of the [University of London] degrees in science, and 56 per cent in technology, were obtained by students attending technical colleges. Moreover, 35 per cent of all internal degrees in technology were awarded to technical college students, mainly at the London polytechnics. Altogether, over 1,000 London University first degrees in science and technology were obtained by technical college students, accounting for 44 per cent of the total.
>
> (Cotgrove 1958, pp. 145–6)

However, as London University changed its regulations and raised the standards of its final examinations during the 1950s, part-time study for its science and engineering degrees became increasingly difficult (Robinson 1968).

In practice, both the establishment of the CNAA in 1964 and the creation of the polytechnics in the late 1960s further encouraged the shift from part-time to full-time provision in the advanced further education sector. For the first few years of its existence, the CNAA – with its committees heavily loaded with university staff – only validated full-time and sandwich courses, and the subsequent growth of part-time degree provision was inhibited by a continuing focus on science and technology subjects (Lane 1975). The polytechnics, for their part, frequently sought to mimic the practices of the universities, wishing also to enjoy their status and resources: engaging in the process termed 'academic drift' (Pratt and Burgess 1974). These trends have been somewhat reversed in recent years, as is suggested by the final column of Table 2, and as will be discussed further in Chapter 3.

Conclusions

What conclusions can be drawn from this brief account of higher education history as seen from the perspective of part-time provision? Two interim conclusions suggest themselves.

First, though they have been overlooked or ignored by many historians, there have always been substantial numbers of part-time higher education students: at least since the foundation of Edinburgh University in the late sixteenth century. Indeed, in simple numeric terms, it is probably true to say that there have been more part-time than full-time students in higher education throughout much of this period, certainly since the mid-nineteenth century.

Second, part-time study patterns have varied considerably over the last century and a half, differing between institutions, sectors and levels of study. Part-time higher education students have typically been involved in lower status aspects of provision: in the further education sector rather than the universities; taking extra-mural or short courses; studying by correspondence, in the evening, or privately; working towards higher national certificates or professional qualifications.

Part-time higher education has seldom received the attention paid to full-time provision, and it has never enjoyed the latter's level of resourcing. But it has been, and remains, of considerable value to those who have experienced it and who could not engage in full-time study. The modern equation of higher education with full-time study, especially as practised in the majority of present-day British universities, is misleading and unreal.

3

The Current Position

Introduction

In 1986/7 – the most recent year for which national statistics had been published at the time of writing – 358,900 students were recorded as studying part-time at higher education institutions in the United Kingdom. In the same year there were 612,900 full-time higher education students, of whom 57,100 were overseas students. Part-time students therefore accounted for 37% of all higher education students, or 39% of all home students (Central Statistical Office 1989, tables 3.16 and 3.17).

By comparison, in 1970/71, there were only 164,700 part-time higher education students, making up 27% of all higher education students (or 28% of home students). Part-time higher education expanded at a markedly quicker rate than full-time provision over those 16 years, with part-time numbers increasing by 118% compared to a rise in full-timers of only 34%. The relative decline in the importance of part-time provision which occurred after the Second World War (noted in the previous chapter) has been reversed. One of the most notable developments – perhaps *the* most notable – in British higher education in the period since the 1960s expansion has been the re-invigoration of part-time provision.

However, the statistics just quoted relate only to long award-bearing courses, and they exclude a number of areas of provision which are of interest in the present context. Few students studying for external degrees or for nursing qualifications, for example, will have been included in these statistics; and none of those following extra-mural, adult education, or short post-experience courses at an advanced level should have been.

In 1986/7, there were 22,175 students registered for London external degrees, of whom 10,084 were based in the United Kingdom. The great majority of these would have been pursuing their studies on a part-time basis (Tight 1987c; University of London Committee for External Students 1988). In the same year, some 95,000 students were enrolled on nursing and paramedical courses at Department of Health and Social Security establishments (Central Statistical Office 1989, table 3.17). There were 299,269 enrolments on university extra-mural courses, all of which are taught at a higher level, and a further 271,248 students were enrolled on short post-experience courses run by other university departments (USR 1988a, table 25). A small number of students at local authority adult education centres would also have been pursuing studies at this level.

Virtually all of these enrolments may be considered to be part-time. Even allowing for some double-counting, therefore, it can safely be stated that rather more people are currently involved in part-time higher education than in full-time provision.

There are also, of course, a considerable number of people studying part-time at a higher level in the private or independent sector: that is, in private institutions of higher education or, much more significantly, with their employers. Unfortunately, no reliable estimates of the numbers involved are available, though it is evident that much of this involvement is part-time (Williams *et al.* 1977). Others may be engaged in higher level study on a self-directed basis, making little or no use of institutional resources.

In the remainder of this chapter, the nature and significance of part-time higher education in the United Kingdom will be examined using the available published national statistics. I will focus in turn on sectors, levels and subjects of study, and then briefly review the characteristics of the students involved. In Chapters 5 and 6, many of the issues raised by this analysis will be explored in more detail – from the perspectives of both providers and clients – using results from my own and others' researches.

Sector

Table 3 disaggregates the national statistics for both the 1986/7 and 1970/71 academic years, by mode and sector. It usefully illustrates three key points.

First, it confirms the observation already made that part-time higher education has grown much quicker than full-time higher education over the last two

Table 3 Home higher education students by mode and sector, United Kingdom, 1970/71 and 1986/7.

Mode	Sector	1970/71	1986/7	Change %
Part-time	Open University	19,600	79,700	+307
	Universities	23,800	44,600	+ 87
	Polytechnics and colleges	121,300	234,600	+ 93
	Total	164,700	358,900	+118
Full-time	Universities	217,200	273,300	+ 26
	Polytechnics and colleges	215,100	282,400	+ 31
	Total	432,400	555,700	+ 29

Source: Central Statistical Office 1989, tables 3.16 and 3.17.

decades. Part of this growth has been due, of course, to the fourfold expansion of the Open University, which had only just begun enrolling students in 1970/71. Yet the numbers of part-time students in both the conventional universities and the public (polytechnic and college) sector nearly doubled over the period concerned. This rate of increase was more than three times greater than that experienced in full-time provision. In the case of the universities, the expansion in part-time numbers took place from a relatively low base level; but in the public sector the absolute growth in part-time enrolments exceeded the rise in full-time students by 46,000.

Second, the table shows that, whereas full-time higher education is split fairly evenly between the university and public sectors, part-time higher education is dominated by the latter. In 1986/7, the polytechnics and colleges accounted for 65% of all part-time enrolments, with the conventional universities contributing only 12%, and the Open University making up the balance of 22%. The expansion of the Open University has only marginally affected this dominance.

Third, the table demonstrates that the balance between full-time and part-time provision differs considerably within the three sectors identified. At one extreme, all of the Open University's students, studying at a distance in their spare time, are by definition part-time. At the other extreme, in the conventional universities, only 14% of students were studying part-time in 1986/7, though this proportion had risen from 10% in 1970/71. In the public sector, full-time and part-time student numbers are almost equal, with 45% studying part-time in 1986/7. This represents a significant change from the position in 1970/71, when only about one-third of public sector students were part-time.

The dominance of full-time provision in the conventional university sector would not be affected much if the 10,084 London external degree registrations based in the United Kingdom were added to the part-time statistics in the table. Including those enrolled on extra-mural and post-experience courses would alter the pattern considerably, though – since these students are rather more part-time than those on long award-bearing courses – not in terms of the resources devoted to the different forms of provision.

Level

Table 4 details higher education student numbers for 1986/7 in terms of mode, sector and level of study. This shows that, just as the balance between full-time and part-time study varies between sectors, so it also differs between different levels of study. Overall, 31% of students were studying at other advanced level, 56% at first degree level and 13% at postgraduate level.

At other advanced level – that is, on courses leading to professional qualifications, higher national certificates or diplomas, and other sub-degree awards – part-time forms of provision dominate, accounting for more than two-thirds of students. The great majority of provision at this level, some 92%, is made by the polytechnic and college sector; more than two-thirds of it is in the colleges alone. Three-quarters of the part-time sub-degree students in the public sector are

Table 4 Higher education students by mode, sector and level of study, United Kingdom, 1986/7.

Level	Sector	FT	PT	PT%
Postgraduate	Open University	—	1,000	100
	Universities	56,200	35,100	38
	Polytechnics and colleges	14,300	18,000	56
	Total	70,500	54,100	43
First degree	Open University	—	66,200	100
	Universities	253,200	6,100	2
	Polytechnics and colleges	194,900	27,100	12
	Total	448,100	99,400	18
Other advanced	Open University	—	12,400	100
	Universities	6,800	3,400	33
	Polytechnics and colleges	87,700	189,400	68
	Total	94,500	205,200	68

Source: Central Statistical Office 1989, tables 3.16 and 3.17; Department of Education and Science *et al.* 1988, table 28; Open University 1989, table 1. It should be noted that the statistics given by these sources are not precisely consistent.

recorded as studying during the day, one-quarter in the evening (Central Statistical Office 1989, table 3.17).

By contrast, full-time provision dominates at first degree level, with 82% of students studying in this way. The bulk of the Open University's students are registered at this level. All of the polytechnics and major colleges have significant numbers of part-time students enrolled on first degree courses, with three of them – South Bank, Manchester and Trent Polytechnics – registering more than 1000 each in 1986/7 (Department of Education and Science 1987a, table 33). Nearly three-quarters of these students are following courses accredited by the CNAA (CNAA 1988a, table 2), with the remainder taking courses accredited by local universities. Not all of the conventional universities have part-time undergraduates themselves, however, and most have relatively few. Indeed, only four universities – Ulster (the larger part of which was until recently a polytechnic), London (mainly at Birkbeck College), Glasgow and Belfast – account for 59% of all such students in the university sector (USR 1987, table 15).

At postgraduate level, there is more of a balance between full-time and part-time forms of provision, though the part-time students differ in character between the sectors. The conventional universities account for 73% of the students recorded at this level. About half of their part-time postgraduate students are undertaking research rather than taught courses. In the public sector, however, most postgraduates are following taught courses.

If three other kinds of part-time higher education – external, extra-mural and post-experience provision – were to be added to Table 4, part-time students would be seen to be of greater importance, but their distribution between levels of study would be relatively little affected. Some 95% of the external students registered with the University of London in 1986/7 were studying for first degrees, with the remainder seeking postgraduate qualifications (University of London Committee for External Students 1988). The much greater numbers following extra-mural courses could, most logically, be added to the figures for other advanced students. Post-experience provision, which can be difficult to distinguish statistically from extra-mural work, is probably best placed in a category of its own. In other words, the effect of these additions to the table would be to slightly reduce the dominance of full-time study at first degree level, while emphasizing further the importance of part-time study at pre-degree and post-degree levels.

Subject

Table 5 disaggregates higher education student numbers by mode, level and subject of study, using the eleven subject groups adopted by the Department of Education and Science. These figures are for the conventional universities, polytechnics and colleges only: that is, they are confined to face-to-face forms of provision.

The table shows that part-time higher education students are concentrated in a small number of subject areas. The percentage of part-time students is above average in only three of the eleven subject groups: education; engineering and technology; administrative, business and social studies. These three groups together account for nearly 80% of all part-time higher education students, though part-time students do not form the majority in any of them.

Each of these three subject groups is somewhat unusual. Education, with 48% of students studying part-time, has above-average numbers of postgraduates: 26% of the total, compared to the overall figure of only 14%. In-service study – that is, by teachers studying part-time while they continue working – is of major importance in this subject area. In the case of engineering and technology, where 42% of students are part-time, an above-average number are studying at other advanced level: 48%, compared to the overall average of 32%. A similar pattern is found in administrative, business and social studies. This is the largest single subject group, accounting for 29% of all students, of whom 42% are studying part-time and 42% are studying at other advanced level.

In all of the other subject areas, part-time students represent less than a quarter of the total, and in some cases – agriculture; music, drama, art and design – the proportion falls below 10%. In most of these subjects, first degree provision (which, as noted in the previous section, is mainly full-time) dominates. It accounts for 83% of all those studying languages, literature and area

Table 5 Higher education students by mode, level and subject of study, United Kingdom, 1986/7.

Subject group	Postgraduate FT	PT	First degree FT	PT	Other advanced FT	PT	Total FT	PT
1	13,500	10,700	29,400	5,900	5,100	27,200	48,000	43,800
2	4,200	3,900	34,300	1,100	5,700	8,400	44,200	13,400
3	9,900	4,700	64,600	5,100	20,000	58,200	94,500	68,000
4	1,200	400	5,200	—	1,800	200	8,200	600
5	14,800	6,600	91,200	4,400	11,100	11,600	117,100	22,600
6	15,100	18,000	107,500	9,700	29,000	81,600	151,600	109,300
7	3,400	1,900	15,900	900	9,300	3,200	28,600	6,000
8	3,200	3,000	39,700	1,700	800	1,100	43,700	5,800
9	2,100	2,600	25,700	2,500	1,500	800	29,300	5,900
10	2,200	1,300	32,600	1,800	10,000	600	44,800	3,700
11	900	—	2,100	—	200	—	3,200	—
Total	70,500	53,100	448,100	33,200	94,500	192,800	613,200	279,100

Source: Department of Education and Science *et al.* 1988, table 28.
Note: All figures are rounded. They also exclude the Open University. The subject groups are as follows:
   (1) Education
   (2) Medicine, dentistry and health
   (3) Engineering and technology
   (4) Agriculture, forestry and veterinary science
   (5) Science
   (6) Administrative, business and social studies
   (7) Architecture and other professional and vocational subjects
   (8) Languages, literature and area studies
   (9) Arts other than languages
   (10) Music, drama, art and design
   (11) Other

studies, 80% of those studying arts other than languages, 71% of those studying music, drama and art and design, and 68% of those studying science. These proportions are all well above the national average of 54% of higher education students on first degree courses.

The subject split of the extra-mural and post-experience courses organized by universities is rather different. Since all of the students taking these courses are effectively part-time, this to some extent redresses the imbalances between modes of study shown in Table 5. Of the 299,269 extra-mural enrolments recorded in 1986/7, 25% were in arts other than languages, 21% in administrative, business and social studies, 16% in languages, literature and area studies, 13% in science and 13% in music, drama, art and design. In other words, they were mainly in subject areas which have relatively few part-time students on long award-bearing courses. Similarly, of the 271,248 post-experience enrolments, fully 43% were in medicine, dentistry and health, with 18% in education and 16% in administrative, business and social studies (USR 1988a, tables 25, 26 and 27).

The majority of those studying for University of London external degrees would be classified under 'architecture and other professional and vocational subjects' if they were included in Table 5. Over two-thirds, 68%, of the 10,084 home registrations recorded in 1986/7 were for one subject, law (University of London Committee for External Students 1988).

Students

Only two student characteristics are recorded in the nationally published statistics: sex and age (more detailed information on students is analysed in Chapter 6).

There are relatively more women in full-time higher education in the United Kingdom than there are in part-time higher education: in 1986/7, the proportions were respectively 44% and 38%. However, while the full-time proportion has risen slowly from 40% in 1970/71, the percentage of women in part-time higher education has risen dramatically from only 14% in that year. Indeed, the absolute increase in the number of women studying part-time, 113,400 over the period in question, exceeds the rise of just 80,800 in the male numbers (Central Statistical Office 1989, tables 3.16 and 3.17).

The proportion of women students in higher education is nearest to parity at first degree level, and is lowest, at just over one-third of the total, at both postgraduate and other advanced levels. Women outnumber men in some subject areas in the universities and in the polytechnics and colleges sector. These are mainly subjects with relatively few part-time students, such as languages, literature and area studies (66% female), music, drama, art and design (57%), and medicine, dentistry and health (57%). They also dominate education (65%), the subject area with the highest proportion of part-time students, but fall to only 9% in engineering and technology, another area in which part-time study is important (Department of Education and Science *et al.* 1988, table 28).

Part-time higher education students tend to be significantly older than their full-time counterparts. Only 14% of part-time students are aged 20 years old or less, while 67% are aged 25 or more; the comparative figures for full-time students are 54% and 17% respectively (Central Statistical Office 1989, tables 3.16 and 3.17). Or, to put it another way, 235,000 (76%) of those aged 25 or more on higher education courses were studying part-time in 1986/7 (Department of Education and Science *et al.* 1988, table 22). Full-time higher education mainly recruits school-leavers, while part-time higher education is a more adult activity.

Conclusions

Many of the characteristics of part-time higher education which were identified in the previous, historical, chapter remain true today. There are still substantial numbers of part-time students in higher education. Indeed, part-time recruit-ment has grown much quicker than full-time numbers over the last twenty years. If those currently registered for external degrees, or studying for nursing and paramedical qualifications, or taking extra-mural or post-experience courses are taken into account – let alone those studying at a higher level outside public institutions of higher education – then there are clearly many more people in part-time than full-time higher education.

Part-time higher education is mainly provided by the public sector insti-tutions and the Open University; the conventional universities have a small but growing role in this area. Part-time provision dominates at other advanced or sub-degree level, mainly involving daytime study. Full-time provision domi-nates at first degree level, with a more balanced pattern at postgraduate level. Part-time study for award-bearing courses is concentrated in the subjects of education, engineering and technology, and administrative, business and social studies. Considerable numbers take short post-experience courses in medical subjects or follow extra-mural courses in the arts. Part-time students tend to be older than full-timers, and the proportion of women studying part-time has increased dramatically in recent years.

4

International Comparisons

Introduction

This chapter describes and compares the higher education systems of a selection of Western developed countries. The main body of the chapter contains a series of brief national analyses. On the basis of these, a comparative examination of the major characteristics of different higher education systems – and, in particular, of the nature and importance of part-time forms of provision within them – is then undertaken. Comparisons are also made with the position in the United Kingdom, as described in the previous chapter.

Taking an international perspective can usefully shed light on practices at home, and may suggest alternative approaches to similar kinds of problems. In the case of part-time higher education, this approach is likely to be particularly revealing, since, so far as I am aware, no comparative analysis extending beyond more than a few countries has yet been attempted.

There are, of course, a number of problems associated with comparative analyses. It is relatively easy for an English speaker to research the higher education systems of former British colonies. These countries inherited British educational practices, and, though they may subsequently have developed in different directions, the shared language and traditions aid comprehension considerably. Elsewhere, however, great differences in language, culture and history bedevil interpretation. Countries of similar sizes at similar stages of development may have very dissimilar educational systems, or they may have characteristics which appear similar on the surface but hide underlying differences in practice or assumptions.

Given what was said in Chapters 1 and 2 regarding the difficulties with both current and historic definitions of 'higher education', it should not be surprising to discover that this term is interpreted in subtly different ways by different governments and societies. The methods and definitions used in the collection of statistics also vary from country to country. And so does the distinction drawn between full-time and part-time higher education; that is, where such a distinction is made at all! Great care is necessary, therefore, in making international comparisons.

There are few existing comparative analyses upon which to draw. Many studies of individual educational systems, or of specific aspects of them, are available, either in English or in the native language. These are rarely presented in a standardized form, however, and studies which synthesize and compare information on two or more systems in any great depth are not common. Where comparative studies have been carried out, they tend to focus on 'mainstream' concerns, such as full-time first degree study in universities, rather than on part-time study. Many analyses which deal specifically with part-time higher education are concerned only with correspondence or distance study (e.g. MacKenzie *et al.* 1975; Rumble and Harry 1982).

In order to restrict the scope of the discussion in this chapter, I have confined my attention to the Western developed societies of North America, Australasia, Japan and Western Europe. Part-time higher education is of considerable significance in many other countries, both amongst the command economies of the Communist Bloc and in the developing nations of the Third World, but these societies are probably too dissimilar from the United Kingdom for immediate and useful comparisons to be made. The analysis which follows is based mainly on secondary sources available in English, supplemented by national statistics and reports and the publications of international agencies.

North America

Canada and the United States share many characteristics. They were both once British colonies (and were, at other times, French and/or Spanish colonies), and inherited many English or Scottish educational practices. Subsequently, higher education developed faster on the western side of the Atlantic and American ideas began to influence European practice. Since the Second World War, the American and Canadian higher education systems have expanded further to enable mass participation in higher learning. Going to college or university is now seen as normal rather than exceptional in these countries, not just for school-leavers but increasingly for adults as well (Paquet 1987; Wagner 1987).

In both Canada and the United States, the major responsibility for the determination of educational policy is exercised at the regional – that is, province or state – level rather than nationally. This allows for, and encourages, a diversity of approaches to the organization of higher education. Both countries are vast, so a decentralized approach is sensible, and both have low population densities when compared to Western Europe. This has encouraged a considerable development of distance forms of educational provision (Wedemeyer 1981; Mugridge and Kaufman 1986).

Canada

In 1986/7, when Canada had a population of 25,309,330 people, there were 1,245,471 enrolments in higher education. In other words, with a population less than half that of the United Kingdom, Canada enrolled rather more higher education students. Of these enrolments, 762,914 (61%) were in universities, with 482,557 in community colleges offering career or university transfer programmes. Some 449,072 students (36%) were recorded as studying part-time, defined in terms of their relative course load: 38% of those in universities and 33% of those in community colleges. The great majority of university students, 88%, were studying at undergraduate level. The proportion of part-time enrolments was almost exactly the same at undergraduate and graduate levels (Statistics Canada 1988, table 5).

Part-time enrolment in Canadian higher education has increased dramatically since the Second World War. In the 40-year period between 1939 and 1979, the number of part-time university students rose from 6200 to 229,900. At the beginning of this period, they made up only 14% of all university students; by the end of it, the proportion was 38%. Between 1954 and 1964, part-time student numbers were growing at an average rate of 50% a year. The major reasons for this increase have been the relative cost (i.e. cheapness) of part-time study for students and the expansion of female participation (Belanger *et al.* 1982, tables 1, 5 and 6). The growth in part-time numbers is expected to continue for the foreseeable future, with part-time students perhaps outnumbering full-timers by the end of the century.

Currently, slightly more than half, 53%, of all Canadian higher education students are female; and women account for 59% of those studying part-time compared to 50% of those studying full-time (Statistics Canada 1988, table 8). Part-time students tend to be significantly older than full-timers as well, with 64% of part-time university students aged 30 years or over, compared to only 9% of full-timers (Canadian Organization of Part-time University Students 1987, table A1). Part-time students are also disproportionately concentrated in certain subject areas. At undergraduate level in the universities, 40% of those part-time students for whom subject data was recorded in 1986/7 were studying social sciences, and 20% were taking general arts/sciences degrees. At graduate level, 39% of part-time students were in the social sciences and 30% in education (Statistics Canada 1988, tables 16 and 17).

Part-time study opportunities and participants are not evenly distributed throughout Canada. In 1986/7, the two provinces of Ontario and Quebec – which together contain 62% of Canada's population – accounted for 75% of all part-time higher education enrolments. Quebec is the only province with more part-time than full-time university students (ibid, tables 5 and 8). It is, of course, the major French-speaking area of Canada, and its people have traditionally been disadvantaged when compared to those in Ontario and other provinces. Its students also tend to be significantly older than elsewhere, with school-leavers typically entering higher education a year or two later (Bertrand 1982).

Evidence from two postsecondary student surveys carried out in 1974/5 and 1983/4 indicates that students from less privileged backgrounds (in terms of their parents' formal educational achievement) are more likely to study part-time than others. This may be because of their inability to afford full-time study, most of the costs of which are borne by the student (and their family or employer) rather than by the state as in Britain. Part-time students are also less likely to borrow to finance their education, though this may be due to their difficulty in meeting the eligibility criteria for the loans available. Yet:

> While part-time students may constitute a relatively new clientele in Canadian postsecondary education they are increasingly becoming hetero-geneous ... there are younger and older male and female part-time students; part-time students with few and many academic qualifications; part-time students that are employed full-time as either blue- or white-collar workers and part-time female students that are both employees and housewives.
>
> (Canadian Organization of Part-time University Students 1987, p. 30; see also Anisef 1989)

This heterogeneity is illustrated in a number of recent institutional surveys. These surveys have also shown that obstacles to part-time and adult partici-pation in higher education remain, and that improvements in the organization and delivery of provision are needed (Waniewicz 1976; Pike and Creet 1978; Devlin 1989).

At York University in Toronto, a committee was set up in the mid-1980s to review provision for mature and part-time students. Atkinson College had been established within York University in 1962, with its own full-time staff and faculty status, to deal with part-time students (cf. the position of Birkbeck College within the University of London). Its student profile has changed significantly since then. The number of unqualified teacher entrants has declined, while those entering with degrees have increased. A course credit system has been created to enable conventional undergraduates to study part-time for part of their course (Abner and Tacon 1988). In 1985, York University had 19,861 full-time and 13,625 part-time enrolments. The review committee recommended that there should be a greater development in future of community outreach and distance education techniques, and that more attempts should be made to shape studies to students and their needs (York University 1987).

The University of Ottawa, to take a second example, is located in the capital city on the Ontario/Quebec border. It has no specific college or faculty for part-time students, who make up 40% of the total enrolment. These students were surveyed by the University in 1987. The main concerns uncovered related to the lack of consideration, consultation and recognition given to part-time students. Getting information or assistance, when academic and administrative staff kept standard office hours, was a particularly common problem (Noble 1989).

United States of America

The United States has the largest and most comprehensive higher education system in the Western world. In 1985, 12,247,055 students were enrolled in its institutions of higher education. Of these enrolments, 5,171,834, or 42%, were part-time, defined in terms of their study load (Center for Education Statistics 1987, table 101). However, some of those registered as 'full-time' students are not full-time in the sense understood in the United Kingdom. Many of them have regular part-time jobs, and a significant minority are in full-time employment.

Part-time students are enrolled in a diverse set of institutions: some of them public (84% of enrolments in 1985), some private; some offering four-year courses and others, mainly community colleges, offering two-year courses. Part-time students are commonest at the highest and the lowest levels of study. In 1985, they accounted for 54% of the 1,650,381 enrolments on postbacca-laureate (i.e. graduate and 'first professional') programmes, and for 87% of unclassified students below baccalaureate level (i.e. at sub-degree level). By comparison, 40% of the 10,596,674 undergraduate students, the mainstay of the system, were recorded as part-time (ibid, table 104).

As in Canada, part-time higher education has become more important in recent years. Between 1972 and 1982, part-time enrolments rose by two-thirds while full-time numbers increased by less than one-fifth. There have been related rises in the participation rates of older students, women and those from minority groups (Cross 1987; Trow 1989b). The market for higher education in the United States is changing:

> At least half of all undergraduates interrupt their studies for a minimum of one year ... the proportion of part-time enrollment in colleges and universities is steadily increasing, and ... the average age of students on our urban, commuter campuses is now twenty-seven or twenty-eight. The 'nontraditional' student is becoming the norm.
>
> (Lynton and Elman 1987, p. 97)

Again, as in Canada, part-time students in the United States tend to be older than full-time students, and are more commonly female. In 1985, 64% of full-time students were aged 21 years or less, and only 9% were 30 years or older; for part-time students, the proportions are almost reversed, at 14% and 48% respectively. And while 49% of full-time students are women, the proportion of part-time students is significantly higher at 57% (Center for Education Statistics 1987, table 103).

Similarly, part-time students are concentrated in certain parts of the country and in particular kinds of institutions. There were more part-time than full-time enrolments in seven of the 50 American states in 1985: Alaska, Arizona, California, Florida, Illinois, Maryland and Nevada. The part-time proportion of the total varied from 70% in Nevada down to 21% in North Dakota. Part-time enrolments are generally low in the less densely populated parts of the Great Plains area and in the Bible Belt, and are highest in the urbanized areas of the Midwest, the North-East and the West Coast (ibid, table 117). Part-time students are most commonly found in community colleges and in the larger and more diversified state universities, such as Georgia State and the University of

Wisconsin. They are less common in the prestige institutions, such as Harvard or Berkeley.

Standards within the American higher education system are more varied than in the United Kingdom. Consequently, both the elite and the popular functions of higher education can be pursued, though not necessarily in the same institutions:

> The popular functions fall into two general categories. First, there is a commitment on the part of the system as a whole to provide places somewhere for as many students as can be encouraged to continue their education beyond high school . . . the second is the provision of useful knowledge and service to nearly every group and institution that wants it.
>
> (Trow 1969, pp. 183–4)

This approach to higher education, coupled with a widespread adoption of modular study and accreditation systems, offers a great deal of flexibility to students. They may interrupt and resume their studies if desired, and can transfer with credit between courses, campuses and institutions. The student funding system encourages (indeed necessitates) such flexibility, with national support based now on loans rather than grants, so that most students now work during the period of their studies.

Some institutions have made notable efforts to recruit more part-time and non-traditional students. The City University of New York, for example, has had a completely open admissions policy since 1970 (cf. the British Open University: Lavin and Alba 1983). And, since 1972, the State University of New York has operated an external degree system, offering qualifications by examination only – but with supporting study courses available – to students wherever they live (cf. the University of London external degree system: Nolan 1977). In other cases, however, and particularly where part-time students are mixed together with full-timers on large, anonymous campuses, their integration and support have presented problems (Chickering 1974; Boyer 1987).

In both Canada and the United States, therefore, substantial provision is made for part-time students within comprehensive higher education systems designed to serve the mass of the population. The different institutions involved offer a variety of kinds and levels of provision. Part-time student enrolment in these countries has become increasingly heterogeneous in character, and is significantly different from the full-time school-leaver intake. Part-time enrolment is growing to the extent that part-time students may soon be in the majority.

Australasia and Japan

Australia and New Zealand were both, like Canada and the United States, British colonies, and they also inherited many British educational practices. Thus, the former University of New Zealand was based explicitly on the model of the University of London (Beaglehole 1937). Both countries have since developed rather different systems of provision. They have, for example, responded to their large areas and relatively low population densities by adopting distance forms of provision (Braithwaite and Batt 1975; Dahllof 1977; Bynner 1985).

Japan, on the other hand, has never been colonized, but based the development of its higher education system during the twentieth century on ideas imported from a variety of sources. Since the Second World War, the American model of provision has become particularly influential (Nakayama 1989); it has also had a major impact on practice in Australia and New Zealand.

Australia

In 1987, out of a total population of some 16 million people, there were 393,734 enrolments in Australian higher education. This represents a lower participation rate than those for Canada and the United States, but it is still significantly higher than in the United Kingdom. Of this total, 59% are recorded as studying full-time, 29% part-time and 12% externally; giving an overall part-time proportion of 41% (Commonwealth Tertiary Education Commission 1987, table T1).

The Australian higher education system has, like that in England and Wales, been organized for the last few decades on a binary basis, with university and advanced education sectors, though this is now changing as institutions enter a period of rationalization and amalgamation (Beswick 1987). In 1987, 46% of the total enrolments were in the university sector with 54% in the advanced education sector. The university sector currently has slightly smaller proportions of part-time and external students. Though university enrolments have expanded sixfold since the Second World War, the balance between full-time, part-time and external students has remained fairly constant. In the advanced education sector, however, the relative importance of full-time provision (cf. the experience of the British polytechnics) and, to a lesser extent, external provision, has grown considerably (ibid, table T1; Anderson and Vervoorn 1983, pp. 151–2).

As in North America, part-time students tend to be significantly older than full-time students, and this difference is becoming more pronounced. In 1987, while 48% of full-time students were aged 19 years or less, only 7% of part-time and 3% of external students were that young. Conversely, while only 10% of full-timers were aged 30 years or over, the proportions for part-time and external students were 47% and 64% respectively. Women students, though until recently in the minority, now account for almost exactly half of the total students studying by each of the three modes (ibid, pp. 37–9; Commonwealth Tertiary Education Commission 1987, tables T1 and 4).

Full-time students make up the majority of enrolments in most Australian higher education institutions. Part-time face-to-face students are not in the majority in any institution, but constitute a substantial presence in most colleges of advanced education and universities, typically sharing teaching and other facilities with full-time students. The institutional distribution of external students is uneven. Only 24 out of 65 colleges and universities had no external enrolment in 1987, but only 14 institutions were recognized as major providers. At four colleges of advanced education – Armidale, Mitchell and Riverina-Murray in New South Wales, and Gippsland in Victoria – and two universities – New England in New South Wales and Deakin in Victoria – external enrolments accounted for more than 60% of the total students (ibid, table 1).

Like part-time face-to-face students, external students are typically in full-time employment, but they differ little from full-time students in their other socio-economic characteristics. In educational terms, however, external students tend to be better qualified on entry than others, and they are likely to have had previous experience of higher education: 'It is no exaggeration to say that external studies is dominated by middle class professionals upgrading or updating their knowledge' (Anwyl and Powles 1989, pp. 11–12). While external studies does recruit unsuccessful applicants to mainstream higher education, those living in rural or remote areas, and other non-traditional or disadvantaged groups, these are by no means its priority clienteles (Anwyl *et al.* 1987). Its main focus is on meeting much the same needs and on serving much the same (albeit now older) customers as conventional higher education.

Australian higher education is now going through a period of reorganization, in which expansion of output, value for money and equity appear to be the key themes (Australian Government Publishing Service 1988). The student funding system is being remodelled as part of these changes – cf. the changes which have taken place in the United States over the last decade or two, and those currently planned in the United Kingdom (see Chapter 9) – with the burden of state support shifted away from grants towards loans, which will subsequently be recovered through a graduate tax (Committee on Higher Education Funding 1988).

New Zealand

New Zealand is a relatively small country, but its 1986 total of 105,796 home higher education enrolments represents a higher participation rate than that for Australia. The majority, 55%, of these students were studying part-time (Department of Education, New Zealand 1988, table 2). The seven university institutions in the country together enrolled 64,781 students, or 61% of the total: 57% of their students were registered as full-time, with 23% part-time and 20% external. Most non-university higher education is provided by polytechnics or by the Technical Correspondence Institute.

The vast majority, 97% in 1986, of the external students in the university sector are enrolled by one institution, Massey University. Six of the seven university institutions, including Massey University, recruit substantial numbers of part-time students for face-to-face study. The proportions studying by the three modes are broadly similar at undergraduate and postgraduate levels, but part-time forms of study dominate at sub-degree level amongst those seeking to gain the Certificate of Proficiency (ibid, table 61).

Historically, part-time study has dominated higher education in New Zealand, though numbers of politicians and academics have wished it had been otherwise. The 1924/5 Royal Commission, for example, objected to:

the extent of part-time study. Concessions rightly made, in the commis-
sioners' view, to meet the needs of a small and special group of potential
students had been taken advantage of by others who could, by the exercise
of a modest self-denial, take the better part of full-time study. Excessive
part-time study was catered for by the evening lecture classes, which while
not unique to New Zealand, were only here found to dominate the system.
In two at least of the New Zealand colleges, there were virtually no lectures
at the pass (first year) level between 9 a.m. and 5 p.m.

(Parton 1979, p. 45)

Despite this, concessions continued to be made: potential part-time students were clearly not a 'small' group, though they remain special.

As in the other countries considered so far, part-time students tend to be older than full-timers. In 1986, while 38% of full-time university students were aged 19 years or less, only 11% of part-timers and 4% of those studying externally were in this age group. And, while only 6% of full-timers were aged 30 years or over, 41% of part-time students and 58% of external students came into this category. Unlike in Australia, there are also significant differences in the numbers of males and females studying by alternative modes. The proportions of males and females enrolled in the universities are virtually equal overall; but, while females make up 59% of part-time students and 62% of those studying externally, they account for only 43% of full-timers (Department of Education, New Zealand 1988, table 58).

The majority of part-time internal university students are in employment, split fairly evenly between education (24%), government (20%) and the private sector (31%), with 9% recorded as 'housepersons' and 13% unemployed. Only a minority, 16%, of these students receive any direct government assistance towards the costs of their studies; though the majority, 84%, of full-time students get such support, mainly in the form of study and accommodation grants (ibid, tables 77 and 78).

There are notable differences between subject areas in the proportions studying by alternative modes. At first degree level, medicine, engineering, law, science and commerce – all subjects which recruit a disproportionate number of males – are dominated by full-time students. Education, where female students are in the majority, is mainly studied part-time, while business studies has a majority of external students. Arts and social sciences also recruit higher than average numbers of part-time students (ibid, table 67). These differences are partly explained by the somewhat restricted curriculum offered to external students by Massey University (Bewley 1982).

Japan

The Japanese educational system is far less familiar to British academics than any of the others described so far, due to the obvious linguistic, cultural and historical barriers. Yet it is widely believed to offer a model worthy of study and emulation, because of the high levels of educational attainment achieved by a large proportion of Japanese youth and the post-war success of the Japanese economy. As already noted, the Japanese educational system owes much to the American model, though it differs from it in a number of ways, notably in the intensity of student commitment.

Japan has a population of over 120 million people, about half that of the United States and more than twice that of the United Kingdom. Its higher education system contains three main types of institutions: universities, junior colleges and technical colleges. In May 1985 there were 2,268,081 students enrolled in these institutions, 82% of them in the 460 universities (Ministry of Education, Science and Culture, Japan, 1987). The system is also split between public and private provision: 10% of junior college, 27% of university and 93% of technical college enrolments are in public sector institutions. Though the private sector dominates in terms of overall enrolment, the public sector includes most of the acknowledged elite institutions.

About half of all higher education enrolments are concentrated in the Tokyo metropolitan area. Most students, 79%, are studying at first degree level, with 18% enrolled at sub-degree level and only a small proportion, 3%, at post-graduate level. Women students remain in the minority, accounting for only 34% of total enrolments, and they are to be found disproportionately at the lower levels of study in the junior colleges (Department of Education and Science 1987b, tables 3 and 4).

Unfortunately, information on the numbers of these students who are studying part-time is not readily available. In 1975, 15% of university students and 27% of junior college students were quoted as studying part-time, either face-to-face or by correspondence (Kato and Postgate 1975). Many private institutions currently offer evening and correspondence study programmes in addition to daytime provision. Some of the students following these pro-grammes are, in terms of their commitment, effectively studying full-time. A national University of the Air was recently established: in May 1985 it had enrolled 17,038 students (Muta 1985; Ministry of Education, Science and Culture, Japan, 1987).

Western Europe

Like Japan, and for much the same reasons, European higher education is poorly understood and appreciated in the United Kingdom. The continuing emphasis in Britain's international higher education relations on the United States and the countries of the Commonwealth seems surprising when it is remembered that the United Kingdom has been a member of the European

Community for nearly twenty years. Closer links are now being forged with other European countries through COMETT, DELTA, ERASMUS and similar schemes, and a steady reorientation of the British higher education system towards Europe is to be expected.

European systems of higher education vary considerably from country to country, but there are also similarities. In several European countries, the 1970s and 1980s witnessed the beginning of a transition from elite to mass higher education: a transition akin to that already achieved in North America, but yet to be undertaken in the United Kingdom (Neave 1985b; Richter 1988). A series of related trends, linked to changes in demography, work patterns and individual expectations, have been widely observed. Numbers of part-time, adult and employed students have been increasing, and there has been a growth in short-cycle higher education (i.e. study not for full degrees). These developments have been reported from, for example, Austria (Kellermann and Sagmeister 1988), France (Cerych 1983), Italy (Ciucci 1984), The Netherlands (de Goede and Hoksbergen 1978), Norway (Kyvik and Skoie 1982), Spain (Pedro 1988), Sweden (Abrahamsson 1984, 1986) and West Germany (Ritter 1986; Huber 1987).

In his comparative analyses of European higher education, Neave has identified three different national approaches to policy: demand-led policies, as in France, Greece, Italy and Spain; expenditure-driven policies, as currently pursued in Denmark, The Netherlands, Sweden and the United Kingdom; and policies transitional between these two approaches, as in Belgium, Ireland and West Germany (Neave 1984). The expenditure-driven systems tend to be characterized by strong public control over admissions, relatively high public expenditure, high full-time staffing costs and an emphasis on full-time students. The demand-led, or Mediterranean, systems exhibit weak public control over admissions, very low student fees, low per capita expenditure and large numbers of part-time students: 'there is a substantial proportion of the student body which is made up of part-timers, either because they have part-time or full-time jobs' (ibid, p. 114). It is regrettable, therefore, that the numbers and characteristics of part-time higher education students are rarely recorded in the statistics compiled by Western European countries. Indeed, the distinction made between full-time and part-time study in the United Kingdom, North America and Australasia is simply not recognized officially in much of Western Europe. Such information as is available on part-time higher education comes largely from occasional institutional or national surveys.

The brief reviews which follow focus on six of the largest Western European countries: France, Italy, The Netherlands, Spain, Sweden and West Germany.

France

In 1986, France had a total population of 55,279,100 people, just slightly less than that of the United Kingdom. In that year there were 969,099 enrolments in the 78 French universities; and 1,213,799 enrolments in the higher education system as a whole, including the various specialist institutions (Ministère de l'Education Nationale 1987, tables 1.3, 10.1). Recent reforms have led to an expansion of the system, and the majority of school-leavers who gain the baccalaureate, some 30% of the age group, now go on to higher education. There are now rather ambitious plans to expand participation by a further 50% by the year 2005 (Neave 1988; Rontopoulou and Lamoure 1988).

Information on the study patterns of French students is patchy, but what there is indicates that there are significant numbers of part-time students within the higher education system:

> According to a recent survey covering six French and two Italian univer-
> sities, nearly 60% of students declared that during their last year of
> undergraduate studies, they had been full-time, part-time or occasionally
> employed. If only the first two of these three job categories are considered,
> about 37% of the French students and 35% of the Italian students had
> part-time or full-time work and, therefore, almost by definition, studied on
> a part-time basis. Fragmentary information suggests that this percentage is
> rapidly increasing. For example, according to another survey undertaken
> in France, it amounted to 18% in 1973, almost exactly one half of the 1982
> figure.
>
> (Cerych 1983, p. 137)

In particular institutions or departments, the proportion of students who are effectively part-time may be higher than these figures suggest. The University of Paris VIII-Vincennes, for example, enrols a substantial number of adult students, from France and other countries, without the standard entry quali-fications. Evening classes are available in most subjects. Out of a total enrol-ment of some 30,000 students, between 30% and 85% of those in different departments are wage-earners. Of the French students, who make up only 53% of the total, 50% work full-time and a further 26% part-time. Only a minority of these students, therefore, are in a position to devote themselves to their studies full-time (Berger *et al.* 1985).

Italy

Italy's population is slightly larger than that of either France or the United Kingdom. In 1987/8 there were 1,096,200 enrolments in the Italian higher education system, the vast majority of them in the universities (Luzzatto 1988). Entry is open to all those with the school-leaving qualification, the *maturita*, and there is little competition between institutions for students. Non-completion rates are much higher in Italian higher education than in the United Kingdom. About 28% of students are estimated to drop out during their first year of study, and less than a third of the first-year enrolments eventually succeed in gaining a degree (Moscati 1985).

As with France, there is no comprehensive data available on alternative study routes. One published survey of enrolment patterns at Milan State University, the third largest in the country, clearly shows that many Italian students are using higher education as a 'waiting room': something to enter as an alternative to unemployment, but with no real intention of sitting examinations (de Francesco 1986). Many other students combine their studies with full-time, part-time, or occasional employment:

> Although Italian university students are always classified in international statistics as 'full-time students', in reality they seem to be much more often part-timers not only because many of them work regularly full-time, but also because even those who do not work often appear to attend university on a part-time basis.
>
> (de Francesco 1984, p. 175)

De Francesco found that 17% of first-year students at Milan State University had full-time jobs, and a further 33% had regular part-time work or temporary jobs. The remaining 50%, the 'full-time' students, were discovered on average to spend only 26 hours a week attending university and studying.

The findings of a 1982 survey of two universities, which tends to confirm these patterns, have already been quoted in the section on France. A review of earlier studies on this theme came to a similar conclusion:

> The incidence of student-workers in universities should not be under-estimated; one is dealing mainly with male students, in many cases married students, who hold a 'steady' job while reading for a degree. This particular type of student, taken as a proportion of the total university population, varies by between 16% and 20% in the different regions. There is a clear correlation between the year of the course and the incidence of student-workers: the number appears to be low in the first years, but increases in the final period with a strong concentration . . . among students who fail to finish within the appropriate time.
>
> (Ciucci 1984, p. 306)

Ciucci also found that the numbers of student-workers were increasing, and he suggested that greater emphasis should be put on short-cycle higher education to relieve some of the resultant pressures.

The Netherlands

The Netherlands is one of the smaller countries in Western Europe, but, with a population of about 15 million people, it is more densely settled than the United Kingdom. Higher education is provided by universities and vocational colleges. In 1981/2, there were 369,733 enrolments in these institutions, 150,359 (41%) of them in the universities and 219,374 in the vocational colleges. Nearly two-fifths of the latter, some 85,389 students, were studying part-time. Of the university students, 12,127 (8%) were registered only for examinations, and a smaller – undefined but growing – proportion were reported as studying part-time (Ministry of Education and Science of The Netherlands 1985).

In the mid-1970s, a survey found that 10% of Dutch university students had full-time jobs (de Goede and Hoksbergen 1978). Between 1979 and 1985, there was a fourfold increase in the number of part-time first-year students in the universities, rising from 3% to 8% of the total intake. The majority, some 60%, of these students were under 30 years of age (van Enckevort and Leibbrandt 1988). Courses for part-time students are concentrated in subjects such as law, social sciences, education, theology and biology; with limited or no provision in most sciences, engineering, agriculture and medicine.

In 1984, the Open University of The Netherlands opened. Modelled in part on the British example, it operates an open access system and enrolled 35,000 students in its first two years. These students, all of whom are effectively part-time, have an average age of 32, and are predominantly male (67%) and in paid work (70%). The Open University's advent has already stimulated competition in the conventional universities, so that the number of part-time students in The Netherlands is likely to increase significantly in the near future (ibid).

Spain

In 1986, Spain enrolled some 940,000 students in higher education from a population of 38,818,355 people. This represented a more than fivefold increase in just 25 years, indicating a rapid transition from an elite to a demand-led mass higher education system (Neave 1984; Pedro 1988). As in Italy, periods of study tend to be longer than in the United Kingdom, though a two-cycle system of higher education is practised. Dropout rates are much higher than in Britain, and a greater proportion of the enrolment is made up of mature students.

Once again, though, there is no reliable, comprehensive information available on students' patterns of study. A substantial proportion of the student body are pursuing their studies part-time, however, combining them with full-time or part-time employment. This state of affairs is clearly reflected in the organization of teaching sessions:

> Usually every university has at least two sessions per day: the first one, in the morning, is attended mainly by young, full-time students; the second one, in the evening, is attended by older, part-time students who work in the morning. And in many colleges and faculties evening course students outnumber morning attenders, mainly in the field of humanities, social sciences, law and business administration.
>
> (Pedro 1988, p. 132)

Spain also has an Open University, the Universidad Nacional de Educación a Distancia, which was chartered in 1972. This now accounts for 10% of the total student body. Courses are offered for the admissions qualification and for degrees in law, philosophy and letters, economics and business administration, science and engineering. A survey carried out in 1979/80 revealed that 63% of its students were aged 26–40 years old; nearly all were in full-time employment, and fully 65% were public servants. Most were middle-class professionals, with nearly half already holding a degree or equivalent qualification (James 1982).

Sweden

Sweden is the only one of the six countries considered here which is not a member of the European Community. It is also, with a population of just over 8 million people in an area nearly twice the size of the United Kingdom, sparsely populated. Not surprisingly, therefore, it has, like Australia, Canada and the United States, developed the use of distance teaching (Dahllof *et al.* 1978); though, unlike The Netherlands, Spain, the United Kingdom and West Germany, it has not established a single national Open University.

In 1983, there were a total of 177,800 students enrolled in Swedish higher education. The great majority, 93%, of them were studying at undergraduate level in one of the six universities or 27 other higher education institutions. All together, these students made up a full-time equivalent load of 124,500 (*Higher Education in Europe* 1986). Postgraduate education, in particular, is a very part-time activity. In 1984, about 35% of postgraduate students were classified as 'non-active', and 60% of the active students devoted less than 70% of their working time to study (Zetterblom 1986).

Swedish higher education has attracted a great deal of attention during the last decade (e.g. Dahllof 1977; Boucher 1982; Cerych and Sabatier 1986; Jansson 1986). In 1977, a series of policy changes were introduced with the aim of further increasing the vocational relevance and accessibility of higher education. As part of these changes, alternative admissions criteria – the 25/5 scheme and its successors – were brought in, enabling those aged 25 years or more with 5 years of work experience to enter higher education alongside those with conventional qualifications. These reforms resulted in a rapid and substantial 'adultification' of Swedish higher education, and stimulated the growth of shorter, part-time and evening programmes of study.

By the early 1980s, adults were in the majority on many higher education programmes. In 1980, for example, 63% of the 130,300 students in conventional higher education were aged 25 years or more, with 23% aged 35 years or older (Abrahamsson 1984). By 1983, 47% of applicants, and 63% of those who were enrolled, qualified for entry either wholly or partly on the basis of work experience. Though it remains the case that: 'the concept of part-time student is not used in common higher education statistics' (Abrahamsson 1986, p. 20), surveys show that, towards the end of the 25/5 pilot programme, about 50% of those enrolled wished to study part-time and 80% did not intend to take a full degree. Of those who enrolled on the basis of school-leaving qualifications, 30% wished to study part-time and 50% did not intend to take a full degree (Jones 1985).

Though more recent policy changes have, to some extent, reduced the importance of age and work experience as entry qualifications, there can be no doubt that there has been a fundamental change in the nature of the student role in Sweden:

> Today, Swedish students in higher education have a number of obligations parallel to their studies. Both young and adult students combine higher studies and work. Others have to find their learning strategies in a context of social restrictions and contradictory obligations, i.e. a limited time budget caused by family, work and other activities. Thus, many of these students have a part-time identity as a student. They are not isolated from society, but, rather, an integrated part of it.
>
> (Abrahamsson 1986, p. 72)

West Germany

The Federal Republic of Germany is the most populous country in Western Europe, with 61,139,000 inhabitants recorded in 1986. It also has the largest higher education system, enrolling 1,410,789 students in 1987. Some two-thirds, 953,839, of these enrolments were in universities, with the remainder in advanced training colleges of various kinds (Hufner 1987; Statistisches Bundesamt 1988, table 16.10). West Germany, like Britain, Spain and The Netherlands, has an Open University, the Fernuniversität, which was chartered in 1974. It enrolled 36,669 students in 1981, the majority of whom were studying part-time for a degree or taking a short course (Keegan 1982).

Like many Western nations, West Germany has experienced a substantial decline in its birth-rate over the last two decades. This has had a significant impact on institutions of higher education, encouraging them to extend their recruitment to non-traditional groups – most notably adults – and to make changes in provision and practice to attract and serve these groups effectively (Brandes and Raters 1981). From the student's point of view, higher education has increasingly become something to balance against employment, unemployment and other activities:

> In 1960, only about 16% of all students were 26 years or older. Since then, the proportion has doubled, not only because of the high average length of study or because of the strategy of using 'academia' as a waiting room while trying to secure employment, but also because of a relatively late entry into higher education, one sometimes being sought after periods of vocational training and/or work.
>
> (Peisert 1985, pp. 19–20)

Though, once again, there are no official statistics available on the split between full-time and part-time modes of study, recent research demonstrates that there are now substantial numbers of part-time students in the German higher education system:

> The traditional concept of the student role saw much of his life centrally determined through the very fact and process of studying: the place where

he lived, the way he was accommodated, his status regarding family and his social relations, most of all and through all his time budget . . . Today for a substantial proportion of students, studies and the fact of being a student loses its central place in life . . . They are persons who among other things are studying.

(Huber 1987, p. 165)

Our universities, without knowing it or doing anything about it, are already teaching to part-time students, and an increasing percentage of our students are working at the same time as they go to university . . . full-time students become the exception rather than the rule at least for most large city universities . . . Already today more than 60 percent of the students are part-time students in our big city universities and up to 30 percent hold a full job.

(Ritter 1986, pp. 114, 119)

Despite the differences between the Western European systems of higher education that I have considered, there seem to be trends common to most of the countries considered. Many of these trends have also been identified in the United Kingdom (see Chapter 3). Pre-eminent amongst them, from the point of view of the present study, are the themes stressed in the last three quotations above:

• the recruitment of increasing numbers (in both absolute and relative terms) of adult students;
• the changing student role; now frequently incorporating part-time or full-time employment, domestic responsibilities and other activities alongside study;
• the growing number of *de facto* part-time higher education students.

And, as the sections on North America and Australasia have indicated, these trends are by no means confined to Western Europe but are relevant to many, probably most, developed countries.

Comparisons and conclusions

We are now in a position to make some general comparisons between the higher education systems of the eleven countries which I have just reviewed and that of the United Kingdom (as described in Chapter 3). Before doing so, it is important to re-emphasize the reservations I expressed in the introduction to this chapter. The most important of these, for present purposes, concerns the failure of many national systems to make a clear distinction between full-time and part-time provision for students. In addition, most national statistics, like those for the United Kingdom, omit or only make limited reference to students who are registered with correspondence colleges or with certain kinds of private institutions. All the statistics, so far as I am aware, ignore those who are pursuing their education outside the formal educational system. Since the great majority of such students will be studying part-time, the relative importance of part-time higher education will typically be underestimated by the official figures.

We should also bear in mind the variations in the characteristics of the formal higher education systems in different countries. These differences include critical aspects such as the length of study, the relation between student inputs and outputs (i.e. dropout and qualification rates), and the national resources devoted to institutional and student support. Then there are the aspects that are not easily measured, most notably the quality or standard of the provision that is offered. More than one author has argued that higher education systems that enable mass access may be failing their students through inadequate preparation, provision and support, resulting in high dropout rates and/or the establishment within the system of an elite sector (e.g. de Francesco 1984; Silber 1987). And, finally, the wide differences in background or societal variables, such as area, population and economic production, should not be forgotten.

Despite these problems, a number of international comparisons between higher education systems have been carried out in recent years (e.g. Organization for Economic Co-operation and Development (OECD) 1971, 1981, 1983; Cerych 1983; United Nations Educational, Scientific and Cultural Organization (UNESCO) 1983. Most of these analyses have been restricted to overall enrolment figures for successive levels of study, however these may have been defined. In a few cases, though, limited comparisons have been attempted between modes of study where this data has been readily available – as for Australia, Canada, the United Kingdom and the United States of America; and also for the Republic of Ireland, The Netherlands and Yugoslavia (see Advisory Council for Adult and Continuing Education 1980; OECD 1971, table A4; OECD 1983, table A4).

Tables 6 and 7 contain selected comparative data for a number of developed nations, recently compiled by UNESCO and the Department of Education and Science (DES) respectively. In neither case does the information provided extend to part-time provision, but the similarities and differences revealed usefully support the analysis presented here. Table 8, which follows, then summarizes some of the findings for the eleven countries just reviewed and for the United Kingdom.

Table 6 lists 1985 (or 1984) data for these twelve countries (UNESCO 1987). It confirms that they vary markedly in size, population and population density. It also shows that, although all twelve countries are Western developed nations, there is a near fourfold difference between the poorest, Spain, and the richest, the United States, in terms of gross national product per capita. The United Kingdom comes towards the bottom of this range, though it is above Spain, Italy and New Zealand.

Student enrolments reflect both the population of the countries concerned and their relative wealth, as well as other factors. The two nations with truly mass higher education systems, recording more than 5000 enrolments per 100,000 of the population (i.e. over 5% overall participation in a given year), are

Table 6   Selected national and educational characteristics, twelve countries, 1985.

Nation	1	2	3	4	5	6
Australia	16	2	10,830	370,320	2,462	48
Canada	25	3	13,680	1,294,194	5,090	46*
France	55	101	9,540	1,255,538†	2,310†	50†
Italy	57	190	6,520	1,181,953†	2,065†	45†
Japan	121	324	11,300	2,403,371†	2,006†	34†
Netherlands	15	355	9,290	390,244†	2,704†	41†
New Zealand	3	12	7,010	95,754†	2,910†	44†
Spain	39	76	4,290	830,664†	2,167†	48†
Sweden	8	19	11,890	220,947†	2,650†	47†
United Kingdom	57	231	8,460	1,006,969†	1,795†	45†
United States	239	26	16,690	12,247,055	5,145	52
West Germany	61	245	10,940	1,550,211	2,546	42

Source: United Nations Educational, Scientific and Cultural Organization 1987.
Key to columns:
   1 Estimated population in millions;
   2 Population density in persons per square kilometre;
   3 Gross national product per capita (US dollars);
   4 Student enrolment at third level (i.e. higher education);
   5 Students per 100,000 inhabitants;
   6 Percentage of students who are female.
* Relates to full-time students only.
† Statistics for 1984.

also the richest: the United States and Canada. All but one of the other countries fall within the 2000–3000 range in terms of this measure. The sole exception is the United Kingdom, which has only 1795 higher education students per 100,000 people, about one-third of the proportion in North America. All, with the exception of Japan, now have female enrolments at or approaching half of the total.

Table 7, which has been extracted from a recent DES statistical bulletin (DES 1987b), summarizes 1984 (or 1983 or 1982) data for seven of the twelve countries. Though the basic data used here is much the same as for the UNESCO source, some rather more involved analyses have been carried out with the aim of better illustrating the relative position of the United Kingdom in the higher education stakes world-wide. Some of the variations in the structure and organization of the different systems considered show up clearly. The universities dominate enrolment in France, Italy, Japan and West Germany, with a more balanced institutional split evident in The Netherlands, the United Kingdom and the United States. First degree level provision accounts for the substantial majority of enrolments in the former group of nations, although many of those enrolled may not get beyond the early part of their courses. In the United Kingdom and the United States, first degree level study absorbs only about half of the total students, with sub-degree and postgraduate provision assuming a much greater significance.

In Table 7, enrolment rates are expressed in relation to the size of the 18–24 age group, which accounts for most of the full-time student population in most higher education systems, rather than in terms of the total population. Nevertheless, the United States is still ahead of the field, and the United Kingdom again brings up the rear with about one-third of the American enrolment rate. The last two columns show the British higher education system in a rather different light. The United Kingdom performs relatively well in terms of qualifications achieved per 100 of the relevant entry age group. It surpasses Italy, The Netherlands and West Germany, but still lags (but not far) behind Japan and the United States. This reflects the lower dropout rates experienced in Britain, particularly when compared to some of the mass entry systems operating in Europe. In terms of public expenditure on higher education, the United Kingdom comes third behind The Netherlands and the United States, despite its comparatively poor gross national product. These figures reflect state funding of both institutions and students: for the latter, the British system is far and away the most generous of those studied.

Though the DES analysis did not attempt any statistical comparison of different modes of study, it did make some general observations:

Part-time study is not recognised formally as a distinguishable mode in some countries although students often work whilst studying thus lengthening their course. The distinction is firmly made in the UK where some two-fifths of higher education students are classified as part-time, including trainee nurses; the USA level is similar. Of the other countries [i.e. the seven considered] only the Netherlands records significant numbers of students as studying part-time. In Italy, although all students

Table 7 Selected higher education statistics, seven countries, 1984.

Nation	1	2	3	4	5	6
France	1,144,000*	19*	82*	71*	32†	42†
Italy	1,182,000	18	99	92	11	25*
Japan	2,403,000	21	81	79	37	23†
Netherlands	384,000*	22*	42*	—	23†	98†
United Kingdom	1,007,000	15	42	54	31	57*
United States	12,468,000	44	62	54	41*	168†
West Germany	1,503,000	20	87	85	23*	37*

Source: Department of Education and Science 1987b, tables 3, 5 and 8. See also Department of Education and Science 1985b.
Key to columns:
  1 Student enrolment in higher education;
  2 Enrolment per 100 of the 18–24 age group;
  3 Percentage of enrolment in universities;
  4 Percentage of enrolment at first degree level;
  5 Qualifications achieved per 100 of relevant age group on entry;
  6 Public expenditure on higher education per capita, upper estimate, at 1983 prices.
*Data for 1983.
†Data for 1982.

Table 8   Selected higher education characteristics, twelve countries, mid-1980s.

Nation	1	2	3	4	5	6
Australia	1987	393,734	41	—	51/49	10/51
Canada	1986	1,245,471	36	38	50/59	9/64
France	1986	1,213,799	(30–40)	—	—	—
Italy	1987	1,096,200	(40–50)	—	—	—
Japan	1985	2,268,081	(20–30)	—	—	—
Netherlands	1981	369,733	(30)	—	—	—
New Zealand	1986	105,796	55	39*	43/61*	6/49*
Spain	1986	940,000	(40–50)	—	—	—
Sweden	1983	177,800	(40–50)	—	—	—
United Kingdom	1986	971,800	37	18	44/38	17/67†
United States	1985	12,247,055	42	40	49/57	9/48
West Germany	1987	1,410,789	(30–40)	—	—	—

Sources: see text for details. A dash (—) signifies that no information is available.
Key to columns:
  1 Year to which statistics apply;
  2 Total student enrolment in higher education;
  3 Percentage of students studying part-time (figures in brackets are estimates);
  4 Percentage of enrolled undergraduate/first degree students studying part-time;
  5 Percentage of full-time/part-time students who are female;
  6 Percentage of full-time/part-time students aged 30 years or more.
* Statistics for university students only.
† Statistics for 25 years or more.

are classified as full-time, some two in three combine study with work. In France some one in three students are estimated to have a job.

(ibid, p. 2)

Table 8 attempts to remedy some of the deficiencies of the previous two tables by drawing on the national analyses presented in this chapter to provide data on part-time higher education. The information given in this table should be treated with caution, particularly that included in the third column. For only five of the twelve countries listed – Australia, Canada, New Zealand, the United Kingdom and the United States – can this data be regarded as reliable, since in those cases it derives directly from published national statistics. The figures quoted for the other seven countries are estimates based on the sources discussed in the text. These are probably reasonably accurate in the cases of Japan, The Netherlands and Sweden, but are less so for France, Italy, Spain and West Germany.

These reservations aside, the table enables us to make some general conclusions. First, part-time students make up a substantial proportion, typically between a third and a half, of the total enrolment of *all* Western developed systems of formal higher education. This is the case whether the system specifically allows for and recognizes part-time study, as in Australasia, North America and the United Kingdom, or whether part-time students are forced to adapt themselves to the constraints of a nominally full-time system, as in much of Western Europe. In the latter case, part-time students are both unrecorded and underrecorded, with the potential demand for part-time study likely to be substantially depressed by lack of recognition.

Second, as already noted, these statistics exclude certain kinds of provision which are overwhelmingly part-time, and thus underestimate the overall significance of part-time higher education. Correspondence or distance provision is not included in many national statistics, especially when it is privately organized. Five of the twelve countries considered here – Japan, The Netherlands, Spain, the United Kingdom and West Germany – have national Open Universities; and all but two have substantial numbers of higher education students studying at a distance. If all of these, and other kinds of part-time students, were included in the national statistics, it is probable that part-timers would outnumber full-timers in most (if not all) of the countries under consideration.

Third, the relative importance of part-time provision is reflected at each level of higher education. Part-time provision tends to be particularly common at sub-degree level, especially when this focuses on preparation for degree course entry, and at postgraduate level. But it also accounts for one-third to one-half of enrolments in the mainstay of higher education: first degree of undergraduate courses. This is demonstrably the case in North America and Australasia. It is implicitly so in Western Europe, where undergraduate provision dominates the higher education system, even if many students there are not aiming for or will not achieve a degree qualification. The one exception to this conclusion appears to be the United Kingdom, where less than one-fifth of first degree students are studying on a part-time basis; and even this percentage is inflated by the inclusion of the Open University's students in the calculation.

Fourth, some general conclusions may be drawn about the characteristics of part-time students. Part-time students are a much more heterogeneous group than full-time students. They appear, where this information is available, to be disproportionately female (though, again, not in the United Kingdom) and significantly older than full-time students. Clearly, part-time provision appeals more to women and to adults, who are less likely than young men to be able to devote themselves to long periods of full-time study. There is also evidence from a number of countries – though it has not been included in Table 8 – of part-time courses recruiting a greater proportion, but still a minority, of their students from lower socio-economic groups. Similarly, part-time provision tends to recruit more people with either relatively low or relatively high entry qualifications: these groups might be termed 'second chance' and 'second bite' respectively.

Fifth, there is evidence that part-time provision in most higher education systems tends to be concentrated in particular subjects and in particular parts of the country. Arts, humanities and social science subjects, and professional courses in business studies, education, health studies and law, tend to be the most readily available and the most studied on a part-time basis. By contrast, engineering, science and medicine are rarely offered by part-time study. Part-time face-to-face provision is, not surprisingly, mainly to be found in densely populated urban areas; sometimes in specific institutions, but more commonly as part of the general provision of a multi-purpose university or college. In less densely populated and rural areas, part-time provision is mainly through distance means, though distance education is by no means confined to such areas.

Finally, there is plentiful evidence to suggest that part-time higher education is increasing in importance in Western developed countries, both in absolute terms and in relation to full-time provision. This trend is likely to continue for the foreseeable future. Part-time provision is the most pragmatic means for expanding access to higher education – a goal in all of the countries considered – enabling students to combine study with work, domestic and social responsibilities.

5

Providers and Provision

Introduction

In Chapter 3 I presented a brief analysis of the current position of part-time higher education in the United Kingdom. This looked at provision in terms of the sectors, levels and subjects involved, and briefly considered student characteristics, drawing on published national statistics. The aim of the present chapter, and of the following one, is to examine these patterns in more detail. The focus of this chapter will be on providers and provision; or, in other words, on courses, the institutions that offer them, and their characteristics. Chapter 6 will then discuss the students and other clients of part-time higher education.

The main themes which will be considered in this chapter are:

- the different providers and awarding bodies involved in part-time higher education, and the numbers of courses that they provide;
- the various modes of study available;
- the availability of different subjects for study;
- course entry and exit arrangements;
- course length and structure;
- course contents, resources and teaching methods;
- the location of the providers and of the provision they offer; and
- the costs associated with this provision.

The analysis is organized in four sections in terms of the main levels of study available: first degree, sub-degree or other advanced, postgraduate and post-experience. Particular attention will be paid to first degree provision, the core of higher education, which has been the subject of most research. Some general conclusions will be drawn at the end of the chapter.

The primary source for the analysis contained in this chapter is my own research (e.g. Tight 1982, 1986, 1989b). This has been supplemented by information from a number of national databases, notably those produced and maintained by the Council for National Academic Awards (CNAA), the Careers Research and Advisory Council (CRAC), the Committee of Vice-Chancellors and Principals (CVCP) and the Educational Counselling and

Credit Transfer Information Service (ECCTIS) (CNAA 1988b, 1988c; CRAC 1988; CVCP 1988; ECCTIS 1989a); and by data from other recent studies.

First degree provision

Overall numbers of courses and providers

In total, 712 part-time first degree courses were offered by 128 institutions of higher education in the United Kingdom during the 1988/9 academic year. A similar survey carried out during the 1985/6 academic year found 615 part-time first degree courses (Tight 1986). The overall increase of 97 courses (a rise of 16%) in just three years – and, with a considerable turnover, rather more than this number of new courses were established in this period – confirms the recent growth of provision shown by the national statistics (see Table 3).

These courses have been identified from the prospectuses and other publications of the institutions concerned. The details were then checked with the available national guides and databases, and, where necessary, with the institutions themselves. It is quite possible that some of the courses included in the 1988/9 total folded during that year, and that some others may have been overlooked. Such cancellations and omissions are likely to be relatively few in number, however, and should not affect the general patterns observed.

The courses identified vary a great deal in size, ranging from single-subject degrees with few students to broad, multidisciplinary or combined degree courses. At one extreme is the Open University's BA degree course, which accounts for two-thirds of all part-time first degree students in the United Kingdom (Table 4), yet comprises a *single* course. At the other extreme are courses which allow part-time students to attend full-time courses alongside conventional full-time students, and which may admit few or no students in any one year.

Table 9 shows the distribution of the courses identified by type of provider. Nearly half, 335 or 47%, of the courses were provided by the 30 polytechnics in England and Wales. A further 229 courses, 32%, were offered by 34 university institutions; and the remaining 148, 21%, by 64 colleges. More than half of the total, 422 courses or 59%, were accredited by the CNAA; including all but two of the courses offered by the polytechnics, plus 89 courses in 41 of the colleges. The other 290 courses were accredited by universities: all of those provided by the universities themselves, plus 2 in two polytechnics and 59 in 28 colleges.

Part-time courses now account for 22% of all the first degree courses accredited by the CNAA, though part-time students only make up 11% of their first degree students. This is because part-time courses tend to recruit fewer students, and have more difficulty in retaining those they do recruit. In 1986/7, there were an average of 65 students on each part-time CNAA course, compared to 148 on each full-time or sandwich course (CNAA 1988a, tables 1 and 2; see also Bourner 1983). Part-time courses in the conventional universities tend to be

Table 9   Numbers of part-time first degree courses by type of provider, United Kingdom, 1988/9.

No. of courses	University	Type of provider Polytechnic	College	Total
1	9	—	26	35
2	5	1	20	26
3	3	—	8	11
4	2	2	4	8
5	1	1	2	4
6	4	1	1	6
7	1	4	1	6
8	1	2	—	3
9	—	2	1	3
10	2	3	1	6
11	—	3	—	3
12	1	—	—	1
13	1	4	—	5
14	1	—	—	1
15+	3	7	—	10
Total institutions	34	30	64	128
Total courses	229	335	148	712
Courses/institution	6.7	11.2	2.3	5.6

smaller, averaging about half the number of students on part-time CNAA courses (Smith and Saunders 1988, table 2).

The extent of the part-time provision made by the 128 institutions identified varies considerably, as Table 9 indicates. All 30 polytechnics offered part-time first degree courses, and most offered a substantial number, averaging 11.2 each. Seven polytechnics provided more than 15 courses each: Coventry, South Bank, Wolverhampton (17 each), Sheffield (19), Thames (21), Manchester (22) and Liverpool (23). In some cases, such as Liverpool and North London – where a major evening degree programme has been built up over the last decade (Johnson and Hall 1985) – this has been a recent development. At the present time, the majority of part-time first degree students who are studying face-to-face are enrolled at one of the polytechnics. This was, after all, one of the intentions when the polytechnics were first established twenty years ago (see Chapter 2 and: Robinson 1968; Pratt and Burgess 1974).

Part-time first degree provision is less extensive in the university sector, though a significant expansion is taking place at a number of institutions (see, for example, Byrd and Schuller 1988). The major operator in this sector, in terms of the number of students recruited, is, of course, the Open University. During the last twenty years, the Open University has established itself as a national provider of high quality, multi-media, part-time distance teaching (Scupham 1975; Perry 1976; Rumble 1982). Twenty-nine of the 45 universities funded by the Universities Funding Council (UFC) also offered some part-time first degree provision in 1988/9. This total includes both of the federal universities, London and Wales; with four component parts of the former and two of the latter making some provision. Indeed, the University of London as a whole offered more than one-third, 77, of all the part-time first degree courses in the university sector.

Nine of the 34 university institutions that offered part-time first degree courses, including the Open University, only provided one course each, and half offered three courses or less. Four university institutions offered 14 or more courses, however, raising the overall average to 6.7. Each of these four institutions is somewhat unusual. Ulster University, which provided 14 courses, some of them on more than one of its four main sites, was only recently established through the amalgamation of Ulster Polytechnic with the smaller New University of Ulster. It currently recruits more part-time face-to-face students at first degree level than any other university (Bishop 1989). Southampton University, which offered 22 courses, achieves this by admitting limited numbers of part-time students to its existing full-time courses. Birkbeck College, part of the University of London, which provided 23 part-time degree courses, specializes in evening provision for employed mature students. It does not offer full-time courses, and has long been the 'brand leader' in the university sector for part-time face-to-face provision.

The fourth of these institutions, the External Division of the University of London, is in many ways the most unusual. In 1988/9, it offered 45 courses by examination only. The university provides students with a syllabus, specimen examination papers and some notes for guidance, and it is left to the students themselves to organize their own studies. A few institutions, notably correspondence colleges, provide tutorial support in the more popular subjects; and in a handful of cases face-to-face courses are available which follow the external syllabuses.

Half of the institutions providing part-time first degree courses are colleges, but most operate in this area only on a very limited scale. Twenty-six of the 64 colleges involved only offered one course each, and a further 20 only offered two courses each. The largest college provider, Humberside College of Higher Education, an institution with many of the characteristics of a polytechnic, provided 10 courses in 1988/9.

The colleges are a diverse group of institutions. Nearly half of those involved in part-time first degree provision are former colleges of education which have diversified their provision over the last decade or so: for example, Edge Hill, South Glamorgan and West London. Most of the rest are multi-faculty institutions, such as Bolton, Ealing and Luton; or, in Scotland, polytechnic-type central institutions, such as Dundee, Glasgow and Napier. A few of the colleges, such as Doncaster and Norwich, focus at least as much on further as on higher education. There are also a limited number of monotechnics – institutions that specialize in one subject area – offering part-time provision. Examples of this group include Loughborough College of Art and Design, Moray House College of Education and the private sector Holborn Law Tutors. Finally, there are a few private correspondence colleges – the National Extension College, Rapid

Results College and Wolsey Hall – which offer part-time tuition for London external degrees.

Mode of provision

Table 10 summarizes the information on the timing or mode of provision by type of provider. Two-thirds of part-time first degree courses were available only by daytime study. In a handful of cases, this provision is organized on a block release basis, with students studying full-time for brief periods (cf. sandwich provision). A few courses are organized on a 'short day' basis (e.g. 10 a.m. to 3 p.m.), so as to appeal to women and others with young children or other domestic responsibilities (Michaels 1979). In other cases, particularly in the university sector, daytime provision may be shared with full-time students.

One-quarter of the courses were available by evening study, either on an evening-only basis (121 courses, 17%) or by day or evening (57, 8%). It should be noted, however, that evening study options tend to be underreported, so the actual proportions may be greater than recorded here. Evening study also tends to be more popular with part-time students: a survey of part-time students on CNAA-accredited first degree courses in 1985 found that 45% of respondents were studying on an evening-only basis (Bourner *et al.* 1990, chapter 1).

The remaining 62 courses, 9% of the total, were not offered by face-to-face study. Forty-five of these were examination-only courses made available through the University of London external degree system. The other 17 courses were offered by correspondence. Fourteen of these are provided by private correspondence colleges for London external degree students; and one each is provided by the Open University (the·largest course of all by far!), Reading University (in estate management) and University College Aberystwyth (a degree in the medium of Welsh).

When these figures are looked at in terms of providing institutions, it can be seen that the polytechnics offer only face-to-face study, mainly during the day (day-only courses account for 76% of their subtotal). The figures for the colleges broadly reflect the modal split for all institutions combined. Just over one-half,

Table 10 Numbers of part-time first degree courses by type of provider and mode of provision, United Kingdom, 1988/9.

Mode of provision	Type of provider University	Polytechnic	College	Total
Day only	118	254	100	472
Day or evening	19	26	12	57
Evening only	44	55	22	121
Correspondence	3	—	14	17
Examination	45	—	—	45
Total	229	335	148	712

52%, of the courses provided by the universities are offered on a daytime basis only. About one-fifth, 19%, are available in the evenings only (Birkbeck College accounts for most of these), and another fifth are provided by the University of London external degree system.

Where institutions offer both full-time and part-time courses in the same subject, and particularly where provision is organized on a modular or interdisciplinary basis, students may be able to alternate or mix periods of part-time and full-time study. Such arrangements are not common at present, but are likely to become of increasing significance (Hubert 1989).

Perhaps more surprisingly, no significant attempts have been made until now to mix elements of distance and face-to-face study, exploiting the advantages of each of these modes for part-time higher education in a flexible way (Tight 1987a). Since its foundation, the Open University has offered a predominantly distance form of study, with only limited opportunities for personal contact between students and tutors during tutorials and summer schools. The other institutions that offer part-time courses have focused almost exclusively on face-to-face tuition, with only limited resources made available to support self-study outside class. Some use has been made of Open University materials in other universities, polytechnics and colleges, but few collaborative developments have been pursued (Lee and Bibby 1986). The advent of the Open Polytechnic – which plans to offer courses with a roughly equal mix of face-to-face and distance study through the existing polytechnics – will, if it is successful, change this state of affairs over the next few years.

Subject availability

The variation in the availability of part-time first degree courses in different subjects is revealing. This is illustrated by Tables 11 and 12, which use a 26-subject classification adapted from the CNAA and USR schemes. The subjects are arranged in four 'faculty' groups: engineering, science, professional and arts/humanities/social sciences. These four groups account for 14%, 15%, 27% and 41% respectively of the total number of courses offered. A cross-faculty group, 'other/combined studies', makes up the remaining 3%. Engineering and science subjects are clearly underrepresented here by comparison with full-time provision (cf. Table 5).

The most prominent single subject amongst those identified, education, accounts for 71 courses or 10% of the total, with more than half of this number being provided by the colleges. This is indicative of a number of factors. First, a significant (though declining) proportion of part-time provision is orientated towards the teaching profession, both in education and in other subject specialisms. Second, teachers can still get work release and/or financial support from their employers relatively easily. Nevertheless, Table 12 does show that one-third of the courses in education are offered during the evening. And, third, education is of continuing importance as a subject of study in the, now diversified, ex-colleges of education.

Table 11 Numbers of part-time first degree courses by type of provider and subject area, United Kingdom, 1988/9.

	Type of provider			
Subject area	University	Polytechnic	College	Total
1 Architecture, building & surveying	4	32	4	40
2 Civil engineering	1	7	1	9
3 Electrical engineering	—	11	2	13
4 Materials studies	—	7	—	7
5 Mechanical engineering	—	11	3	14
6 Other/combined engineering	2	11	1	14
Subtotal: Engineering	7	79	11	97
7 Biological sciences	7	14	3	24
8 Chemistry	2	16	2	20
9 Computer studies	2	11	2	15
10 Mathematical sciences	4	8	1	13
11 Physics	4	6	—	10
12 Other/combined science	12	9	2	23
Subtotal: Science	31	64	10	105
13 Business studies	10	36	14	60
14 Education	11	22	38	71
15 Health studies	5	16	14	35
16 Law	1	17	9	27
Subtotal: Professional	27	91	75	193
17 Art, design, performing arts	10	10	10	30
18 English language/studies	13	7	2	22
19 West European languages/ studies	19	2	5	26
20 Other languages/studies	24	3	—	27
21 History	17	4	2	23
22 Philosophy/theology	21	—	2	23
23 Economics/geography/ politics	17	17	8	42
24 Psychology/sociology	17	16	2	35
25 Combined arts/humanities/ social sciences	17	35	15	67
Subtotal: Arts/humanities/ social sciences	155	94	46	295
26 Other/combined studies	9	7	6	22
Grand total	229	335	148	712

Relatively large numbers of courses are also available in the three other subjects identified in the professional group: business studies (60 courses, 8% of the total), health studies and law. These courses are mainly offered by the polytechnics; though in the case of law 9 of the 27 courses offered are for the London external degree. The courses in health studies are all in nursing or paramedical subjects; medicine as such is not available by part-time study.

Part-time provision in engineering and science subjects is also dominated by the polytechnics, with the architecture, building and surveying subject area being particularly strongly represented. The position is different in the arts, humanities and social sciences, which have been the main growth area in part-time degree provision in recent years. Here, the universities offer most of the provision available, except in the case of combined degrees.

Combined subject degrees are worthy of particular attention. They account for 18% of all the part-time courses available, with combined arts/humanities/ social sciences degrees alone accounting for 9%. They also tend to be larger courses, with all of the single-subject areas identified available for study in one or more of them. Many of these courses allow for considerable flexibility in patterns of study, with specialization possible in one, two or more subjects drawn from a wide range of options.

A rather different perspective is given by Table 12, which relates subject availability to mode of provision. In engineering, part-time provision is made almost exclusively during the day (95% of courses), and this predominance is only slightly less marked for science subjects (81%). By contrast, evening study is quite widely available in many arts, humanities, social sciences and pro- fessional subjects. In the case of law, day-only study accounts for just 6 out of 27 courses.

A comparison of the 'correspondence' and 'examination' columns of Table 12 indicates that correspondence courses are only provided for the more popular London external degrees, notably law, economics and some Western European languages. Home-based students are largely left to their own devices so far as the wide array of external syllabuses in other languages and literatures are concerned. These include such rarities as Bulgarian Language and Literature, and Pali (with Sanskrit), which are seldom offered by any institution even on a full-time basis.

Entry and exit arrangements

Almost all of the courses identified were geared to the traditional academic year, September/October to June/July, and have a long summer break. Only two courses, one of them the Open University's, were found to start at a different time: at the beginning of the calendar year. In the case of correspondence and examination-only provision, of course, this distinction is not important. A few courses advertise the fact that they do not have an intake every year, though this may well be true of others if recruitment is less than satisfactory.

Over three-quarters, 548, of part-time degree courses have entry

Table 12 Numbers of part-time first degree courses by mode of provision and subject area, United Kingdom, 1988/9.

Subject area	D	D/E	E	C	Ex	Total
			*Mode of provision***			
1 Architecture, building & surveying	38	1	—	1	—	40
2 Civil engineering	8	1	—	—	—	9
3 Electrical engineering	12	1	—	—	—	13
4 Materials studies	7	—	—	—	—	7
5 Mechanical engineering	14	—	—	—	—	14
6 Other/combined engineering	13	1	—	—	—	14
Subtotal: Engineering	92	4	—	1	—	97
7 Biological sciences	21	1	2	—	—	24
8 Chemistry	19	—	1	—	—	20
9 Computer studies	13	1	1	—	—	15
10 Mathematical sciences	7	2	4	—	—	13
11 Physics	7	1	2	—	—	10
12 Other/combined science	18	2	3	—	—	23
Subtotal: Science	85	7	13	—	—	105
13 Business studies	30	12	13	2	3	60
14 Education	46	2	23	—	—	71
15 Health studies	32	2	1	—	—	35
16 Law	6	3	14	3	1	27
Subtotal: Professional	114	19	52	5	4	193
17 Art, design, performing arts	19	2	6	1	2	30
18 English language/studies	13	2	5	1	1	22
19 West European languages/ studies	11	—	4	4	7	26
20 Other languages/studies	4	—	3	—	20	27
21 History	12	3	5	—	3	23
22 Philosophy/theology	15	1	3	1	3	23
23 Economics/geography/ politics	29	1	6	2	4	42
24 Psychology/sociology	18	5	11	—	1	35
25 Combined arts/humanities/ social sciences	44	9	13	1	—	67
Subtotal: Arts/humanities/ social sciences	165	23	56	10	41	295
26 Other/combined studies	16	4	1	1	—	22
Grand total	472	57	121	17	45	712

*D = day only; D/E = day or evening; E = evening only; C = correspondence; Ex = examination.

Table 13   Numbers of part-time first degree courses by faculty and entry level, United Kingdom, 1988/9.

Faculty area	A	H	D	I	N	Total
			*Entry level**			
Engineering	57	40	—	—	—	97
Science	79	26	—	—	—	105
Professional	99	3	2	89	—	193
Arts/humanities/						
social science	293	—	2	—	—	295
Other	20	—	1	—	1	22
Total	548	69	5	89	1	712

*A = A level; H = HNC/HND level; D = diploma; I = in-service; N = no qualifications required.

requirements which are expressed primarily in terms of A-level passes or their equivalent (see Table 13). By contrast, only one course, again the Open University's, is advertised as open to all adults whatever qualifications they might, or might not, have.

Of the other courses, 89, or 13% of the total, were designed to be taken in-service by people with appropriate work experience as well as qualifications. The majority of these, 67 in all, are in education, and are designed for teachers with a few years' experience. The others are in health studies, and are mainly intended for experienced nurses. A further 69 courses, 10% of the total, were geared to Higher National Diploma or Certificate (HND or HNC) entry. These courses are mostly in engineering, where they account for 41% of the courses on offer, and science subjects. The remaining five courses required specific professional qualifications or diplomas for entry, or were only available to part-time students after one year of full-time study.

Table 13 gives a somewhat misleading impression of entry qualifications, however, since it deals only with the standard requirements. Most of the institutions involved allow for the possibility of entry with non-standard qualifications, particularly for courses pitched at A-level or equivalent entry standard. Some institutions have introduced special schemes to attract students lacking the standard entry requirements (e.g. Percy 1988). In such cases, each applicant's maturity, experience, qualifications and ability to benefit from the course in question will be carefully assessed through interviews and/or written tests.

An increasing number of students who enter part-time higher education with non-standard qualifications now come through access courses (Tight 1987b; Woodrow 1988). Access courses have been around for at least two decades (Hutchinson and Hutchinson 1978), but have become widely available only in the last few years. Well over 500 such courses are now offered in the United Kingdom (Lucas and Ward 1985; ECCTIS 1989b). Access courses are designed to improve students' confidence, study skills and subject knowledge for entry to further education, higher education or employment. They typically involve up to a year or more of part-time study.

Despite these developments, the importance of non-standard entry should not be exaggerated. Until recently, only a dubious 4.5% of admissions to first degree courses accredited by the CNAA came into this category, and these students were concentrated in relatively few institutions (Evans 1984). Up until 1984, only 5% of the intake to the Polytechnic of North London's evening degree scheme came through its linked access course, though an additional 5% made use of the learning development units offered as part of the degree scheme (Johnson and Hall 1985). A survey of 55 CNAA-accredited part-time degree courses carried out in the mid-1980s found that only 15% had an associated access course, with a similar proportion claiming to offer the possibility of entry with advanced standing. Half, however, operated associate student schemes, enabling students to take individual modules of courses, and allowing them to enrol for the full course if their progress was satisfactory (Barnett 1987).

Eighty-seven of the part-time first degree courses identified in 1988/9, 12% of the total, only led to ordinary or pass degrees; at least in their part-time forms (see Table 14). Most of these pass degree courses are accredited by the CNAA. Most are in engineering and science subjects, where they account for nearly one-quarter of all the part-time courses provided. Full-time pass or general degree courses are widely available in the Scottish universities, and in a growing number of cases these have been made available to part-time students as well.

More than one-third, 261, of all the courses led only to an honours degree, and a further one-third, 248, led to either pass or honours degrees. In total, therefore, 84% of all part-time first degree courses only allow for their students achieving a full degree qualification at either pass or honours level. The possibility of students leaving their courses before completion with an intermediate certificate or diploma qualification is only allowed for in the

Table 14 Numbers of part-time first degree courses by faculty area and intermediate/end qualifications, United Kingdom, 1988/9.

| Faculty area | | Qualifications available* | | | | |
	Honours	Pass	Pass/ honours	One inter- mediate	Two inter- mediate	Total
Engineering	12	23	58	4	—	97
Science	15	26	41	15	8	105
Professional	78	15	75	16	9	193
Arts/humanities/ social science	155	16	69	29	26	295
Other	1	7	5	5	4	22
Total	261	87	248	69	47	712

* Honours = honours degree only available; Pass = pass/ordinary/general degree only available; Pass/Honours = pass and honours degrees available; One intermediate = one intermediate qualification (i.e. certificate or diploma) available in addition to pass and/or honours degree; Two intermediate = two intermediate qualifications (i.e. certificate and diploma) available in addition to pass and/or honours degree.

minority of cases: 116 courses, or 16% of the total. Almost half of those courses are in the arts, humanities, or social sciences.

In a few other cases where institutions offer 'parallel' free-standing certificate or diploma courses (such as for the Diploma in Higher Education – Bruce *et al.* 1989), course transfers to gain an intermediate qualification may also be possible. In the future, with more and more courses being organized on a modular basis, transfer between courses and/or institutions with credit is likely to become increasingly possible (CNAA 1987; Schuller *et al.* 1988).

Length and structure

The minimum registration period required to complete a full honours degree by part-time study varies between two and six years. The overall average of about 4.5 years is not that much longer than the full-time average. The maximum period allowed for completion may be very indefinite, notably for courses based on credit accumulation: the periods specified vary between six and ten years.

In a small but increasing number of cases, exemptions and credit given for previous study and/or experience may enable suitable students to complete a course in less than the minimum time specified. Minimum lengths of two or three years of attendance are common for in-service and post-HND/HNC courses. A preliminary year may be spent in preparatory study on the job in the former case. For post-A-level courses, four, five, or six years of study are the most common patterns.

The amount of contact and study time required by degree courses is also variable. The Robbins Committee and the UGC jointly examined this subject in the early 1960s (Committee on Higher Education 1963, appendices 2A and 2B; UGC 1964b). They found that the majority of part-time students who followed daytime courses attended for one whole day a week, while the most popular pattern for evening-only study was three evenings a week. In each case, the total weekly contact time would be about nine to twelve hours. Full-time university undergraduates, by contrast, spent an average of 14.8 hours a week in attendance; varying between 7.2 hours for humanities students at Oxbridge and 23.2 hours for pre-clinical medicine in Wales.

More recently, Bourner's 1985 survey of CNAA-accredited part-time degree courses found that students spent an average of 7.7 hours a week in course attendance, with an additional 9 hours in private study. There was an inverse relationship between the amount of time spent in attendance – which ranged from 5.1 hours for education students to 10.6 hours for engineers – and the time taken up by private study (Bourner *et al.* 1990, chapter 5). The Open University, for its part, assumes that students on full credit courses will spend 14–20 hours per week in study, and those on half credit courses 8–12 hours per week (Open University 1982).

In other words, there is considerable variability, and also something of an overlap in terms of study time between the least intensive full-time courses and the most intensive part-time ones. This makes a mockery of the neat financial distinction between full-time and part-time study drawn by the British government (see Chapter 1). In a sense, there is really no such thing as a full-time student. All students are effectively part-time, more or less. They vary in the time they devote to their studies, and to their other activities, but it would be difficult to find a student who genuinely devoted all of their waking hours to study.

Where the institution involved offers both part-time and full-time degree courses in the same subject, their structure tends to be broadly similar. In recent years, there have been a number of developments in course structures which, though they are applicable to full-time as well as part-time provision, are particularly pertinent to part-time and mature students (see also Chapter 1 and 7). The use of modular forms of provision – splitting courses up into discrete units of standard length, which can then be taken individually or combined in a variety of ways – and their extension through schemes of credit accumulation and transfer have already been mentioned (Toyne 1979). Such schemes have already been widely implemented in a number of institutions, such as Newcastle and Oxford Polytechnics (Slowey 1988; Watson *et al.* 1989; see also Banfield 1990).

Modularization can, of course, have disadvantages. It may, for example, reduce the coherence of the educational experience for both student and teacher if it is developed in an inappropriate fashion. But, for part-time students, the advantages will usually outweigh any disadvantages:

> Part-time and mature students can derive particular benefit from many of the key features of modular courses . . . including flexibility, wider access and credit accumulation and transfer. Part-time students are able to study at their own pace and to alter the amount of study they undertake by choice of suitable modules. Credit can be built up over time to achieve an award. This may be especially helpful to mature students with work and domestic responsibilities. It may also be helpful to mature students to be able to sample subjects of which they have limited experience and to delay final choices. Students may also move more easily between full-time and part-time modes within a modular structure.
>
> (Ram 1989, p. 12)

Another structural development of relevance here is independent learning, as practised at North East (now East) London Polytechnic and, to a lesser extent, at Lancaster University (Percy *et al.* 1980; Stephenson 1980; Cunningham 1981). These schemes allow both part-time and full-time students to put together their own programmes of study and assessment for recognized awards. The students make use of the courses and facilities available within and outside their institutions, and they are supported and advised in their studies by both staff and fellow students. Such a student-centred approach is particularly appropriate for non-traditional students with their widely varying experience and needs.

Contents, resources and teaching methods

There is, as some of the comments made in the previous section imply, a divergence of opinion amongst providers of part-time degrees regarding approaches to teaching and learning. On the one hand, there are those who argue that part-time provision should be equivalent in all respects – that is, in the breadth and depth of the syllabus, in the nature of the teaching methods used, in the relative freedom allowed to the individual student, and in the forms of assessment employed – to full-time provision if it is to be accepted as being of equal standard (see, for example, Smith 1983).

On the other hand, there are those who argue that education should be based primarily upon the needs and characteristics of the students concerned. Part-time and mature students – with their greater heterogeneity, experience and responsibility – typically demand and benefit from a different approach to teaching from that used with young, full-time school-leavers. This is not to say that student-centred approaches to learning are not appropriate to younger or full-time students, but to recognize their greater applicability to mature and part-time students (Entwistle 1983).

It might be expected that the latter view would be prevalent in institutions which deal only with part-time mature students, like Birkbeck College and the Open University. Even in these cases, however, there are strong pressures towards conformity and the maintenance of equivalence with full-time courses. Birkbeck College is restricted by its position within the federal University of London. The Open University has always been concerned to emphasize its equal standing with more conventional universities. It has, perhaps inevitably, given much more attention to the technology appropriate for mass distance education (e.g. Lewis 1971; Bates and Pugh 1975; Perry 1976; Marris 1977) than to the individual learning needs of its many students.

There are, of course, considerable practical problems in adapting higher education to the needs of part-time students, most notably the limited time which many of them have available for study (Trotman-Dickenson 1988; Smith 1989). Particular attention needs to be given, therefore, to ensuring that library (Payne 1983), computing, laboratory, counselling, catering and other facilities are available to part-time students when they want to make use of them. The provision of additional support through course guides and handouts and the use of appropriate information technology can supplement what the student re-ceives through direct staff contact. Unfortunately, there is plenty of evidence that these fairly obvious responses to the needs of part-time students have not always been made (Barnett 1987; Noble 1989; UCACE 1990).

Independent learning was mentioned in the previous section, and might equally well have been discussed here, since it impinges on course content and method as well as on structure. Experiential learning can be thought of as a related concept, though it is sometimes taken to refer to just the accreditation of prior experience and the learning derived from it (Evans 1983, 1988). In its more general sense, experiential learning has to do with the use of that experience as a basis for higher learning and the development of the higher education curriculum (Usher 1986; Weil and McGill 1989). Like independent learning, it appears to be of particular relevance to part-time higher education, since it builds on the links between higher education institutions and the employers and community organizations with which part-time students are involved through their work and other activities.

Location

One of the most interesting aspects of part-time first degree provision is the locational pattern of course availability. Given the massive investments which

Table 15 Numbers of part-time first degree courses and providers by regions and population, United Kingdom, 1988/9.

Region*	No. providers	No. courses	Population† (millions)	Courses/ million
1 Greater London	20	148	6.6	22.4
2 South-East England	14	51	5.3	9.6
3 North Thames	8	29	4.7	6.2
4 South-West England	6	34	4.3	8.0
5 East Anglia	4	12	2.4	5.0
6 East Midlands	8	51	3.2	15.7
7 West Midlands	8	68	5.1	13.3
8 Wales	5	10	2.8	3.6
9 Yorkshire & Humberside	11	58	4.8	12.1
10 North-West England	14	101	6.4	15.9
11 North England	6	36	3.1	11.7
12 Scotland	15	35	5.0	6.9
13 Northern Ireland	3	17	1.6	10.9
Total face-to-face	122	650	55.1	11.8
14 Correspondence/ examination	7§	62	—	—
Grand total	128	712	55.1	12.9

* The regions are as follows:
    South-East England = Hampshire, Isle of Wight, Kent, Surrey, East and West Sussex.
    North Thames = Bedford, Berkshire, Buckingham, Essex, Hertford, Oxford.
    South-West England = Avon, Cornwall, Devon, Dorset, Gloucester, Somerset, Wiltshire.
    East Anglia = Cambridge, Lincoln, Norfolk, Suffolk.
    East Midlands = Derby, Leicester, Northampton, Nottingham.
    West Midlands = Hereford & Worcester, Shropshire, Stafford, Warwick, West Midlands.
    Yorkshire & Humberside = Humberside, North, South and West Yorkshire.
    North-West England = Cheshire, Greater Manchester, Lancashire, Merseyside.
    North England = Cleveland, Cumbria, Durham, Northumberland, Tyne & Wear.
† Population figures are taken from the 1981 Census, 'usually resident population' (Office of Population Censuses and Surveys 1984).
§ One of the institutions counted as offering part-time face-to-face provision also offers a correspondence course.

have been made in student residences during the last forty years, location has come to be seen, falsely, as largely irrelevant for full-time students (McDowell 1981; Richardson 1981). This is obviously not the case for part-time face-to-face students, for whom physical accessibility is of paramount importance. Table 15 summarizes the spatial distribution of the 650 part-time face-to-face degree courses identified in terms of thirteen regions.

The greatest concentration of part-time degree study opportunities, 148 courses or 23% of all face-to-face provision, is in Greater London. On average, there are nearly twice as many courses available in Greater London as there are throughout the country as a whole. Of course, this is a rather simplistic way of looking at the matter, since these study opportunities are available to other than local residents. Indeed, provision in the two regions bordering London, South-East England and North Thames, is below average. Clearly, residents of Surrey and Buckinghamshire are, by and large, expected to travel into London (where they may also work) if they wish to attend a part-time degree course.

Outside the London area, there is above-average provision of part-time degree courses throughout the Midlands and the North of England. In some parts of these areas, providers are in competition with each other, and with the Open University, and potential students may have some choice between alternative courses (Overell 1984). In Wales, East Anglia and Scotland (see Gallacher *et al.* 1989), however, provision is well below average; with, for example, only 10 degree courses available on a part-time basis throughout the whole of Wales. In these regions, students will have little or no choice if they wish to study part-time for a degree: for most, the effective choice will be between the Open University and nothing. These patterns are largely confirmed if a more detailed analysis based upon student numbers rather than courses, and on counties and urban areas rather than regions, is carried out (see Tight 1987e and pp. 99–101 below).

There are a series of interrelated reasons for these variations in locational supply, of which actual demand is not the most significant. The most important explanatory factors appear to be institutional size, location and character. The role of the polytechnics is the key factor, as they are the institutions most likely to offer a range of part-time degree courses. All of the polytechnics are located in or near large urban areas; there are none in East Anglia. This is not the case for many universities and colleges, some of which were established at a time when there was a fashion for greenfield campuses and small-town sites. Institutions located outside the major conurbations are unlikely to recruit part-time face-to-face students in large numbers.

Costs

A number of economists have attempted to estimate the costs of different kinds of higher education provision, in order to provide the inputs necessary for comparative cost–benefit analyses (e.g. Selby Smith 1970; Wagner 1972, 1977; Laidlaw and Layard 1974.) Until recently, however, few have attempted to calculate the true costs associated with providing courses in specific subjects and by particular formats; or to relate these costs to the fees charged to students, and to national and institutional resourcing policies.

Institutions of higher education have, of course, long been aware that the costs of part-time provision can be treated in different ways. When part-time students are recruited in limited numbers to existing full-time courses, it may be most appropriate to treat them as a marginal cost. When free-standing part-time provision is offered, it needs to be costed on a more separate basis. A survey of 43 institutions that offered part-time advanced further education in vocational subjects in the mid-1980s, carried out by Her Majesty's Inspectorate (HMI), took the former approach in arguing for a modest expansion of provision: 'the major conclusion of this report is that increased enrolments on many courses could be accommodated at relatively marginal cost and with advantages for the quality of the education of the workforce in general' (Department of Education and Science 1985c, p. 34).

In a survey carried out at much the same time, Smith found that the fees charged to part-time degree students varied significantly between different institutions and sectors. They averaged £175 per year in polytechnics, £193 in colleges and £231 in universities (Smith 1987; Smith and Saunders 1989). Even more revealing, however, was the response when providers were asked about the estimated costs of provision per part-time student. The great majority of respondents – course tutors – admitted that they did not know, while those that claimed to know quoted widely differing figures: for example, £335 and £995 per student for two similar courses in the same subject. Smith concluded that a range of course resourcing models were in operation, the most popular of which, departmental fudge, was based largely on historical precedent and immediate needs.

Clearly, more work is needed in this area, both to increase understanding and to improve practice. Such work is already under way in many institutions, as new, more explicit and more competitive funding regimes take effect (see Chapter 9).

Sub-degree provision

Sub-degree or other advanced provision – that is, higher education provision that terminates at a level below the final part of a first degree course – takes different forms in the public (polytechnics and colleges) and university sectors (see Chapter 3).

In the public sector, sub-degree provision has two main elements: courses leading to Higher National Certificate (HNC) or Higher National Diploma (HND) qualifications, and those preparing students for the examinations of the various professional bodies (Cantor and Roberts 1986). Courses for HNCs and HNDs are validated in England, Wales and Northern Ireland by the Business and Technician Education Council (BTEC); and in Scotland by the Scottish Vocational Education Council (SCOTVEC). Professional courses are concentrated in the areas of accounting, administration, banking, commerce, management and other aspects of business studies; and, to a lesser extent, in other vocational areas (Jarvis 1983a). In addition, some courses are offered which lead to certificates or diplomas awarded by the polytechnics or colleges themselves. These are mainly in subject areas in which the institutions concerned have particular specialisms.

In the university sector, sub-degree provision is of less significance, being largely confined to the liberal adult education programmes organized by departments of extra-mural studies, adult education, or continuing education (Legge 1982). Not all universities have such departments, but most make some provision in this area. Unlike in the public sector, few of the courses offered lead to a formal qualification. Not surprisingly, therefore, this aspect of university provision is not given much prominence in the national statistics.

In this section of the chapter, rather than attempt a comprehensive analysis of part-time sub-degree provision, I shall focus on two areas. First, I will examine the dominant form of sub-degree provision in the polytechnics and colleges sector, HNC and HND courses. Second, by way of contrast, I will look at the position in the university sector as regards extra-mural or adult education provision.

Higher National Certificates/Diplomas

Unlike first degree courses, most of the courses that lead to an HNC or HND qualification are provided on a part-time basis. Indeed, the distinction between these two qualifications is largely based on the mode of study pursued. The HNC is the main part-time qualification route: it involves a course of study of less breadth than that for the HND, but of equal standard. In some cases, the HND may also be available by part-time study as a second stage, but it is usually available only on a full-time basis, while the HNC is seldom ever offered full-time. This arrangement – offering alternative part-time and full-time qualifications which, at least in theory, are of equivalent standing – is unusual, if not unique, in the British higher education system.

In total, 1506 part-time HNC/HND courses were offered by 316 institutions of higher education in the United Kingdom in the 1988/9 academic year (see Table 16). This information has been gathered in the same way as that for part-time first degrees, and the same reservations apply as to its absolute accuracy. There were more than twice as many part-time HNC/HND courses available as part-time first degree courses; and more than twice as many institutions were involved in their provision. And, as the student enrolment statistics indicate (see Table 4), these courses also tend to be significantly larger.

Over four-fifths, 83% or 1254, of these courses were offered by 287 colleges; with most of the balance, 245 courses or 16% of the total, provided by 28 of the 30 polytechnics. Only one university, Ulster, makes any provision in this area, and this is something of a historical anachronism. The largest single provider, Kirkcaldy College of Technology, offered 20 part-time HNC programmes.

Table 16 Numbers of part-time HNC/HND courses by type of provider, United Kingdom, 1988/9.

No. of courses	University	Type of provider Polytechnic	College	Total
1	—	1	61	62
2	—	—	55	55
3	—	3	44	47
4	—	2	22	24
5	—	2	19	21
6	—	3	26	29
7	1	—	6	7
8	—	3	12	15
9	—	2	12	14
10	—	3	8	11
11	—	—	6	6
12	—	2	6	8
13	—	2	5	7
14	—	—	2	2
15+	—	5	3	8
Total institutions	1	28	287	316
Total courses	7	245	1,254	1,506
Courses/institution	7.0	8.8	4.4	4.8

On average, the polytechnics offer twice as many part-time HNC/HND courses each as the colleges, with means of 8.8 and 4.4 courses per institution respectively. More than half of the colleges offered three courses or less. As in the case of part-time first degree provision, the college group includes a diverse collection of institutions, ranging from large polytechnic-type colleges to monotechnics specializing in one subject area. In this case, however, colleges whose main business is further rather than higher education form the dominant subgroup.

The main mode of provision for part-time HNC/HND courses, far more so than for part-time first degrees, is daytime study (Table 17). Three-quarters,

Table 17 Numbers of part-time HNC/HND courses by mode of provision, United Kingdom, 1988/9.

Mode of provision	No. of courses	Total %
Day only	1131	75
Day or evening	289	19
Evening only	19	1
Day or block release	28	2
Block release only	22	1
Day or correspondence	13	1
Correspondence only	4	0
Total	1,506	100

1131, of the courses offered were only available by this means. Courses are commonly organized on the basis of one full day (i.e. day *and* evening) of study per week, which normally involves day release from employment. Only one-fifth, 308, of all the courses were available by evening study, mostly as an option on the normal daytime pattern. Small numbers of courses were available by either block release or correspondence study.

The subject areas available for HNC/HND study are more restricted than those offered for first degrees. Provision is essentially confined to vocational subjects: engineering, applied science and business studies. HNC/HND courses are offered in only 16 of the 26 subject areas identified earlier in the chapter (Table 18; Cf. Table 11). The most prominent single subject amongst those identified, business studies, alone accounts for nearly one-fifth, 19%, of all the

Table 18   Numbers of part-time HNC/HND courses by subject area, United Kingdom, 1988/9.

Subject area	No. of courses	Total %
1 Architecture, building and surveying	228	15
2 Civil engineering	65	4
3 Electrical engineering	186	12
4 Materials studies	59	4
5 Mechanical engineering	200	13
6 Other/combined engineering	197	13
Subtotal: Engineering	935	62
7 Biological sciences	34	2
8 Chemistry	67	4
9 Computer studies	71	5
10 Mathematical sciences	11	1
11 Physics	21	1
12 Other/combined science	29	2
Subtotal: Science	233	15
13 Business studies	285	19
15 Health studies	36	2
16 Law	2	0
Subtotal: Professional	323	21
17 Art, design, performing arts	15	1
Subtotal: Arts/ humanities/ social sciences	15	1
Grand total	1,506	100

part-time courses on offer. If sub-degree courses leading to professional quali-fications were also included in this table, the dominance of this subject area would be even more apparent. Little provision is made at this level in this form in other professional areas.

Engineering as a whole accounts for nearly two-thirds, 62%, of all provision. Large numbers of part-time courses are offered in all of the major engineering disciplines: building services, building studies, civil engineering, electrical and electronic engineering, mechanical and production engineering, and motor vehicle engineering. Most of the remaining courses are in the applied sciences. The only HNC/HND courses offered in the arts, humanities, or social sciences are in the field of design.

The standard entry requirement for admission to an HNC/HND course is the possession of an Ordinary National Certificate (ONC) or Ordinary National Diploma (OND) in an appropriate subject. In some cases, other qualifications, including combinations of GCSE and A-level passes, may be acceptable. So far as exit arrangements are concerned, the great majority of the part-time courses considered, 1308 or 87%, only lead to the HNC qualification. Almost all of the remainder, 196 courses or 13% of the total, lead also to the HND, but two part-time courses are designed to lead to the HND qualification only. Part-time courses for the HND are concentrated in business studies, electrical engineer-ing, mechanical engineering and computer studies. As noted in the previous section, a significant number of part-time first degree courses in the engineering and applied science areas are designed for entry at HNC/HND level (see Table 13).

The length of HNC/HND courses is fairly standardized. Two years of part-time study are normally required to obtain an HNC (the same period of full-time study is required for the HND), with a further one or two years of part-time study needed for the HND where available. All courses are organized on a modular basis, with the contents of the modules agreed with either the BTEC or the SCOTVEC. This system is particularly well developed in Scotland, and it allows flexibility for both institutions and students. Within an institution, related courses may share modules in common, with some modules taught simultaneously to both full-time and part-time students. Students may opt to study specific modules or combinations of modules, and can gain credit for modules studied at other institutions.

Part-time HNC/HND courses are much more evenly distributed around the country than are part-time first degree courses (Table 19; cf. Table 15). This is not surprising given the larger number of courses on offer, and the greater number of institutions involved. In England, Wales and Northern Ireland, the number of courses on offer relative to the local population does not vary much from region to region. In all cases, provision is at or above the levels recorded for part-time degrees. Provision in Scotland is rather more extensive, reflecting its different educational system and validation arrangements, and probably also a greater degree of module-sharing between named courses.

As in the case of degree-level study, only limited information is available on the costs of providing part-time HNC/HND courses, and on the relative costs of

Table 19   Numbers of part-time HNC/HND courses and providers by regions and population, United Kingdom, 1988/9.

Region*	No. providers	No. courses	Population (millions)	Courses/ million
1 Greater London	39	147	6.6	22.3
2 South-East England	25	122	5.3	23.0
3 North Thames	31	129	4.7	27.4
4 South-West England	23	105	4.3	24.4
5 East Anglia	9	50	2.4	20.8
6 East Midlands	14	78	3.2	24.4
7 West Midlands	31	106	5.1	20.8
8 Wales	16	82	2.8	29.3
9 Yorkshire & Humberside	22	110	4.8	22.9
10 North-West England	33	174	6.4	27.2
11 North England	20	102	3.1	32.9
12 Scotland	40	250	5.0	50.0
13 Northern Ireland	11	47	1.6	29.4
Total face-to-face	312	1,502	55.1	27.3
14 Correspondence	4	4	—	—
Grand total	316	1,506	55.1	27.3

*For key to regions, see Table 15.

alternative forms of provision. A review carried out by the Association of Polytechnic Teachers in 1985 suggested that sub-degree provision was being subsidized to some extent by first degree provision (which tends to be better funded) in some institutions (Association of Polytechnic Teachers 1985). A more detailed examination of alternative modes of HNC provision was carried out in one institution, South West London College, in the late 1970s. This found that directed private study – that is, short periods of block release supported by correspondence study – was the cheapest form of part-time provision for the institution to make, and that evening courses were also less expensive than day release (Jones and Wylie 1979).

University extra-mural provision

This section is mainly based on the annual report of the Universities Council for Adult and Continuing Education (UCACE) for 1987/8, the existence of which makes the direct collection of data unnecessary (UCACE 1989). This report records a total of 11,542 extra-mural courses for that year. Compared to the figures quoted for part-time first degree and HNC/HND courses, this sounds like a great deal – and it is. But it has to be remembered that extra-mural courses are typically much shorter and less intensive, averaging about 25 hours in contact time and enrolling an average of 21 students each (ibid, tables 1, 4, 5).

The majority of these courses were organized by the extra-mural, adult education, or continuing education departments concerned (the names adopted vary) on their own, but some were run in conjunction with the local branch of the Workers' Educational Association (WEA). Twenty-nine of the 45 universities funded through the UFC made extra-mural provision in the year concerned. Nottingham University was the largest single provider, putting on a total of 864 courses, more than twice the average of 398 per institution.

Virtually all of the courses offered were part-time. Some 516 courses, 4% of the total, are actually classified in the report as full-time, but these are almost all short full-time courses lasting for a few days at most: in other words, they are, so far as this study is concerned, part-time. A larger proportion, 10% of the total, involved residential attendance for a short period, typically a weekend, a few days, or a week. Residential study is a feature upon which some adult educators place considerable stress (e.g. National Institute of Adult Continuing Education 1989).

The subjects available for study are summarized in Table 20 (cf. Tables 11 and 18). The arts, humanities and social sciences dominate, to a greater extent even than for part-time first degree provision, accounting for 7932 courses or 69% of the total. Most of the remaining courses were in science or professional subjects, which made up 16% and 11% of the total respectively. Only 346 courses were provided in the engineering area, a mere 3% of the total, and most of these were in one subject, planning. The most popular individual subject areas were history – with local history a notable specialism – and art, design and performing arts, which accounted for 18% and 14% respectively of the total courses.

This subject split is largely explained by the audience the courses are aimed at – adults with a limited spare-time interest in learning – and the restricted resources available for extra-mural provision. The entry requirements are also significant: no previous qualifications or specialist knowledge is normally asked for or needed. Indeed, many of those who provide extra-mural courses pride themselves on their responsiveness to the varying interests, experience and needs of their students. Curricula and teaching methods can often be adjusted as appropriate, though this is by no means standard practice (see, for example, Thompson 1980; Jarvis 1983b).

Only 696, or 6%, of the extra-mural courses provided in 1987/8 led to a named award, in the majority of cases a certificate or diploma awarded by the university or department concerned (ibid, table 7). Over one-third of the award-bearing courses, 269, were organized by just one university, London. The successful achievement of such an award is now increasingly accepted as a valid entry qualification for a related degree course. In some cases, advanced standing or credit exemptions may be granted as well.

Most extra-mural courses, 8498 or 74% of the total, involved non-consecutive attendance. Most of this subtotal, 5160 courses (45% of the total), lasted for one term or less; only 732 courses, principally those leading to named awards, lasted for more than one year. The balance, 3044 courses or 26% of the total, were organized on the basis of consecutive attendance, either part-time or full-time.

Table 20   Number of university continuing education courses by provider and subject area, United Kingdom, 1987/8.

Subject area	Extra-mural		Other	
	Courses	Total %	Courses	Total %
Subtotal: Engineering (1–6)	346	3	1,276	10
7 Biological sciences	682	6	126	1
8/11 Chemistry/physics	126	1	167	1
9/10 Computing/mathematics	473	4	441	3
12 Other/combined science	518	4	86	1
Subtotal: Science	1,799	16	820	6
13 Business studies	389	3	1,824	14
14 Education	512	4	1,934	14
15 Health studies	152	1	3,731	28
16 Law	171	1	447	3
Subtotal: Professional	1,224	11	7,936	59
17 Art, design, performing arts	1,666	14	324	2
18 English language/studies	1,128	10	500	4
19 West European languages/ studies	684	6	1,013	8
20 Other languages/studies	105	1	9	0
21 History	2,097	18	264	2
22 Philosophy/theology	475	4	100	1
23 Economics/geography/ politics	463	4	290	2
24 Psychology/sociology	1,052	9	372	3
25 Combined arts/humanities/ social sciences	262	2	361	3
Subtotal: Arts/humanities/ social sciences	7,932	69	3,233	24
26 Other/combined studies	241	2	162	1
Grand total	11,542	100	13,427	100

Source: Universities Council for Adult and Continuing Education 1989, table 6(a); Universities Statistical Record 1988b, table 18.

Here, the largest subgroup, 1506 courses (13% of the total), lasted for a single day; only 138 courses (1%) involved more than one week of consecutive attendance.

It is not possible to provide an analysis of the location of university extra-mural courses in a form directly comparable to Tables 15 and 19, because the departments concerned typically offer courses at a number of locations off-campus as well as at the university itself. In some cases, provision is made in adjacent counties, and at a considerable distance from the institution concerned. On average, there are 209 extra-mural courses available for every million residents throughout the country. This means that about 1 in every 230 people is enrolled on such a course during the year (not allowing for double-counting). The level of provision is highest in the East Midlands, where Leicester and Nottingham Universities both offer substantial programmes; and also, somewhat surprisingly, in Wales. Provision is lowest in East Anglia and the North of England.

Postgraduate provision

This section focuses on taught postgraduate courses, and does not consider research provision. This is not because part-time registration for research degrees is of no interest: though in some ways it is more flexible than taught courses are, it presents similar problems, so far as part-time provision is concerned, to other levels of study (see, for example, Rudd 1985, especially chapter 6). I am excluding it from consideration here because it is difficult to present information on research provision in a way comparable to the other data analysed in this chapter. Opportunities to engage in part-time research are widely available in many subjects, but they are not easily classified. For taught courses, however, information on availability is regularly published (Committee of Vice-Chancellors and Principals 1988, CNAA 1988c).

In 1988/9, there were a total of 1940 part-time taught postgraduate courses available in the United Kingdom at universities or in CNAA-accredited institutions. This is a larger figure than those for either part-time HNC/HND courses or part-time first degree courses. It should be noted, however, that this figure is not entirely comprehensive, since it excludes a few courses offered by colleges which are accredited by universities.

It is also subject to the reservations expressed earlier in this chapter with respect to other kinds of provision. The courses concerned vary considerably in the size of their recruitment. Some institutions specifically identify a series of course titles in a given field, while others offer a single course with appropriate specialisms available within it. Some of the courses identified may have folded or recruited no students in the year in question (a number operate on a biennial basis); others may have been overlooked. These deficiencies are likely to be relatively minor, though, and an analysis of the data presented provides a clear idea of the nature of part-time taught postgraduate provision.

Forty-five universities and 99 polytechnics and colleges were involved in this provision in 1988/9 (see Table 21). All but 2 – Cambridge and Oxford! – of the 45 universities funded through the UFC offer some part-time provision at this level. Two other universities – the Open University and Cranfield Institute of Technology – funded directly by the DES do so as well. All 30 polytechnics make some provision, together with 69 colleges accredited by the CNAA.

Whereas public sector institutions (and the Open University) dominate part-time provision at other levels, the universities account for the majority of

Table 21   Numbers of part-time taught postgraduate courses by type of provider, United Kingdom, 1988/9.

No. of courses	Type of provider		
	University	CNAA	Total
1	0	52	52
2	0	7	7
3	1	7	8
4	2	2	4
5	1	4	5
6	0	3	3
7	1	2	3
8	2	5	7
9	1	1	2
10	0	1	1
11	2	4	6
12	0	1	1
13	0	1	1
14	0	1	1
15+	35	8	43
Total institutions	45	99	144
Total courses	1,512	428	1,940
Courses/institution	33.6	4.3	13.5

part-time postgraduate provision. In 1988/9, they offered 1512 taught courses, or 78% of the total. The average university offered eight times as many part-time taught postgraduate courses as the average CNAA-accredited institution: while most of the latter offered only one course, most of the former offered 15 or more. One university, London, alone provided 320 part-time postgraduate courses, 16% of the total; and three others – Glasgow, Manchester and Wales – offered more than 70 each.

However, only a minority of these courses, 546 or 28% of the total, were offered solely on a part-time basis. The remainder could be studied either part-time or full-time, and usually mixed part-time and full-time students together. Most of these courses are taught during the daytime to suit the wishes of full-time students and staff: exclusively part-time courses are more commonly available by evening study. The courses offered by public sector institutions tend to be exclusively part-time: these account for 67% of their provision, but only 17% of that made by the universities.

By comparison, nearly three times as many courses were offered exclusively full-time: 1490 in the universities and 123 accredited by the CNAA. Nevertheless, there remains a rough balance at this level between part-time and full-time provision (see Table 4), with part-time provision of greater significance in the polytechnics and colleges, and full-time provision of greater significance in the universities.

A substantial number of part-time taught postgraduate courses are offered in most of the 26 subject areas which have been identified (see Table 22). Provision

Table 22   Numbers of part-time taught postgraduate courses by type of provider and subject area, United Kingdom, 1988/9.

Subject area	Type of provider University	CNAA	Total	%
1 Architecture, building and surveying	45	16	61	3
2 Civil engineering	46	2	48	2
3 Electrical engineering	47	12	59	3
4 Materials studies	6	3	9	0
5 Mechanical engineering	25	6	31	2
6 Other/combined engineering	45	22	67	3
Subtotal: Engineering	214	61	275	14
7 Biological sciences	24	14	38	2
8 Chemistry	16	11	27	1
9 Computer studies	31	12	43	2
10 Mathematical sciences	39	8	47	2
11 Physics	21	10	31	2
12 Other/combined science	28	5	33	2
Subtotal: Science	159	60	219	11
13 Business studies	108	148	256	13
14 Education	196	49	245	13
15 Health studies	112	13	125	6
16 Law	34	2	36	2
Subtotal: Professional	450	212	662	34
17 Art, design, performing arts	63	40	103	5
18 English language/studies	68	2	70	4
19 West European languages/ studies	79	3	82	4
20 Other languages/studies	79	3	82	4
21 History	76	13	89	5
22 Philosophy/theology	102	4	106	5
23 Economics/geography/ politics	114	6	120	6
24 Psychology/sociology	90	13	103	5
25 Combined arts/humanities/ social sciences	18	10	28	1
Subtotal: Arts/humanities/ social sciences	689	94	783	40
26 Other/combined studies	0	1	1	0
Grand total	1,512	428	1,940	100

is concentrated in the arts, humanities and social sciences (40% of the total number of courses), and in professional subjects (34%). The Engineering and science account for relatively small proportions of the total (14% and 11% respectively). The most important single subject areas identified are business studies and education, which each account for 13% of the total provision. In both of these areas, the client groups concerned have a tradition of engaging in part-time postgraduate study, frequently with support provided by their employers. The relative importance of education would be slightly increased if the part-time postgraduate courses provided by colleges, but accredited by universities rather than the CNAA, were included in this survey, since most of these are in this subject area.

This subject distribution partly reflects the tendency for science and engineering courses, particularly in the universities, to be offered mainly on a full-time basis (see also Lee *et al.* 1979). The majority of the taught postgraduate courses in these subjects – 57% in the case of engineering, 61% in science – are available only by full-time study. The reverse is true for professional subjects and the arts, humanities and social sciences, for which 64% and 59% respectively of taught postgraduate courses are offered on a part-time basis.

The standard entry requirement for undertaking a taught postgraduate course is, of course, as the term 'postgraduate' implies, the possession of a first degree of an appropriate standard or an equivalent qualification. In some professional subjects, such as business studies and education, relevant experience is at least as important. In other areas, such as some arts, humanities, or social science subjects, non-standard qualifications may be acceptable. As at first degree level, some providers have experimented with novel teaching methods or more flexible course structures, recognizing the greater maturity of their clients. Such developments have, however, been little studied or reported upon (see Hargreaves and Searle 1981; de Winter Hebron 1983a; Horner 1986).

Most part-time taught postgraduate courses, 1224 or 63% of the total, lead only to a Masters degree qualification (see Table 23). A further 403 courses, 21% of the total, can lead to either a Masters degree or a diploma. The distinction is usually that the Masters qualification involves slightly longer

Table 23   Numbers of part-time taught postgraduate courses by faculty area and end qualification, United Kingdom, 1988/9.

Faculty area	End qualification			
	Diploma	Dip/Masters	Masters	Total
Engineering	28	112	135	275
Science	20	67	132	219
Professional	202	105	355	662
Arts/humanities/social sciences	63	118	602	783
Other	0	1	0	1
Total	313	403	1,224	1,940

Table 24 Numbers of part-time taught postgraduate courses and providers by regions and population, United Kingdom, 1988/9.

Region*	Providers	Courses	Population (millions)	Courses/ million
1 Greater London	26	508	6.6	77.0
2 South-East England	11	126	5.3	23.8
3 North Thames	15	131	4.7	27.8
4 South-West England	13	64	4.3	14.9
5 East Anglia	6	21	2.4	8.8
6 East Midlands	7	96	3.2	30.0
7 West Midlands	12	147	5.1	28.8
8 Wales	5	79	2.8	28.2
9 Yorkshire & Humberside	12	180	4.8	37.5
10 North-West England	13	214	6.4	33.4
11 North England	5	68	3.1	21.9
12 Scotland	16	210	5.0	42.0
13 Northern Ireland	2	81	1.6	50.6
Total face-to-face	143	1,925	55.1	34.9
14 Correspondence	6†	15	—	—
Grand total	144	1,940	55.1	35.2

* For key to regions, see Table 15.
† Five of the institutions which offer correspondence courses also offer face-to-face provision.

study and includes a significant project or dissertation element. In some cases, lower entry requirements may be set for the diploma stream. The remaining courses, 313 or 16% of the total, lead only to a postgraduate diploma. Two-thirds of these are in professional subjects: indeed, 73 of them lead to the CNAA's Diploma in Management Studies (DMS) qualification.

Taught postgraduate courses are shorter than first degree and many sub-degree courses. While full-time taught postgraduate courses typically last for just one academic year, the part-time equivalent usually takes two years. This allows for cohorts of part-time and full-time students to be mixed together fairly conveniently, particularly where much of the second part-time year is taken up with project work. Some courses last longer – up to five years of part-time study in extreme cases – or permit students to take longer than the standard period over their studies.

The location of part-time taught postgraduate courses is summarized in Table 24. Part-time provision at this level is even more spatially concentrated than at first degree level (cf. Tables 15 and 19). More than a quarter of all provision, 508 courses, is to be found in the Greater London area. This region hosts nine times as many courses, relative to its resident population, as East Anglia, the region which is the poorest provided for. Above-average levels of provision are also made in Northern Ireland (concentrated in Belfast), Scotland (concentrated in Glasgow and, to a lesser extent, Edinburgh) and Yorkshire and Humberside (concentrated in Leeds and Sheffield). Indeed, more than half of all part-time taught postgraduate courses are to be found in just six metropolitan areas: London, Manchester, Glasgow, Belfast, Leeds and Birmingham. This concentration undoubtedly reflects the fact that postgraduate provision has an international as well as a national market.

Post-experience provision

Post-experience provision – that is, higher level short-course provision designed to update or extend the knowledge and skills of people with relevant work and educational experience – is an important and fast-growing aspect of British higher education. Particular attention has been given in recent years to its role as a link between, on the one hand, universities, polytechnics and colleges, and, on the other, industry, commerce and the professions (Connor and Wylie 1985; Department of Education and Science 1989a).

In spite of its increasing significance, post-experience provision has been little studied as yet. The available statistics are neither comprehensive nor entirely reliable. Given the nature of this provision, this state of affairs is not altogether surprising. A good deal of it is organized outside institutions of higher education – for example, by employers or professional bodies – and much of it is offered on a one-off basis. In this section, therefore, I will focus on the available information relating to established institutions of higher education, and, in particular, to the universities. Most polytechnics and colleges also offer a range of post-experience courses, but these are not recorded as such in the national statistics.

In 1987/8, according to the published statistics, a total of 13,427 post-experience courses were provided by universities in the United Kingdom (USR 1988b, table 18; UCACE 1989, table 1). These statistics are undoubtedly not a full record, and it should be noted that the two sources quoted organize them in rather different ways. The Open University is excluded from these figures, though it offers a range of short courses in the form of study packs; in 1987, 73,063 such packs were sold (Open University 1989, table 1).

Most, though not all, of the post-experience courses provided by the conventional universities were vocational in orientation. About one-fifth of them were provided by postgraduate medical or dental departments; the remainder, 10,552 courses, on which I will concentrate, were offered by other university departments. Like the extra-mural courses considered earlier in this chapter, the bulk of this provision was in the form of quite short courses. Non-medical post-experience courses averaged 34 hours in contact time, and enrolled a mean of 25 students each. One-third of these courses, 3577, involved full-time attendance for the period of study concerned; and nearly one-quarter, 2448, were organized on a residential basis (UCACE 1989, tables 1, 2 and 4).

In contrast to extra-mural courses, most post-experience courses, 8109 or 77% of the total, involved consecutive attendance. In one-third of these cases, the course only lasted for one day, and in two-thirds it lasted for three days or less. Rather surprisingly, given the frequently expressed unwillingness of employers to release their staff for more than a day or two at a time, one-eighth of these courses involved consecutive attendance over a period of 15 days or more. The remainder, 2443 courses or 23% of the total, were arranged by non-consecutive attendance, with nearly two-thirds of them lasting for one term or less. Only 8% of the courses led to a named award, either a university certificate or one awarded by an external body.

The subject split of university post-experience provision also contrasts sharply with that made by the extra-mural departments (see Table 20). The majority of the provision offered, 7936 courses or 59% of the total, is in professional subjects, clearly indicating its overriding vocational orientation. Over one-quarter of the total, which here includes the provision made by postgraduate medical and dental departments, is in just one subject area: health studies. This reflects the successful development by the health service of a well organized and funded system of continuing education during the period since it was nationalized. Business studies and education each account for 14% of the total provision. All in all, the subject distribution recorded here has more in common with that for postgraduate taught courses (cf. Table 22) than it has with extra-mural provision.

In the year in question, all 45 of the universities funded through the UFC made some non-medical post-experience provision, ranging from 807 courses at Manchester down to just 44 at Bath. Three other universities ran more than 500 courses: London, Edinburgh and Birmingham (ibid, table 1). Only 20 of these universities were involved in post-experience medical or dental provision, with more than one-fifth of these courses provided by one university, London (USR 1988b, table 18).

In the public sector, the CNAA accredits a growing range of courses which are best classified as post-experience. During the 1986/7 session, 97 courses were operated leading to its Diploma in Professional Studies qualification. Most of these courses, 90 in all, were in the field of education, with the remainder in nursing (CNAA 1988a, table 14). The Diploma in Management Studies (DMS), discussed in the previous section under postgraduate provision, might also have been considered here, as might the Certificate in Further Education. None of these are short courses, however: each requires up to two years of part-time study.

Conclusions

The analysis of part-time provision presented in this chapter largely confirms, but also considerably adds to, the brief statistical account given in Chapter 3. Four main conclusions may be drawn from this analysis.

First, and perhaps most obviously, there is a great deal of part-time higher education currently provided in the United Kingdom, and the indications are that it is of growing importance (see also Chapter 9). The characteristics of 712 part-time first degree courses, 1506 part-time HNC/HND courses, 11,542 university extra-mural courses, 1940 part-time taught postgraduate courses and 13,427 university post-experience courses have been examined in this chapter. And it should be remembered that this analysis has not been fully comprehensive, but has been limited to some extent by the information available. Taken together, these courses add up to a substantial body of provision, outweighing in sheer numbers the (admittedly better resourced) opportunities available for full-time study.

Second, many of the characteristics of part-time higher education provision vary significantly from level to level. Part-time first degree study, which is very limited when compared to full-time provision, is provided mainly by the public sector institutions and the Open University. The courses are mostly in the arts, humanities and social sciences, and in professional subject areas. These courses typically last for a minimum of four or five years. Provision is concentrated in Greater London, the Midlands and the North of England.

For HNC/HND qualifications, part-time study is the main route. These courses are offered almost exclusively by public sector institutions, and mainly by day release. They are confined to vocational subjects in the engineering, applied science and business studies areas. Part-time HNC courses typically last for two years, are organized on a modular basis, and are widely available throughout the country.

Part-time taught postgraduate courses are of similar length to HNC courses. They are also more widely available than part-time first degrees, but are similarly concentrated in the major metropolitan areas. Provision at this level is dominated by the universities, and is mostly offered in the daytime, with part-time and full-time students frequently mixed together. As at first degree level, the arts, humanities and social sciences, and the professional subjects account for the majority of the provision available.

The bulk of the extra-mural and post-experience provision made by the universities is in the form of short courses. Virtually all of these are effectively part-time. Extra-mural provision is primarily in the arts, humanities and social sciences, and is mostly taught by non-consecutive attendance over a term or less. Post-experience courses, by contrast, are mainly in professional subjects, and tend to involve consecutive attendance for one to three days.

Third, the characteristics of part-time courses tend to differ from those of comparable full-time provision, particularly when they are separately organized. These differences are clearest in the case of the length and structure of the courses concerned. Part-time study typically takes rather longer, but is more flexibly organized than full-time study. A partial exception to this conclusion is to be found at HNC/HND level. Here, the part-time route is of equal length and equivalent standard, but involves study of less breadth than the full-time route.

Other significant differences between part-time and full-time provision are less well documented. In many cases, it is evident that the contents of part-time courses, and the teaching and learning methods which they employ, take into account and make use of the greater maturity and experience typically possessed by part-time students. It is not clear, however, just how prevalent these practices are.

Fourth and finally, as the last comment indicates, it is apparent that more research needs to be carried out into the provision of part-time higher education. The areas requiring most study are the costs associated with different kinds of provision, and the different approaches to learning which they employ. The lack of information on these topics is not, however, confined to part-time provision, but extends throughout higher education as a whole.

6

Students and Clients

Introduction

This chapter, like the preceding one, aims to examine in rather more detail some of the issues which were briefly considered in Chapter 3. The focus of the last chapter was on the providers of part-time higher education, and on the characteristics of the provision they make. Here, the attention will be concentrated upon the students and clients of part-time higher education. As in the previous chapter, particular attention will be paid to those taking part-time first degrees, partly because this is the key level of provision in higher education, and partly because more information is available on those studying at this level.

I will begin by reviewing the existing sources of information on part-time higher education students: national surveys and statistics, institutional research and local studies. This review will serve to illustrate the heterogeneity of the users of part-time higher education, the breadth of information available on them, and its limitations. This information will then be systematically analysed in the main body of the chapter in terms of the following key user characteristics:

- age, sex and other demographic characteristics;
- social background;
- previous educational experience and qualifications;
- motivation;
- employment and employers;
- location;
- expenditure;
- reactions to courses;
- educational performance.

Where possible and appropriate, information on part-time students will be compared with that for full-time students. Some general conclusions will be drawn at the end of the chapter.

Sources of information

National surveys and statistics

The national statistics available on the characteristics of part-time higher education students – from sources such as the CNAA, the DES and the USR – have already been referred to in Chapter 3. These statistics, and the various analyses based upon them (e.g. Farrant 1981), are of limited use for this chapter. They provide good basic information on the numbers of students, their sex and the type of course and qualification they are pursuing, and give some data on their age and location. They do not, however, enable any useful insights to be drawn into the backgrounds, lives, activities, aspirations and experiences of the students concerned.

It is fortunate, therefore, that a series of surveys and studies have been undertaken during the last two decades which fill in many of these deficiencies, and permit a more rounded picture of the users of part-time higher education to emerge. These surveys have tended to focus on different levels and modes of study, or on particular sectors or subject areas. Four main clusters of relevant research will be briefly described.

First, the most useful general source of information on part-time first degree students is the survey of 2876 such students on CNAA-accredited courses carried out by Bourner and his colleagues in 1985 (Bourner *et al* 1988, 1991). This provides a great deal of pertinent data on students' demographic, social and educational characteristics; and on their motivation, experience of and satisfaction with their courses. Comparisons are made between the face-to-face students included in the survey and those studying at a distance with the Open University.

Bourner's study can be supplemented by a number of others. Historically, it may be related to earlier work by Whitburn and others, who surveyed 9035 students in 28 polytechnics in 1972/3 (Whitburn *et al.* 1976). Their study allows comparisons to be made between the characteristics of part-time and full-time students. Spatially, Bourner's work is partly complemented for Scotland by that of Gallacher and his colleagues (Gallacher *et al.* 1989). They provide data on the demographic, social and educational characteristics of part-time degree students in 1987/8. And, in terms of level, the CNAA study can be compared with the reports on advanced further education in England and Wales prepared by Her Majesty's Inspectorate (HMI). These give general details of students' characteristics and performance, and offer insights regarding links with employers and other local organizations (DES 1985c).

The second cluster of relevant research centres on postgraduate students, and is mainly associated with the work of Rudd and his colleagues. Two surveys are of particular interest here: the first carried out in the early 1970s and involving about 240 part-time postgraduates; the second, in the late 1970s, involving 507 science and technology students (Rudd and Simpson 1975; Lee *et al.* 1979). Together, these surveys give a useful picture of the characteristics, motivations, employment and performance of the students concerned. A more recent study provides some supplementary information, notably regarding financial aspects of study (Roweth 1987).

Third, there is a distinct research literature relating to correspondence and distance study. Glatter and his colleagues surveyed 4942 correspondence students who enrolled for selected London external degrees and professional qualifications in 1967. They focused on the students' background, experience and performance, and carried out follow-up surveys at later dates (Glatter *et al.* 1971; Harris 1972). Since then, British research in this area has concentrated almost exclusively on a single institution, the Open University, which is discussed in the next section.

Fourth, and included here partly to provide a more general context, there are a series of studies dealing with adult education in general. Four national surveys carried out during the last two decades are of especial interest here (National Institute of Adult Education 1970; Advisory Council for Adult and Continuing Education 1982b; Munn and MacDonald 1987; Woodley *et al.* 1987). These surveys can be complemented by more detailed analyses of the position of adult students in higher education (e.g. Jones and Williams 1979; Squires 1981).

Institutional and local studies

The Open University is pre-eminent so far as institutional research into part-time higher education in the United Kingdom is concerned. Its latest annual statistical report, for 1987 (Open University 1989), provides information on 89,491 undergraduate, postgraduate, associate and short-course students. Much relevant data is included on their demographic, educational and employment characteristics, and on their location. This data is effectively complemented by internal reports on, for example, why people choose to study with the Open University, how they organize their studies and how they progress (e.g. McIntosh *et al.* 1976, 1980; Woodley and Parlett 1983).

The other British institution most closely associated with part-time higher education is Birkbeck College, part of the University of London. It is much smaller than the Open University, with 2716 students registered in 1987, and has not undertaken institutional research on anything like the same scale. Useful information on its students' demographic characteristics, occupations and performance is, however, available from college and university sources (e.g. Academic Advisory Committee on Birkbeck College 1967; Birkbeck College 1989).

The Polytechnic of North London is also located in the inner London area, and is increasingly in competition with Birkbeck College for part-time students. An evening degree scheme was established here in 1979, and this now has several hundred students enrolled. A report on the scheme published in 1985 contains an extensive analysis of 672 of its students. Information is provided on their demographic, educational and employment characteristics, on their aims and expectations, and on their subsequent experience of study (Johnson and Hall 1985; see also Ashman and George 1980).

Outside London, there are two recent institutional studies of particular relevance. A 1984 study at Sheffield City Polytechnic contains an analysis of 5101 mature students, 72% of whom were studying on a part-time basis. The study focuses on their perceptions and experiences of higher education and on how the institution responds to them (Johnston and Bailey 1984). A study carried out at the University of Ulster also allows comparisons to be made between part-time and full-time students. It provides information on student motivations and performance, and on their attitudes to the provision offered by the institution (Woodward *et al.* 1985; see also Penhallurick 1988).

Other studies of part-time students which will be discussed in this chapter are of more limited application, referring to single courses or small groups of students. Researchers at Newcastle Polytechnic have studied part-time students at a number of levels: on the associate student scheme at undergraduate level, and on postgraduate and post-experience courses in management (de Winter Hebron 1983a, 1983b; Slowey 1988). In London, reports have also been produced on part-time degree students at Goldsmiths' College (Vinegrad 1979, 1980; Caulcott 1983) and Middlesex Polytechnic (Bourner 1983).

As in the case of the national studies referred to, these institutional and local studies can also be usefully supplemented by reference to related analyses of adult students in higher education (e.g. Roderick *et al.* 1981, 1982; Smithers and Griffin 1986a).

User characteristics

Demographic characteristics

The national statistics analysed in Chapter 3 showed that, in 1986/7, 38% of part-time higher education students were women, compared to 44% of full-time students. In terms of age, only 14% of part-time students were aged 20 years or less, with 67% aged 25 years or more; compared to proportions of 54% and 17% respectively for full-time students. Similar figures were reported for other Western developed nations in Chapter 4.

These statistics are confirmed and considerably augmented by Bourner's 1985 survey of CNAA part-time first degree students. His respondents had a mean age of 30 years: 47% were aged 20–29 years, 35% were 30–39 and 14% were 40–49. Nearly two-thirds, 65%, were male. The majority, 60%, of respondents were married, and over 40% had children. Both age and gender varied significantly with the subject studied (see Table 25). The percentage of students aged under 30 years rose to over 90% in the cases of chemistry and quantity surveying, but fell to 11% for education and humanities. Men dominated all the engineering subjects, accounting for at least 95% of students in each case, but were in the minority for social studies (38% of students) and humanities (29% of students – Bourner *et al.* 1991, chapter 2).

Open University students, by contrast, tend to be older and are more commonly female. The 1987 statistics show that 19% of their undergraduates

Table 25   CNAA part-time first degree students by subject, age and gender (1985 survey data).*

Subject	Under 30 (%)	Women (%)
Quantity surveying	93	5
Electrical/electronic engineering	70	3
Metallurgy/materials studies	82	4
Mechanical engineering	66	2
Other engineering	66	1
Biological sciences	83	61
Chemistry	92	21
Computer studies	52	25
Mathematics	35	31
Physics	82	8
Business studies	51	33
Education	11	54
Law	31	39
Art/design	27	41
Humanities	11	71
Social studies	27	62
All subjects	47	35

*The subject classification used in this table is analogous to, but not identical with, that used in Chapter 5 (see Tables 11, 12, 18 and 20).
Source: Bourner *et al.* 1991, chapter 2.

were aged 21–29 years; 44% were 30–39, 23% were 40–49 and 13% were aged 50 years or more. Nearly half, 46%, were women; which represents a significant increase from 27% in 1971, the first year of the University's operation. More than half, 53%, of the Open University's associate students – those taking a single undergraduate course rather than a full degree – were women. As with the courses accredited by the CNAA, gender was closely linked to the subject studied. The proportion of female students taking undergraduate-level courses in the University's faculties varied from 16% in technology to 68% in education (McIntosh *et al.* 1976, p. 77; Open University 1989, tables 4 and 7).

Other studies confirm that the demographic characteristics of part-time first degree students vary widely from course to course. Gallacher and his colleagues found that the proportion of women on the four Scottish degree courses they examined varied from 58% to 77%. Age was a much more variable factor. On a life sciences course, 92% of the students were aged 30 years or less, compared to only 11% on an arts and social sciences degree. The proportions who were married ranged from 32% to 73%, and those who had children from 12% to 58% (Gallacher *et al.* 1989, pp. 50–52).

The majority, 54%, of the students who enrolled on the Polytechnic of North London evening degree scheme were female. This percentage varied between 69% for English studies and 24% for mathematical studies. Just over half, 51%, were aged 30 years or less on entry, with a further 41% aged 31 to 45 years, and an overall mean age of 32 years (Johnson and Hall 1985, p. 8). Vinegrad, to give one further example, found that 52% of the 347 students who had taken the part-time psychology degree at Goldsmiths' College were men. The same proportion were aged between 20 and 29 years on entry, with a further 34% aged between 30 and 39 years, and 11% aged between 40 and 49 years (Vinegrad 1980, p. 148).

Part-time students taking sub-degree courses tend to be younger than those on degree courses, with the majority aged between 18 and 25 years old (Department of Education and Science 1985c, p. 7). This is mainly because of the lack of support available to older students from their employers. The balance between male and female students again varies widely:

> The proportion of women students on courses usually reflected their relative numbers in the associated occupational groups. For example, only 10 of 700 students on the BTEC higher certificate courses in engineering in a group of Midland colleges were female. On the other hand an increasing number of women are undertaking business studies and construction courses. In one course leading to the Institute of Housing qualification, 50% of the students were female. Nursing courses continue to attract a predominantly female enrolment.
>
> (ibid, p. 8)

At postgraduate level, the 1979 survey carried out by Lee *et al.* found that their respondents were relatively young, with 60% aged 30 years or less. This is largely explained by the restriction of their survey to science and technology subjects, with men making up 88% of the sample. The age distribution of students differed little between taught Masters, M.Phil. and Ph.D. courses' qualifications. Nearly three-quarters, 73%, of the respondents were married (Lee *et al.* 1979, pp. 36–7, tables 25–7). The earlier study of graduate students in all subjects, carried out by Rudd and Simpson, found that 48% of part-time postgraduates were aged 29 years or less, compared to 88% of full-timers (Rudd and Simpson, 1975, p. 130).

Social background

There is a considerable sociological literature dealing with the social or class background of those participating in part-time further and higher education (see, for example: Cotgrove 1958; Hordley and Lee 1970; Hopper and Osborn 1975; Venables 1975; Raffe 1979). Since the Second World War, it has been widely recognized that there are two main routes into and through further and higher education. There is the conventional full-time route through A-level study, leading from independent or selective schools to universities. And there is the alternative part-time route, involving vocational study in further education institutions. Much of the debate in the literature has focused on whether the existence of this alternative route has enabled significant numbers of students from working-class backgrounds to aspire to and benefit from higher education.

It is worth quoting from two of the more recent analyses of this issue:

Looked at in inflow terms, the university is dominantly a service-class institution, part-time further education dominantly working class, and the college of education more evenly based but with its typical student from the intermediate class.

(Halsey *et al.* 1980, p. 183)

Fundamentally, part-time education does not provide an alternative route in either the educational or the social sense, or in the broader sense which takes account of the fact that those disadvantaged in terms of class background are also more likely to attend non-selective schools and to leave school with low levels of qualification.

(Blackburn *et al.* 1980, p. 613)

One conclusion which may be drawn from these studies is that, although the part-time route enables many people to participate in further and higher education who would not otherwise be able to do so, it offers rather restricted opportunities. These opportunities tend to be most heavily exploited by those who are from middle-class backgrounds or are seeking middle-class status. It may be that higher education, in its present form, is essentially a middle-class activity (see also Chapter 8).

Are these conclusions confirmed by the various studies of part-time higher education which have been referred to? Bourner's survey of part-time first degree students on CNAA-accredited courses found that 73% of respondents had entered non-manual employment immediately after finishing their full-time education. By comparison, only 55% of their fathers and 57% of their mothers who were in employment could be so categorized. By the time of the survey, there had been considerable occupational movement, with 92% of the respondents then in non-manual employment. Bourner concluded that:

The findings of this study are consistent with a picture in which taking a CNAA part-time degree course is part of a process of upward social and economic mobility. There is also a suggestion in the findings that a significant proportion of the part-time students are in families in which continuing education is perceived as a route to enhanced economic life chances and that the students were continuing a process of upward socio-economic mobility started by their parents.

(Bourner *et al.* 1988, p. 7)

Gallacher and his colleagues, in their study of Scottish part-time degree students, provide further supporting evidence. They found that, whereas 37% of their sample indicated that their fathers were in non-manual occupations, 83% of the respondents had initially entered non-manual occupations and 93% were in such occupations at the time of the survey (Gallacher *et al.* 1989, tables 6.8 to 6.10). Previous research on part-time degree students studying at polytechnics and with the Open University confirms these trends:

Whereas 39% of Open University students have fathers whose occupations were 'middle-class', this increased to 90% of students when their present occupations were considered. Therefore, while the Open University is undoubtedly used as a vehicle for enhancing upward social mobility, it is obvious that its students have already displayed a considerable degree of upward mobility by the time they enrol on their course of study. The same (albeit to a slightly lesser extent) appears to be true of polytechnic part-time students: whereas 57% of them had fathers in occupational class 1, 2 or 3 [i.e. non-manual occupations], 76% of them were themselves in class 1 to 3 occupations. Only a small percentage (17%) of the part-time students could, therefore, be considered to be 'working class' by the time they began their course of study, whereas use of father's occupation as a basis of classification would have indicated a higher figure of 34%.

(Whitburn *et al.* 1976, pp. 113–14; quoting figures from
McIntosh 1974, p. 61)

A similar pattern of dominance by the middle class has been found in studies of full-time mature students (see, for example, Whitburn *et al.* 1976, pp. 127–9; Smithers and Robinson 1989, table 2.5).

Many part-time first degree students have used the teaching profession as a route towards upward mobility. There are indications that this strategy – coupled with the tendency for teachers to engage in part-time study throughout their careers – has a significant impact at postgraduate level as well. Rudd and Simpson, in their study in the early 1970s, found that 71% of their part-time postgraduate respondents were teachers. Less than one-half, 44%, had fathers who were in clerical or skilled manual occupations. And only one in ten had a graduate parent, compared to a proportion of one in four for full-time post-graduate students (Rudd and Simpson 1975, p. 130).

Previous educational experience and qualifications

Bourner's survey of part-time CNAA degree students found that they tended to leave school at a relatively early age, but that they subsequently made consider-able use of part-time and, to a lesser extent, full-time educational opportunities. Nearly half, 47%, had left school aged 16 years or younger, though only 27% had completed their full-time initial education by that age. Nearly two-thirds, 65%, undertook some form of part-time study after completing their full-time initial education and before starting their part-time degree course. Hence, though only 30% had two A levels or their equivalent – that is, the standard entry requirement for a degree course – at the time they left school, 83% had gained such qualifications before they started their degree courses (Bourner *et al.* 1991, chapter 2).

These patterns are being repeated now. A recent study of young people's intentions to enter higher education found that:

One in two qualified boys who had taken A levels but were not in full-time higher education were either resitting exams or studying part-time whereas the proportion of qualified girls studying part-time or resitting exams was

Table 26   CNAA and Open University part-time first degree students by level of highest previous qualification.*

Qualification	A/H	Soc	Ed	Sci	Eng	Bus	Total	Open Univ.
			CNAA†					
Postgraduate	4	6	2	1	1	2	2	2
First degree	10	9	3	10	3	2	6	8
Professional (degree or above)	6	12	4	4	0	6	5	3
Univ/CNAA Cert/Dip	5	4	7	2	1	1	3	4
Teaching Cert/Dip	29	6	75	4	1	5	15	13
HNC/HND	2	5	1	57	72	28	34	11
Professional (sub-degree)	4	11	6	2	2	8	5	5
A level(s)/Higher(s)	18	24	1	12	14	24	16	17
ONC/OND	4	5	0	3	3	8	4	8
O level(s)	10	11	0	1	0	9	5	20
Other/none	9	8	1	3	4	7	5	7
Totals	100	100	100	100	100	100	100	100

Sources: Bourner *et al.* 1991, chapter 2 (1985 CNAA survey data); Open University 1989, table 2 (1987 data).
* All figures are column percentages.
† A/H = Arts/Humanities;   Soc = Social   Studies;   Ed = Education;   Sci = Science;   Eng = Engineering; Bus = Business Studies.

even higher – almost two out of every three girls . . . One in four said that the part-time course would help them qualify for a higher education course. More BTEC/OND students than those who had studied A levels were pursuing higher education qualifications on a part-time basis.

(Redpath and Harvey 1987, p. 2)

At the time they began their degree courses, more than one-third, 34%, of Bourner's sample were qualified to HNC/HND level: these students were mainly enrolled for degrees in engineering or science (see Table 26). A significant minority, 13%, were 'over-qualified', already possessing qualifications at or above degree level. One-tenth had no qualifications at all, or only O levels – they were mainly enrolled in arts, humanities, social studies, or business studies courses. Three-quarters of those enrolling on part-time degree courses in education had a teacher's certificate or diploma.

These findings parallel the description given in Chapter 5 of the characteristics of part-time degree provision. They also confirm the arguments in the preceding section regarding the importance of the alternative part-time route to and through further and higher education. And they are largely confirmed by the work of other researchers, though variations between courses and providers are also apparent.

Johnson and Hall, for example, in their study of enrolments on the Polytechnic of North London evening degree scheme, found that their students tended to be better educated than Bourner's more general sample. The majority, 60%, had had at least three years of full-time education after reaching the age of 16 years. On entry, 23% of their students already had a first degree, its equivalent, or a higher qualification, and another 23% had a diploma or a professional qualification (Johnson and Hall 1985, pp. 10–12). Slowey, in a study of associate students at Newcastle Polytechnic, found that 63% of entrants had qualifications above A-level standard, and that a further 15% had one or more A levels (Slowey 1988, pp. 312–13). The study of Scottish part-time degree students carried out by Gallacher and his associates found that half of their sample had left school with at least the minimum higher-education entry requirements. Nearly three-quarters, 74%, obtained such qualifications after leaving school (Gallacher *et al.* 1989, pp. 53–5).

The Open University, of course, practises a policy of open entry for students on a first-come, first-served basis. It might be expected, therefore, that its students would have fewer qualifications when compared to those taking part-time face-to-face degrees. The difference is not, however, that great (see Table 26). In 1987, only 5% of its total undergraduate and associate student population possessed no formal educational qualifications on entry. The majority, 70%, had higher education entry qualifications, and 13% already had degrees or postgraduate qualifications (Open University 1989, table 2).

Full-time mature students have broadly similar educational backgrounds (see, for example: Whitburn *et al.* 1976, chapter 6; Roderick *et al.* 1981, chapter 8).

At postgraduate level, the great majority of entrants naturally have a first degree, its equivalent, or higher level qualifications. Lee and her colleagues, in their study of part-time science and technology postgraduates, found that 81% had first degrees. All had at least one tertiary level qualification, with nearly two-thirds, 61%, having more than one such qualification and 18% having three or more (Lee *et al.* 1979, p. 39, table 37).

Motivation

Bourner's study found that the most important motivation of part-time degree students was 'to improve their career prospects', which was mentioned by 76% of respondents as a very important aim. Overall, work-related aims predominated, with subject-related and personal development aims assuming a lesser importance, though they were still highly significant (Bourner *et al.* 1991, chapter 4). These findings are confirmed by a recent survey of adults in all kinds of formal education:

> Two out of every three students taking qualifying courses are studying for instrumental reasons, mainly connected with career improvement. One in six are aiming for 'self-development' and a similar-sized group are primarily interested in the subject matter itself.
>
> (Woodley *et al.* 1987, p. 170)

The reasons given by part-time students for studying part-time rather than full-time, for studying at one institution rather than another, and for taking a particular course, are related to their general motivations and tend to be pragmatic. Part-time courses are seen as being much more convenient when work, domestic and other responsibilities have to be taken into account. In Bourner's study, 93% of respondents identified 'I could study without giving up my job/career' as a very important factor in their choice of course. More than one-half, 55%, similarly noted 'the pattern of attendance fitted in with my domestic responsibilities' (Bourner *et al.* 1991, chapter 4). For the majority of part-time students, full-time study is clearly not a realistic alternative in terms of the time, cost, or dislocation involved (cf. Advisory Council for Adult and Continuing Education 1982a, chapter 4).

Bourner's study also revealed a surprising lack of awareness of part-time study opportunities amongst those who took advantage of them. About three-quarters of those surveyed had been unaware of the course on which they enrolled for more than two years prior to their enrolment. Nearly 80% had rejected the alternative of enrolling with the Open University because they wanted face-to-face tuition, though half expressed an interest in studying partly by distance means (Bourner *et al* 1991, chapters 4 and 5). Many of those who have enquired of, but not enrolled at, the Open University, or who have declined the offer of a place, indicate that they have opted to study at another institution: that is, face-to-face (Woodley 1978).

These attitudes are reflected or reversed in the responses of those studying at a distance. For example, Glatter's 1967 study of correspondence students found that they opted for this format because it fitted in with their other responsibilities. It also offered needed study support when attending classes was not a realistic possibility for reasons of time or cost (Glatter *et al.* 1971, pp. 78–83).

At postgraduate level, Rudd and Simpson's survey found that the reasons given for undertaking part-time study tended to have at least as much to do with subject interest or personal development as with employment. Nearly half, 48%, of their respondents cited interest in or enjoyment of the subject or of research; this proportion rose to 57% for Ph.D. students. Over one-third, 36% (61% of postgraduate diploma students), mentioned better pay or promotion prospects. Rather surprisingly, only 13% (17% of Ph.D. students) mentioned preparation for a university career as a reason, although this is often regarded as a primary aim of postgraduate study (Rudd and Simpson 1975, pp. 132–4).

Employment and employers

Data on the occupations of part-time higher education students confirms many of the conclusions reached in the preceding sections: that these students are predominantly middle-class, that most of them are studying part-time because they are employed, and that many of them are studying subjects closely related to their jobs.

While significant numbers of part-time students on some courses are unemployed, overall they are a small minority. Unemployed people can rarely
afford to participate in part-time higher education, and may find themselves
debarred from receiving unemployment benefit if they do so. Those that are
able to enrol (e.g. those who have a supportive spouse) frequently do so to
improve their chances of securing employment, of course, very often in the
subject they are studying.

Gallacher and his colleagues, for example, found that 85% of the Scottish
part-time degree students they surveyed were in full-time employment, with a
further 8% employed part-time. Only 4% gave their occupation as housework –
though on one of the courses surveyed the proportion was 32% – while the
remaining 3% were described as unemployed, disabled, or retired (Gallacher
et al. 1989, pp. 55, 59).

Birkbeck College enrolled 370 new entrants to its part-time first degree
courses in 1987 (see Table 27). Of this total, 91% were in employment, the great
majority of them on a full-time basis. The most popular occupational groups
recorded are university, civil service, or local government administration (22%

Table 27 Occupations of new entrants to Birkbeck College, 1987/8.*

Occupational group	First degree	Taught postgraduate	Research degree
Schoolteachers	9	9	7
Lecturers	1	3	11
Research assistants	3	3	3
Computer programmers, systems analysts	5	8	3
Technicians, draughtsmen, operators	9	6	6
University/civil service/ local government admin.	22	19	7
Hospital, police, social service	6	7	3
Professional, arts, journalism	10	13	6
Business executive and clerical staff	14	11	6
Sales and service staff	7	1	1
Industrial workers	5	2	0
Parental responsibilities	4	2	3
Retired	1	0	1
Unemployed	4	3	3
Full-time students	0	14	41
Totals	100	100	100
Number of new entrants	370	562	116

Source: Birkbeck College 1989, p. 200.
* Figures are percentages of column totals.

of the total), business executive and clerical staff (14%), professional, arts and journalism (10%), schoolteachers (9%) and technicians (9%). Over the period since the Second World War, there has been a significant change in this recruitment pattern. The numbers of teachers and lecturers enrolled have declined sharply, while there has been a corresponding growth in the importance of other categories (Academic Advisory Committee on Birkbeck College 1967, p. 35).

Similar trends have been noted at other institutions, including the Open University. The proportion of teachers entering its undergraduate programme fell rapidly from a peak of 40% in 1971, the first year of recruitment, to less than 10% in 1987 (Open University 1989, p. 63). The pool of non-graduate teachers who were seeking graduate status – and the extra pay and promotion prospects that come with it – gradually dried up. Compared to Birkbeck College, a greater proportion of the Open University's students are not in employment, which is not surprising given the home-based nature of its courses. In 1987, the leading occupational category amongst its new undergraduates was houseworkers, who accounted for 17% of the total enrolment. The other main groups recorded were technical personnel (13%), health and social workers, other professionals and the arts (13%), clerical and office staff (11%), retired or unemployed (10%), and then teachers (9%) (Open University 1989, table 3).

The CNAA survey found that 89% of its part-time degree students were in paid employment, with 52% in the public sector, 25% in manufacturing and 20% in the service industry. Both manufacturing industry and large organizations were overrepresented amongst the students' employers, when compared to their importance in the national economy. This is indicative of the vocational relevance of many part-time degree courses, and the greater willingness of large employers to support part-time study through work release and/or financial sponsorship. Almost one-third of the survey respondents were members of relevant professional bodies; and nearly half intended to use their degree to join or improve their standing in a professional body (Bourner *et al.* 1990, chapters 2 and 4).

Similar overall levels of employment are found amongst part-time postgraduate students, though both the balance of occupations and the seniority of employment tends to be different. At Birkbeck College, the occupational spread of new entrants to postgraduate taught courses is broadly analogous to that at first degree level, but the pattern alters for research students (see Table 27). In the latter case, more than one-third, 36%, of the part-time enrolment have jobs in teaching or research. Enrolment from the education sector has also been decreasing at this level (cf. Rudd and Simpson 1975, pp. 130–31).

At sub-degree level, most part-time students are employed as technicians, supervisors or junior or middle managers. A recent HMI report on part-time advanced further education identified four main categories of students in terms of their employment:

1. those sharing the same background from a particular industry, who follow a course directly relevant to their everyday employment;

2.   those from an employer who has specified the job-specific needs of his employees which the course is expected to fulfil;

3.   those from an employer who is content for them to undertake a broadly-based course which is not normally job-specific;

4.   those from a range of employers who follow a course in a discipline related to their employment.

(Department of Education and Science 1985c, p. 7)

At this level of study there is usually a close linkage between educators and local employers.

It is somewhat surprising, therefore, to discover that the attitudes of many employers towards part-time higher education – and, in particular, towards the employment of mature graduates – are less than positive: 'a sample survey of a wide range of employers revealed little interest in the private sector as a whole in employing graduates over 30 (although there were some exceptions), but there was a much more liberal attitude amongst public sector employers' (Graham, 1989, p. 2). Another survey, confined to Wales – one of the poorest parts of the United Kingdom in terms of part-time higher education provision (see Chapter 5) – found little evidence amongst employers of demand for part-time higher education (Trotman-Dickenson 1987).

Location

The spatial distribution of part-time higher education provision was considered in the previous chapter. Here, I intend to examine the location of part-time higher education students at both macro and micro levels.

Clearly, at the micro level, for part-time students undertaking face-to-face study, their location cannot be too much at variance with that of the course they are taking. They need to be able to get to the institution concerned without too much difficulty. This is well illustrated in a number of studies, although these also show the lengths to which some students are prepared to go to attend the course of their choice. The HMI report on part-time advanced further education succinctly identifies these extremes:

Almost all the students on BTEC higher certificate courses lived within a 20 mile radius of the colleges they attended. In a few instances, the catchment area for a particular course increased as equivalent provision in neighbouring colleges declined. Degree courses were usually provided on a regional rather than a local basis and, in consequence, some degree course students had to travel a considerable distance to college. In rural areas, particularly in Wales, some students found it necessary to travel much greater distances; round trips of 60 to 100 miles for attendance at a day release course were necessary for students attending one college ... Occasionally, a student would travel some distance in order to attend a particular college if they changed their employment or were posted to another area. In one extreme example, following his transfer to another town by his firm, a student regularly undertook a 400 mile journey, including an overnight stay, in order to attend a higher certificate course in civil engineering at a college near London. (Department of Education and Science 1985c, p. 8)

It is instructive here to compare the experience of three inner London institutions which offer part-time degree programmes – the Polytechnic of North London, Goldsmiths' College and Birkbeck College. At the Polytechnic of North London, the 1984 survey of evening degree course students found that 40% of them lived within just 2.5 miles of the polytechnic (Johnson and Hall 1985, p. 9). At Goldsmiths' College, an analysis carried out in 1977 discovered that 42% of the students on four part-time degree courses had home addresses in one of the six inner London boroughs adjacent to the college site. In all, 46% lived within inner London, 37% in the outer London boroughs and 16% further afield (Caulcott 1983, p. 7). At Birkbeck College, a study of 1980 data found a similar spread, with 44% of part-time undergraduates resident in inner London, 36% in outer London and 20% further afield (Tight 1982, p. 38). Many of these far-flung students are people who commute daily to work in London and then go on to the college after work, but a significant number spend several hours a week travelling just to attend the College.

At a macro level, it is possible to carry out the same kind of analysis for

Table 28 Part-time face-to-face higher education students per million residents by region and institutional type, England, 1984/5.

Region*	Population† (millions)	Students/million residents§ U	P	C	O	Total
1 Greater London	6.6	1,540	3,132	1,835	1,605	8,112
2 South-East	5.3	370	288	1,506	1,007	3,171
3 North Thames	4.7	549	564	2,495	807	4,415
4 South-West	4.3	355	988	968	1,043	3,354
5 East Anglia	2.4	589	0	1,332	748	2,669
6 East Midlands	3.2	599	1,495	877	506	3,477
7 West Midlands	5.1	448	1,899	309	1,142	3,798
8 Yorkshire & Humberside	4.8	634	1,844	1,001	702	4,181
9 North-West	6.4	514	1,506	1,346	990	4,356
10 North	3.1	273	1,949	433	889	3,544
Total	45.8	633	1,486	1,270	1,000	4,389

Source: Tight 1987e, table 1.

*The regions are as defined in Table 15. The analysis is based upon students' institutions rather than on their home addresses. It has been assumed that all University of London internal students are based within Greater London. Figures for independent or private institutions are not included.
† The population statistics ('usually resident population') are taken from: Office of Population Statistics and Surveys 1984.
§ The education statistics are taken from: Department of Education and Science 1985d, Universities Statistical Record 1986, supplemented by additional data from the DES.
U = university; P = polytechnic; C = major college; O = other institution.

students that was carried out for courses in Chapter 5 (see Tables 15 and 19). Table 28 summarizes such an analysis for face-to-face students, using data for all levels of higher education in England during the 1984/5 academic year (see Tight 1987e). This table broadly confirms the course-based analysis reported in Chapter 5. There are nearly twice as many part-time students per resident in Greater London as there are throughout the country as a whole. Part-time student numbers are above or about average in the North Thames, Yorkshire and Humberside and North-West regions, and below average elsewhere. There is a threefold variation between Greater London and the region, East Anglia, that records the lowest relative number of part-time students.

If this analysis is repeated at county level, more variation is apparent, with the numbers of part-time students per million residents ranging from the peak of 8112 in Greater London to just 403 in Northumberland (ibid, pp. 172–4). With the exception of Merseyside, all of the metropolitan counties recorded above-average densities in the year studied. Yet the highest rates outside London were in Avon, Berkshire, Oxfordshire and, most curiously, Bedfordshire – a county without a polytechnic, and with a below-average number of full-time students.

It is interesting, in this context, to examine the Open University's experience. It has always been one of the Open University's aims to reach out to potential students who do not have access to other forms of higher education. One might, therefore, expect to find more of its students in parts of the country lacking in alternative face-to-face provision. This is not, however, the case. The distribution of enrolled Open University students is closely related to the underlying population distribution, due to the quota system employed in processing applications (Open University 1989, table 5, p. 62). Above-average numbers of applications are received from London and the Home Counties, which are relatively well provided with face-to-face courses, and from Scotland; with below-average numbers from much of the rest of the country (Brook 1984). The reasons for this pattern appear to be a mixture of relative affluence and differing educational expectations.

This pattern of applications does not appear to be a temporary one, and it applies to other kinds of distance students as well. The study of correspondence students carried out by Glatter and his colleagues in 1967 found that nearly half of those surveyed lived in the South-East region. More than one-quarter, 26%, lived in Greater London, with lesser concentrations in the North-West and Yorkshire and Humberside regions (these are not exactly the same regions as those used in Table 28 – see Glatter *et al.* 1971, pp. 83–4). Most correspondence students live in large towns or conurbations. They have either chosen to study at a distance rather than face-to-face or they are unaware of the alternatives available.

Expenditure

Over the years a series of studies have surveyed the costs incurred by students participating in part-time higher education, and some have made practical suggestions for improving their position. One analysis in 1976 concluded that unemployed students were better off studying full-time, but that those with significant incomes would lose out if they took this route (Wagner and Watts 1976). Another study, in 1979, argued that part-time mature students could increase their net incomes by taking the final year of their course on a full-time basis, thereby benefiting from the split between the financial and academic years (Bourner 1979). Others have looked at the proportion of study costs borne by part-time students, who, unlike full-time students, have no mandatory right to a grant.

The Open University surveyed the costs and hardship borne by its undergraduate students in 1986. They discovered that their students' annual expenditure on course fees, books, stationery, equipment, postage and other items, over and above any assistance received, averaged £200. The fee for a full credit course then was £152, and the summer school fee stood at £99. Only 38% of students received any support towards these costs, mainly from their employers, and only 9% had all of their course and summer school fees paid for them (Open University 1989, pp. 71–2).

The survey carried out by Bourner and his colleagues in the previous year, 1985, found that the average gross costs incurred by part-time CNAA degree students was £363 per year. Of this total, 42% was absorbed by course fees and 29% by additional travel costs. More than one-fifth of the respondents reported some difficulties in meeting these costs, though about 60% received some financial assistance. Two-thirds of those in paid employment (89% of the total), had all of their fees paid by their employers, and half were given time off with pay to attend their classes (Bourner *et al.* 1991, chapter 6). It seems, then, that students studying face-to-face tend to receive more support than Open University students, probably because of the closer vocational relevance of their studies. Part-time students at sub-degree level also tend to be well supported by their employers where their studies are applied in nature (DES 1985c, p. 9). In a significant minority of cases, however, no support is available.

At postgraduate level, the pattern is more varied and is changing. Lee and her collaborators, in a survey carried out in the late 1970s, found that 67% of their sample of science and technology postgraduates were given some financial help by their employers, with 50% having all of their fees paid and 71% receiving some study-time allowance (Lee *et al.* 1979, pp. 48–51, tables 65–6). In the early 1980s, Roweth studied a similar group of postgraduates, some of whom were receiving bursaries from the Science and Engineering Research Council. She found that 55% received some financial support from their employers, and 65% were given some work release (Roweth 1987).

A more general study carried out at about the same time found that 54% of part-time university postgraduates starting research, and 74% of those starting taught courses, received some support from their employers (Advisory Board for the Research Councils 1982, table 2.4; Whalley 1982). Since then it is probable that the support available to most kinds of part-time higher education students has decreased to some extent.

Students' reactions to their courses

The distribution of evaluation questionnaires to students at the end of their courses is now common practice in many institutions of higher education. More sophisticated evaluation methods are currently being explored by some researchers (Green *et al.* 1989). Such exercises inevitably suffer from a number of disadvantages. They frequently ignore students who do not complete their courses, and the students surveyed may be disposed to tell the questioners what they think they want to hear. De Winter Hebron, reporting on a series of interviews with both students and staff on part-time management courses, concluded:

> Students *say* one thing and *do* another: staff *expect* one thing and *get* another . . . Staff, too, *claim* one thing and *emphasize* another – just like students – while students rank things *in one order* when talking to staff, and *in another order* when responding to questionnaires.
>
> (de Winter Hebron 1983b, p. 23)

If we bear these problems in mind, however, there is a lot of useful information available on students' reactions to their courses. Both positive and negative responses are evident.

In their study of part-time polytechnic students in 1972/3, Whitburn and her colleagues found that only 29% of their respondents believed that the interests of part-time students were adequately considered by their polytechnic's administration. More, 48%, felt that their interests were adequately considered by the teaching staff; less, 14%, by the students' union. This hardly represents a ringing endorsement. Yet, somewhat inconsistently, most part-time students reported that they did not use the polytechnic or student union facilities, mainly because of a lack of interest or time (Whitburn *et al.* 1976, pp. 119–21).

By contrast, Bourner's 1985 survey found a generally more positive response. Over 90% of the respondents rated their courses as either 'roughly as expected' or 'better than expected', and a similar proportion said that they would recommend them to others. Dissatisfaction was most apparent with regard to canteen facilities and childcare arrangements, with many also complaining about student participation and feedback within their courses. Most students reported that they had experienced difficulties of some kind, either directly with their studies, or with the effects on them of their work or domestic responsibilities. For the majority, though, these difficulties had been no worse than expected.

A positive interest was expressed by the majority of those surveyed in making course structures more flexible. The changes suggested included making parts of courses available by distance learning (as the Open Polytechnic scheme intends); permitting the final stage of courses to be taken by full-time study; making intermediate awards available (e.g. certificates or diplomas); and mixing part-time and full-time students for teaching purposes. Perhaps most significantly, a majority of the respondents also expressed an interest in continuing their part-time studies at postgraduate level (Bourner *et al.* 1991, chapters 4, 5 and 6).

Institutional studies largely confirm the findings of these national surveys. The study by Woodward and his colleagues of part-time degree and sub-degree students at the University of Ulster found generally high levels of satisfaction. Yet most of those questioned did not view the library facilities or the student welfare system as being particularly important to them, even when these facilities were designed specifically for them (Woodward *et al.* 1985). The evening degree students at the Polytechnic of North London similarly reported general satisfaction with their courses, the teaching and assessment methods used, and their relations with staff and other students. Problems were noted with access to library and catering facilities, and, in some cases, with their studies and their impact on other commitments. Many said that their participation in the evening degree scheme had substantially affected or changed their lives, often leading to a continuing involvement in study (Johnson and Hall 1985, chapter 4).

Open University students also tend to be very positive in their assessment of their studies. In a survey of graduates carried out in 1985/6, 20% replied that the overall benefit they had obtained from their studies had been 'enormous', 48% said that it had been 'great', and a further 29% said that there had been 'some' benefit. Most judged the effects of their studies on themselves, on themselves as members of society, and on their jobs and careers, as being positive. However, only a minority felt that the impact on their social life or family had been generally positive (Open University 1989, pp. 72–5).

Rudd and Simpson's survey of postgraduates in the early 1970s found rather lower satisfaction levels: a quarter of their respondents described themselves as very satisfied with their courses, with another quarter quite satisfied. Most were happy with their supervision, though some wanted more staff–student contact, and others argued for more facilities to be made available at the times they most needed them (Rudd and Simpson 1975, pp. 139–40). The later study of science and technology postgraduates by Lee and others looked at the gains which students got from their studies. Those most highly rated by their respondents were intellectual, prágmatic, or instrumental in nature. Improvements in status, financial position, or personal relationships, by contrast, were rated lowly (Lee *et al.* 1979, pp. 76–9).

Educational performance

Studies of the performance of part-time higher education students have focused on two related issues: the results achieved in examinations and the extent to which students do not complete their courses. Most analyses have dealt with first degree study only.

A number of recent studies have compared the degree results of part-time and full-time students. One study of CNAA records has shown that part-time students achieve a higher proportion of commendations on pass degree courses, and a greater proportion of first class and upper second class results on honours degree courses (Bourner *et al.* 1988, p. 12). Others have found that there are significant variations in the examination results of part-time students taking different subjects, and on new and older courses (Smith and Saunders 1988, pp. 17–20).

Studies of mature students have also shown that they tend to perform relatively well in their final examinations (see, for example, Smithers and Griffin 1986b, chapter 10). And research suggests that students accepted for degree courses on the basis of qualifications gained through part-time study – for example, Ordinary and Higher National Certificates, City & Guilds examinations – achieve better degree results than those with more conventional entry qualifications. Those with non-standard entry qualifications appear to perform at least as well as those with conventional qualifications (Bourner and Hamed 1987).

These findings, of course, relate only to those students who complete their courses and take the final assessment. It is a commonplace that part-time students are less likely to complete their courses than full-timers: a phenomenon that has been described variously as dropout, wastage, attrition, or non-completion. Some have argued, on these grounds, that part-time courses should be discontinued, at least in certain subject areas (e.g. Venables 1967, 1972). The general reasons for non-completion are fairly well known, and involve both positive and negative factors. Part-time courses tend to be longer than full-time courses. Part-time students do not receive financial support as a right, and they usually have more commitments and responsibilities than full-time students.

While the incidence of non-completion in part-time study tends to be relatively high, it is very variable. A study of 235 part-time degree courses in 1986 found an average wastage rate during the first year – when they are normally highest – of 24%, with one extreme report of 91% (Smith and Saunders 1988, pp. 14–17). Vinegrad, in his study of 347 students who had at various times been enrolled on a single degree course, noted that 65% had dropped out, three-quarters of them during the first year of their studies (Vinegrad 1980, p. 153). Non-completion rates for students taking courses by correspondence also tend to be high, particularly where little personal contact or support is provided (Glatter *et al.* 1971, pp. 49–53, 106–7; Harris 1972). At the Open University, where high-quality learning materials are supported by tutorials and summer schools, the eventual graduation rate of undergraduate students has been estimated at 50–60% (McIntosh *et al.* 1980).

Woodley has identified three main groups of factors contributing to student dropout. First, there are those relating to the course itself or to the institution providing it: for example, badly structured, taught, or supported courses. Second, there are factors relating to the student's study environment: for example, work and domestic problems. And, third, there may be problems with the individual student's motivation. It has to be recognized that students' motivations for taking a course may change, that they may decide that these motivations are better satisfied elsewhere, or that they may conclude that they have been satisfied without completing the course in question (see Woodley and Parlett 1983; Woodley *et al.* 1987, chapter 9).

It is difficult to assess the relative importance of these three groups of factors. Students who have dropped out are difficult to follow up, and may rationalize their reasons for leaving if they can be found and questioned. Nevertheless, check-list approaches for identifying students who are potentially 'at risk' of dropping out have been devised (e.g. Woodley and Parlett 1983, pp. 8–13; Bourner *et al.* 1991, chapter 8). Such methods can help institutions to improve their provision, and the flexibility of their response to students' varied and changing circumstances, but they can never be entirely satisfactory. There is no simple solution to the issue of student dropout, but it is misleading to view it entirely as a problem. Students who enrol but do not complete will usually have learned something, if only about themselves. It would not be feasible or desirable to completely eradicate dropout.

Conclusions

The research discussed in this chapter has enabled us to build up a fairly clear picture of the students and clients of part-time higher education.

Part-time students are different from full-time students, and they form a much more diverse group. They tend to be older, but vary considerably in age, with the majority in their twenties or thirties. The older part-time students naturally tend to be married, and to have children. Most part-time students are male, though this pattern is rapidly changing. Part-time and full-time students are of broadly similar social class – that is, they are overwhelmingly middle class – but part-time students show greater evidence of upward social mobility.

Part-time students have a wide range of educational experience and qualifications. On average, they did not perform as well in their initial education as full-time students. Many, however, enter higher education with relatively high entry qualifications, often gained through part-time study. A smaller but growing group enter higher education with non-standard qualifications. Most are taking their courses for a mix of instrumental, self-development and subject-interest reasons. The first of these reasons tends to be dominant for sub-degree and first degree students, where vocational courses are of great importance. The last two reasons are most significant at postgraduate level and on non-vocational courses.

Students and clients choose part-time higher education because they cannot afford to study full-time: most part-time students are in full-time employment. Employers frequently contribute to the costs of part-time study and/or provide paid release from work. This support is far from universal, however, and a significant minority of students experience financial problems during their studies. Undoubtedly, many more are prevented from studying by such problems.

Part-time students are disproportionately concentrated in the London and South-East regions. Many live at a considerable distance from the institutions they are studying with. They tend to express general satisfaction with their courses, though changes in course structures, teaching methods and support facilities are frequently suggested. For a significant minority, participation in part-time higher education is a life-changing experience. For many, perhaps most, it forms part of a commitment to continuing their education throughout adult life. Non-completion rates for part-time students are relatively high but variable. Those who do complete their courses perform at least as well on average in their final assessment as their full-time counterparts.

Within this heterogeneity, it is possible to identify common or typical kinds of part-time student:

> It seems as if there are two polar kinds of student. There is the student, probably in his early or mid-twenties, receiving support from his firm to attend a course which relates to his work situation. The student is normally male, and probably has few, if any, family responsibilities. At the other end of the spectrum, there is an adult, often with family commitments, in the late twenties or thirties, wishing to have the chance of experiencing higher education. The student is here much more likely to be female, and the course is likely to represent a sharp break from daily experience. This kind of student will often be self-supporting, and will be making a not inconsiderable financial commitment to study on the course.
>
> (Barnett 1987, p. 10)

A similar categorization has been suggested for mature students as a whole:

> There exists a meaningful division between two distinct groups of mature students. The 21–29 age group is predominantly male, studying on a full-time basis in the faculties of Engineering, Science and Business and Management. The older group had more female representation and tends to be studying in the faculties of Humanities, Social Studies and Art and Design.
>
> (Johnston and Bailey 1984, p. 5)

It would be unwise, however, to attempt to summarize the variety of part-time higher education students in too simplistic a fashion.

7

Value and Purpose

Introduction

This chapter has two main aims. First, to examine the value of part-time higher education, comparing it with full-time provision. Second, and more fundamentally, to consider the underlying purposes of higher education as a whole. I will then discuss the question of how higher education should be provided, contrasting the dominant model of provision with its alternatives, in the following chapter. The argument presented here builds extensively on two previously published papers (Tight 1987d, 1989a).

It is something of a paradox that, while there has been a great deal of debate about higher education in the United Kingdom in recent years, there has been relatively little serious consideration of the value and purpose of this activity: what it is and what it is for.

> What have appeared to have been fierce debates in the United Kingdom about higher education have been, with few exceptions, carried on within a narrow range of assumptions, or have been about managerial or administrative decisions.
>
> (Trow 1989a, p. 66)

It seems to be assumed by most academics that the educational opportunities which they provide are of great but immeasurable worth – indeed that they are 'invaluable' – and that this assumption is (or should be) shared by those outside higher education. This is not to say that no attention has been paid to the issues of value and purpose, but that most of it has been superficial or uncritical. In this chapter, I will attempt to probe rather deeper into these questions and suggest some answers.

Value

There are, of course, immediate problems of scope and definition. First, even if it is assumed that higher education is an unproblematical concept (a point I will return to later in this chapter and in the following one), the notion of 'value' is certainly multi-dimensional and subject to a variety of interpretations. It may, for example, be defined in terms of worth, desirability, utility, estimation, equivalence, or purchasing power (*Oxford English Dictionary*). Economists, philosophers and sociologists, to name just three disciplinary groups, could all put forward reasonably coherent theories of value which could be applied to higher education, with the focus of attention placed differentially on product or process, content or context. To allow a suitably thorough exploration, the analysis which follows will need to draw on these and other interpretations as appropriate.

A second problem is that higher education has different value for its different clients: that is, students, academics, institutions of higher education, employers, the exchequer, society in general. All of these interests, and their conflicting relationships, should ideally be borne in mind in an analysis of this kind.

Third, it is difficult to consider the value of part-time higher education in isolation. Some comparison is called for, and two complementary strategies suggest themselves. Different types of higher education may be compared with each other; or the value of higher education as a whole may be related to the values accruing to other activities, especially those competing for the same resources.

I will take the former approach in this section, and compare part-time higher education with full-time higher education. The comparison will be structured around six interrelated themes, chosen to highlight the relationship between higher education and the rest of society:

- demand, access and equity;
- maturity and adulthood;
- employment and activity;
- residence;
- cost-effectiveness and productivity;
- flexibility and innovation.

Higher education undoubtedly has other values more internal to itself which will not be reflected in this analysis, but it seems most appropriate here to focus on the context in which it operates. After examining the purposes or functions of higher education in the second part of the chapter, I will then consider its value as a whole in relation to other activities.

Demand, access and equity

The demand for higher education is, like its value, difficult to assess. It is probably most useful to think of it at two levels: revealed demand, as adjusted to the available (and sometimes very limited) supply, and latent demand, which may be considerably larger. Seen in these terms, access has to do with the extent to which latent demand is recognized and turned into revealed demand, and then satisfied through supply; while equity relates to the justness of the treatment of individual demands.

The evidence of revealed demand over the last two decades is that part-time higher education has been one of the principal growth areas of provision (see Chapters 2 and 3). Within the mainstream of the higher education system, part-time students dominate sub-degree provision and account for nearly half of all postgraduates, though they make up only a minority of those following first degree courses. In other kinds of higher education – such as external degree courses, correspondence courses leading to professional qualifications, short and non-award-bearing courses – part-time study is the norm.

Latent demand is a more problematic concept. Government projections of the future demand for higher education are based primarily on the size of the cohort of young entrants to full-time higher education, their qualification and participation rates, and on anticipated changes in these factors. Demand from other groups, and for other kinds of provision, is treated very much as a secondary issue, with part-time student numbers extrapolated in an arbitrary fashion (see Chapter 9). Provision outside the mainstream is simply ignored. This approach to forecasting carries clear messages about the perceived value of different forms of higher education.

Even so, recent government predictions suggest a situation in which part-time student numbers hold up surprisingly well when compared with projections of full-time numbers (DES 1986). Yet there can be little doubt that, as the National Advisory Body (NAB) has argued, 'part-time demand is a managed phenomenon: to put it very simply, there is no good measure of the students seeking courses that are not offered' (NAB 1984a, p. 13).

There is, however, a considerable range of evidence regarding unfulfilled or potential demand: from national surveys, from the Open University's experience, from requests made locally for provision (Tight 1982; Open University 1986). The recent decline in the full-time participation rate for school-leavers, taken in conjunction with the growing tendency for 'second chance' or 'second bite' education later in life, may also be expected to lead to increased demand in the future. Evidence from other developed countries suggests that the real demand for higher education is a good deal higher than that currently satisfied in the United Kingdom (see Chapter 4). It also indicates that substantially increased demand can only realistically be satisfied by a system which places much greater emphasis on part-time forms of study.

Access to higher education for many people and for many needs can only be made available on a part-time basis. In many other cases it might be better provided, or provided just as well, by part-time rather than full-time means. Full-time provision effectively excludes people who were marginal to the entry system at the conventional age, but who are able to benefit from higher education, and who wish to do so, in later life. Further use of the system by those who have already benefited is also discouraged.

Part-time provision is appropriate for those who are in employment, or who have heavy domestic responsibilities, and who are unable to spare the time to enrol full-time. Many people seeking entry to higher education are also ineligible for grant aid for full-time study, or are unwilling to take the cut in their living standards that accepting it would bring about. Conversely, those who are unemployed, and who are receiving financial assistance, are debarred from undertaking anything but strictly limited study, in case it prevents them from taking up offers of employment. The housebound and those in institutions are clearly unable to attend courses, but can have them delivered through correspondence or distance means.

The notion of equity, embodied in the Robbins principle – 'courses of higher education should be available for all those who are qualified by ability and attainment to pursue them and who wish to do so' (Committee on Higher Education 1963, p. 8) – has been variously endorsed or modified by successive governments. It requires that those able to benefit from higher education are not denied access to it simply because they are unable or unwilling to subscribe to full-time provision designed for late adolescents. If it is accepted that people other than school-leavers – who may not have conventional entry qualifications, and who will have differing characteristics and requirements – have as much right to access to higher education, then part-time forms of provision must inevitably be accorded a greater value.

Maturity and adulthood

These arguments are reinforced when the evidence on adults' educational abilities and experience is considered. The ideal of making educational opportunities available for all those who want or need them throughout life has gained ground since the Second World War. The most eloquent treatment of this subject is probably that to be found in the pages of the Faure Report (Faure *et al.* 1972). The guiding concept has been variously expressed as lifelong education, recurrent education, permanent education, or continuing education. However styled, it contains a firm rejection of the notion that education should be confined to a period of full-time study in childhood, adolescence and early adulthood, with later life structured almost entirely around work and leisure.

People are living longer nowadays, and they are enjoying better health and increased leisure. The frequency and significance of technological, economic and social change is accelerating. There is a growing need for personal, social and cultural development. All of these trends require that greater recognition and value is given to post-initial education: education for adults. Much of this education will not, of course, be higher education, but it will be mainly part-time.

Progress along these lines has been hampered in the past by the mistaken belief that learning is a particularly child-like ability that presents adults with great difficulties. This belief has often been paraphrased as 'you can't teach an old dog new tricks'. For a long time this assumption gained support from psychological research, which has devoted most of its attention to child development. Where adults have been studied, the tendency has been to use methods devised for studying children. More recently, however, it has been shown that mental development does not cease with the attainment of physical maturity, with a subsequent slow and remorseless decline downwards towards the grave. Age does appear to diminish certain intellectual traits, such as short-term memory, and is frequently associated with poorer hearing and eyesight. But in most cases these losses are easily compensated for, and are more than balanced by the maturity of attitude, breadth of experience, greater motivation and more informed choice that adults are able to bring to the learning process (Cross 1981; Allman 1982, 1983).

Recent evidence on the performance of adults in higher education supports this analysis (see also Chapter 6). For example, adults lacking the standard entry qualifications who were admitted, after a careful selection process, to five English universities performed at least as well on average as conventional undergraduate students, and in some respects better (Smithers and Griffin 1986a, 1986b). Providing that the different characteristics and circumstances of younger and older students are controlled for, these findings are confirmed by other studies of both full-time and part-time adult students (Woodley 1981; Bourner *et al.* 1988).

These results should not be too surprising. There is, or should be, something about higher education (or perhaps the highest education) which is peculiarly adult, and, consequently, likely to be organized on something other than a full-time basis. After all, many of the problems of British higher education stem from the fact that most entrants are not fully adult. Our universities, polytechnics and colleges have to take on a semi-parental role, and function in part as a kind of finishing school. There is a need to re-emphasize the *adultness* of higher education, and to remove or ameliorate the various artificial barriers that restrict adult access to higher education: whether they be attitudinal, informational, geographical, financial, structural, situational, or educational (Advisory Council for Adult and Continuing Education 1982a).

Employment and activity

Perhaps the most important difference between full-time and part-time forms of higher education is that, whereas the former gives the dominant role in a particular period of life to higher education – with employment and other activity subsidiary, absent, or deferred – the latter is based on the assumption that students are employed or have other obligations which make them unable to commit themselves full-time to study. Yet, as I argued in Chapter 5, the difference is not quite as clear-cut as this implies. Full-time forms of education typically only involve the student in a part-time commitment to study (Rickman 1981; Carter 1983). Full-time students have a good deal of time free for holidays, leisure and socializing. Many also take up part-time employment as a means of supplementing increasingly inadequate grant awards. The difference between part-time and full-time higher education is, therefore, relative rather than absolute.

It is widely believed that for higher education to be really valuable it has to be full-time. Indeed, this view is so prevalent in this country that many people believe that the only form of higher education available *is* full-time. But this belief is erroneous. There is, on the contrary, a great deal to be said for mixing involvement in education with other aspects of life, notably employment, to the mutual benefit of the different roles. Students can learn while working, and from working, as well as while studying. What is important is determining an appropriate balance between these activities for given aims and particular students or clients.

These arguments have been put forward many times. Within higher education, they are most often heard in connection with sandwich education. There are a number of different models of sandwich education, but they share the common characteristic of interleaving periods of work experience with full-time study. Sandwich courses are not available in all institutions or subjects, but are concentrated in applied science, engineering and business studies. A similar principle operates in the training of teachers, nurses, social workers and other groups, though these are not normally thought of as sandwich education. Many benefits have been claimed for sandwich education. It develops practical experience, skills and self-knowledge in students. It provides stimulation and recruitment advantages for the employers involved. And it helps to create linkages and publicity for educational institutions. Just how valuable these benefits are in practice is a matter of some debate (DES 1985a; Culshaw 1987).

However, the benefits claimed for sandwich education also apply to part-time provision, but in a more general way. Part-time provision meshes higher education together with not just work, but other activities as well. Sandwich education places the onus primarily upon the educator to establish the links, and to arrange for periods of work experience for their students. In the case of part-time education, this relationship is typically reversed. The major responsibility for making the linkages rests with the students themselves and/or their employers.

And the possible patterns are much more varied. Part-time day-release courses in vocational subjects may be explicitly designed to meet the initial training needs of technical and lower managerial grades. Later on in their careers, the need to update or retrain may be met through short courses, with little loss in work time. In-house research and development work may be carried out in liaison with staff from institutions of higher education. Where work release is not possible, or where the educational aims of students do not coincide with those of their employers, evening or distance study can be used. Part-time forms of provision, unlike full-time or sandwich education, also enable study to be combined with domestic responsibility, unemployment, community involvement and other roles.

Since they place more responsibility on the learner, part-time courses can be less satisfactory than sandwich courses in providing a coherent package of education and activity. But this can be compensated for by appropriate guidance and counselling before and during study. The underlying aim should be to facilitate educational development alongside other responsibilities, with each aspect of life – education, work, home, community, leisure – interacting to the extent that the student or client wishes. In this way, the general benefits accruing to students and, through them, to society as a whole, may be maximized.

Residence

A belief in the value of residential provision has persisted in this country alongside the widespread institutional preference for full-time education. The origins of this belief lie in the medieval necessity – consequent upon poor transport and communications – for intending students to move to the vicinity of scholars if they wished to gain an education (see Chapter 2 and Tight 1987e). This monastic pattern of provision was adopted by the public boarding schools, the Oxbridge colleges and the Inns of Court; in each of which the acquisition of an education came to have at least as much to do with residence as with study. These arrangements have been maintained with relatively little change right up until the present day, even though the original reasons for them have ceased to have much relevance.

It is important, however, to remember that there are other traditions. The medieval Scottish university foundations at Glasgow, Aberdeen and Edinburgh were much more closely related to the underlying population distribution than those in England. They gave far less attention to the accommodation of their students, leaving this responsibility to the students and their families. This pattern allowed much greater scope for the admission of local and part-time students. And it was the Scottish model which was adopted when the civic universities were established in major cities south of the border in the nineteenth century.

Subsequently, both the civic universities and the newer foundations moved as far as possible over to the full-time residential pattern of higher education. This took place as they steadily shifted their orientation away from local markets and towards national admissions systems. But their emphasis on the need to accommodate the large majority of their students on campus has proved to be counter-productive in a number of ways. It helped to determine the location of the new universities on greenfield sites outside small towns or cities. It was only in such places that the amount of land deemed to be necessary was available at a reasonable price or by gift. This meant, however, that the local market for students would inevitably be restricted. And, when the UGC proved unable to fund all of the residential accommodation requested, it left the newer universities stuck out on a limb, with a large number of commuting students forced to live off-campus (Jobling 1970).

Somewhat similar developments may be traced in the public sector, where the polytechnics have begun to move away from local recruitment towards national enrolment, though they have less accommodation available. The teacher training colleges, on the other hand, particularly those which were religious foundations, have long stressed the virtues of residence (Dent 1977; Wyatt 1977a, 1977b).

This emphasis on residential provision discriminates against the interests of local, adult and part-time students. It is obviously also expensive to operate. What, then, is its justification? The report of a UGC subcommittee published over 30 years ago concluded that:

> Three forces, then, have led universities in the recent past to build halls of residence – shortage of accommodation; a recognition that all was not well with the student in the lodgings available and with some students living at home; and a belief on the part of many people in the civilising and educative effect of halls of residence.
>
> (UGC 1957, pp. 7–8)

These arguments may have carried great force when they were written, but they hardly stand up to serious consideration today. It is often claimed that there is a shortage of private sector accommodation appropriate for students. But such claims tend to be based on over-expectations, an unwillingness to look beyond the immediate environs of the institution and an ignorance of the workings of the housing market (Rudd 1980). The worries expressed about students' general welfare now seem to be overly maternalistic, particularly as research has failed to reveal any relationship between students' residence and academic perform-ance (Marris 1964; Brothers and Hatch 1971).

The crux of the argument really rests upon the subcommittee's third point, yet even this has been undermined by the trend away from halls of residence and towards self-catering accommodation. We may accept that collegiate accom-modation has a civilizing and educative role. But we should also recognize that the wider world is, or should be, similarly civilizing and educative, though in a different, broader and more realistic way. Halls of residence tend to be inward-looking, denying contact and interchange with those outside. We cannot all live in them, certainly not all of the time, whereas as all have, increasingly, to live in the world.

So long as institutions of higher education continue to devote so much attention to school-leavers, they will continue to have an interest in the provision of residential accommodation, even if greater recognition is given to the potential for home-based study (Morgan and McDowell 1979). The existing residential provision cannot be easily dispensed with.

For part-time and adult students, who normally have established responsi-bilities and life-styles, the cloister is at best irrelevant and at worst dangerously distracting. For them, two alternative models of higher education are particu-larly apposite. The first of these is the community service-station model, which sets institutions within existing centres of population, where they can interact with the local economy and community (Armytage 1955; Abercrombie *et al.* 1974). The second is the outreach model, which takes the personnel and facilities of higher education to wherever students or clients are located, rather than vice versa. In either case, short periods of residential study could be involved where feasible and appropriate, though this would not be the norm (National Institute of Adult Continuing Education 1989).

Cost-effectiveness and productivity

Many of the differences between part-time and full-time forms of higher education are brought into sharper focus when their comparative cost-effectiveness and productivity are considered. Table 29 summarizes the major costs and benefits affecting the different parties involved in higher education. The items included in this table do not apply to every course or institution, or to every type or level of higher education. Their importance, and the directness of their effect, also varies considerably from case to case. Some of the items are not wholly quantifiable, or can only be quantified on the basis of rather dubious assumptions. Nevertheless, the table offers a useful framework for developing an appreciation of the financial and other calculations affecting students, institutions of higher education, employers, the exchequer and society as a whole.

For a part-time student in employment, for example, forgone earnings are likely to be a less important cost than they are for full-time students, though the latter may not recognize this. Fees and other course-related costs will usually be more significant for part-time students, because they benefit to a lesser extent from grants and other forms of financial support. The relative age of the students concerned, and the greater uncertainty associated with the success of part-time study, will affect the probability of them benefiting from increased

Table 29   The major costs and benefits of higher education.

For the student
costs: fees, travel, books and equipment, accommodation, forgone earnings and leisure time
benefits: student grants, work release, other support given, increased potential earnings, personal development and socialization

For the institution
costs: staff (teaching and other), accommodation and social facilities, teaching materials, recruitment and publicity
benefits: fees (from or on behalf of students), institutional grants, contact with employers and the community

For the employer
costs: fees, other support costs, forgone production, potential loss of qualified staff
benefits: increased productivity, employee satisfaction, contact with educational institutions

For the exchequer
costs: student and institutional support, forgone tax revenue
benefits: increased potential tax revenue

For society
costs: student, institutional and employer support, forgone output
benefits: increased productivity, social and cultural development

---

earnings after graduation. The personal development gained during study or research may, however, prove to be much more valuable than any ensuing financial benefit. This is likely to be a particularly important consideration for mature students.

For the institution, the costs and benefits associated with different forms of provision will depend upon their overall mix of provision, the size of the groups being taught, and the resourcing policies applied internally and externally. The position is complicated and some cross-subsidization between courses is almost inevitable. One major cost relating to full-time students, residential accommodation, will be absent for part-time provision; which may also bring greater benefits to institutions through external contacts. Yet – because of the higher dropout rates and the higher support costs associated with proportionately longer courses – it may be more expensive for a given institution to provide for part-time rather than full-time students.

The employer's perspective is most relevant for part-time higher education, particularly where students benefit from work release or have part of their study costs paid for them. For most full-time students, these costs are borne mainly by the exchequer and/or their families. It is difficult to measure the potential benefits of higher education for employers: many of them are long-term. Careful calculations are required if a reasonable balance with the up-front costs of supporting higher education is to be arrived at. However, the costs of supporting full-time students, who will be withdrawn from the workforce during the period of their studies, tend to be considerably greater, though they are usually indirect.

So far as the exchequer is concerned, the balance of advantage between different kinds of provision is purely a matter of expenditure and revenue. Taking a broader view, the costs and benefits of higher education as they affect society as a whole can be seen as a kind of summation of the four preceding perspectives. The conclusions drawn from a system-wide analysis of this nature are likely to be very different from those of the exchequer or of providing institutions.

A comprehensive assessment along these lines would require detailed and extensive research. Fortunately, existing studies provide some useful pointers. Many of these have regarded higher education as an investment in human capital, the pay-off from which will be expressed over time in the salaries earned by those who have experienced it. Such analyses suggest that there are relatively high rates of return, for both students and society, to such investments; at least at sub-degree and first degree levels (e.g. Psacharopoulos 1981; Marris 1983; Leslie and Brinkman 1988). The rates of return to part-time study can be even higher, despite the lower completion rates; particularly if this is undertaken early on in the student's career (Layard *et al.* 1971; Venables 1972; Agnello and Hunt 1976).

It is more difficult to find research which compares institutional support costs with potential revenues, viewing higher education more as a consumption good than as an investment (see pp. 68–9). This is partly due to problems of complexity and confidentiality. It would appear, however, that many providers of part-time higher education in the United Kingdom fund courses by distributing the resources available in response to immediate needs and past practice (Smith 1987; Smith and Saunders 1989).

The particular case of the Open University has been much better documented. It has demonstrated that a large-scale, part-time distance teaching system can – allowing for its higher dropout rates – produce graduates significantly cheaper than conventional full-time, face-to-face provision (Hinchcliffe 1971; Wagner 1972, 1977; Laidlaw and Layard 1974). Less resource-intensive models of distance provision would produce even more favourable results. So do many models of part-time face-to-face provision, particularly where the part-time students are taught alongside full-time students at marginal cost (Selby Smith 1975; Gleeson 1980; Muta 1985).

It would appear – pending further research – that there are good economic arguments for shifting the balance of resourcing and provision away from full-time and towards part-time higher education. This would, of course, need to be done gradually and in such a way as to make the best continuing use of existing facilities. There is also a strong case for basing any future expansion of provision on part-time rather than full-time attendance. Such a strategy would enable as many people as possible to take advantage of higher education for a given level of resourcing.

Flexibility and innovation

Innovations of various kinds – few of which are really new – are continually being introduced into the practice of higher education with the aim of improving provision and increasing flexibility. Some of these innovations, such as interdisciplinary study and alternative assessment methods, have as much relevance for full-time as for part-time provision. Many others, though they have been applied to both full-time and part-time courses, are much more applicable to the latter. Examples include the development of access courses to prepare non-traditional entrants for higher education, the removal of formal entry requirements and the use of independent study or experiential learning methods. These innovations are particularly appropriate for part-time provision because of their orientation towards adult audiences (see also pp. 2–4 and 64–7).

Similarly, while the modularization of courses in many institutions has allowed full-time students greater freedom in putting together programmes of study, the modular or credit accumulation model of higher education is likely to be most relevant for part-time students (Squires 1986; Ram 1989). Part-time study typically takes longer to complete. Part-time students are quite likely to move home or change jobs during their studies, and they may wish to transfer their accumulated credit between institutions or courses. They may also need to alter the pattern or pace of their studies in the light of changes in their other responsibilities.

A further group of innovations, though potentially of general applicability, have so far been largely confined to part-time forms of higher education. The application of correspondence and distance forms of study is one obvious example. These approaches have proved to be particularly useful for professional and 'second chance' education, focusing on adults who are unable or unwilling to attend face-to-face courses. Another example is the timetabling of lectures, seminars and other aspects of face-to-face provision to suit the convenience of the students concerned. For part-time students, this might mean in the evening, in the middle of the day, or at the weekend. Full-time and part-time students could be taught alongside each other at such times, but this possibility has not been exploited as much as might be expected.

The general message here is that developments in course content, structure, presentation and assessment have been more prevalent in part-time provision. Such developments are more relevant to part-time higher education because of its adult focus, inherent diversity and greater market orientation. Flexibility and innovation seem far less important to full-time higher education because of its continuing commitment to a single, standardized activity: the further education of well-qualified school-leavers.

The major conclusion from the analysis presented in the first part of this chapter has to be that part-time higher education is seriously undervalued in the United Kingdom when compared with full-time higher education. I would go further and argue that part-time higher education is *in general* more valuable than full-time higher education: because of the increased and more flexible access it provides; because of its adult orientation; because of its overall cost-effectiveness; and because of the closer and more realistic linkages which it can foster between education, economy and society. A fundamental shift in the balance of our higher education system away from full-time and towards part-time provision is called for.

This conclusion does not deny the value of full-time higher education, but attempts to put it into its proper context. We may readily accept that, for many students, a period of full-time higher education offers a valuable break from other concerns, during which study and reflection can proceed relatively unhindered. In the case of school-leavers, it can also ease the transition between adolescence and full adult responsibility, though it is arguable whether this is really an educational function.

But we should also recognize that full-time higher education, as currently practised in the United Kingdom, is unwarrantedly exclusive. It denies access to the majority of those who could benefit from it. It perpetuates an outmoded school model of provision. And, because it is relatively expensive, it is inconceivable that it could provide the basis for a significantly expanded system in the foreseeable future. Higher education, to have most value for most people in most circumstances, should be predominantly part-time.

Purpose

As I indicated in the introduction to this chapter, there have been few recent British analyses which have seriously considered the fundamental purposes of higher education practice (but see Barnett 1985, 1988). Official statements are not a great deal of help here either. The oft-quoted report of the Robbins Committee, for example, dealt with the aims of higher education in eight crisp paragraphs:

> What purposes, what general social ends should be served by higher education? . . . no simple formula, no answer in terms of any single end, will suffice . . . To do justice to the complexity of things, it is necessary to acknowledge a plurality of aims. In our submission there are at least four objectives essential to any properly balanced system. We begin with instruction in skills suitable to play a part in the general division of labour . . . secondly, while emphasizing that there is no betrayal of values when institutions of higher education teach what will be of some practical use, we must postulate that what is taught should be taught in such a way as to promote the general powers of the mind . . . Thirdly, we must name the advancement of learning . . . Finally, there is a function that is more difficult to describe concisely, but that is none the less fundamental: the transmission of a common culture and common standards of citizenship.
>
> (Committee on Higher Education 1963, pp. 6–7)

The 1985 Green Paper on Higher Education did not mention aims or purposes, though the White Paper which followed did, in response to criticism, address the subject in two paragraphs (Secretary of State for Education and Science *et al.* 1985, 1987). Neither the UGC nor the NAB had much to say on this subject in their submissions prior to the Green Paper (NAB 1984b; UGC 1984b). All of these statements merely gave the Robbins Report a general endorsement. The NAB and UGC documents added a reference to continuing education, while the government placed a greater emphasis on the needs of the economy and the underlying financial constraints.

Despite this lack of analysis, there are still a variety of sources which are of use in considering the purposes of higher education. Research that has been carried out in other countries and in other disciplines helps to provide a framework. This may be supplemented by the available evidence on the expectations of students and the other clients of higher education (see Chapter 6). On this basis, we may identify five main purposes for higher education which are relevant to current practice in the United Kingdom. I shall refer to these alliteratively as:

- skills development,
- selection,
- socialization,
- scholarship, and
- service.

These purposes are, of course, interrelated. There are also question marks associated with each of them.

Skills development

Higher education may aim to develop skills in its participants which are of value to them, to their actual or potential employers, and to society as a whole. The term 'skills' is being used here in a wide sense to cover the first two objectives identified by Robbins. It encompasses both vocational and liberal skills, general and specific skills, and personal-transferable and subject-based skills.

It is possible – following the rather mechanistic logic of some of those associated with the current *Enterprise in Higher Education* initiative (Manpower Services Commission 1987) – to define all of the skills which are of interest to a particular party; and then to specify precisely how and when they are to be developed during a course of study. Whether this strategy is followed or not, it may be that many such skills could be developed better, more appropriately and at less expense outside higher education.

Selection

This is arguably a more important function of higher education, especially where, as in the British system, supply is rationed. Much has been written on the use of education for selection (and socialization) by sociologists, though their attention has been mainly focused at the school level (e.g. Hussain 1976; Bourdieu and Passeron 1977, 1979). Higher education, in these terms, seeks to identify and accredit individuals with higher level abilities of certain kinds. These assessments are then used by employers and others to 'place' the individuals who have benefited from the process.

Yet the certification which higher education gives to its participants is, to a considerable extent, a reflection of their earlier education and social background. And this is reinforced by the hierarchy which operates within the higher education system itself (see pp. 91–3). The direct contribution of higher education to the selection process may, therefore, not be that great. In many cases, the mere fact that someone has had a higher education may prove to be more important for selection purposes than the subject studied or the final grade achieved. After all, in Britain, getting into higher education is rather more difficult than coming out of it with a qualification once you have got in.

Socialization

The third purpose identified is likely to reinforce any bias present in the selection function. Higher education is seen here as responsible for socializing its participants for their future roles. It adjusts and forms their values and behaviour to fit them for their intended professional and personal niches in the economy and in society. This function is, I suspect, similar to what Robbins meant when it spoke of common culture and standards; though, to be rather more honest, you might just as well call it elite culture and standards. This is close to the original, experiential purpose of higher education in this country – that is, the production of well-rounded gentlemen and intellectuals – and it has always been an important part of its purpose.

Scholarship

Scholarship, or the advancement of learning and knowledge, is also a long-standing function of higher education. Its extension to include research is of more recent origin. Newman, for example, though he was by then out of step with the views of his time, believed that research was best carried on outside the university (Newman 1852). This view is now emerging again in a different form: research funding may be removed from certain university departments or institutions, and concentrated in 'centres of excellence'. Yet, regardless of how research is organized, it remains the case that a good deal of scholarship takes place outside higher education institutions: for example, in industry, in public libraries, in private homes.

Service

This function is more commonly recognized outside the United Kingdom: as in the United States (e.g. Trow 1969), the Soviet Union and many Third World countries. Higher education is seen there as having a responsibility to serve local industry and the community through consultancy, applied research and teaching, and even advocacy. The institution of higher education is viewed as part of the wider society, not as in some way separate from it. This attitude is now becoming more prevalent in Britain, at least at the profit-making end of the spectrum. Its importance is implicit in most of the arguments made in the first part of this chapter.

Somewhat cynically, a sixth purpose, shared by most institutions and systems (outside as well as within education), might be added at this point. This function could be seen as either additional or all-encompassing: namely, self-perpetuation. It might then be argued that, whereas none of the purposes outlined above are essential aims for any particular institution of higher education, self-perpetuation almost invariably is.

The expectations of the various clients of higher education, in so far as they are expressed and understood, tend to confirm this broad categorization of purposes. For example, the work of the 'Expectations of Higher Education' project based at Brunel University has produced a considerable amount of evidence regarding employers' attitudes towards first degree study. In Britain, widespread graduate recruitment is a comparatively recent phenomenon (Silver and Silver 1981; Gordon 1983). It is not surprising, therefore, that employers do not share a standard view on the value of degrees:

> For many employers the value of a degree is not something which can be assessed solely in terms of the degree itself, but derives from a comparison

with other available forms of experience and training ... The most straightforward form of evaluation lies in assessing the specific attributes which are gained during degree work, which non-graduates lack. Examples given are the ability to learn, relative maturity, the level of training. However, there is no consensus among employers about this; some argue that such qualities might as easily be developed by non-graduates and indeed some argue that it is preferable for people to undertake forms of training other than degree work, even though they still recruit graduates ... Three factors contribute to the value added by a degree. The majority perceive it as adding some value beyond A levels, though some do not think it is very great. Mostly, this value derives from a mix of academic and non-academic qualities which graduates are believed to acquire. Secondly, a minority put a very high value on the substantive content of the degree. A third perception cross-cuts these. Whereas the first two see values as attributes to the individual graduate, the third sees a value in the degree as a useful (if not wholly accurate) screening device.

(Roizen and Jepson 1985, pp. 63–4)

On this evidence (see also Teichler 1989), employers of graduates seem to be mainly concerned with the skills development and selection functions of higher education. The emphasis is placed firmly on the product and its background rather than on the process and content.

This may not be the case with other kinds or levels of higher education. Day-release and sandwich courses, which are most common at sub-degree level, draw employers into a closer relationship with both the student and the higher education institution during the course. Employers may be involved in course planning, teaching and evaluation. Yet the general support which many employers give to the principle of sandwich education does not necessarily mean that they will select sandwich students for jobs in preference to those with more conventional qualifications (DES 1985a). The widespread prejudice against employing mature students has already been noted in Chapter 6 (see Graham 1989).

Collaboration between employers and higher education also tends to be closer at postgraduate level, notably in applied research projects and in the provision of short post-experience courses. The service function of higher education is being stressed here. Both parties are now being urged into closer partnership in these areas by the government, despite some lingering doubts on each side. At this level, of course, the product involved is rather different. The students (employees) concerned will usually study part-time, remaining on their employer's payroll and under their direction.

Some evidence is also available on students' expectations. Conventional full-time students tend to have a rather underdeveloped perception of the purposes of higher education. A national survey carried out at the beginning of the 1960s concluded that such students displayed a general lack of consideration regarding their reasons for entering higher education, for choosing to study a particular subject and for attending one institution rather than another (Marris

1964). The situation is not much changed now (Higgins and Keen 1988), though it may be that student attitudes were different during the late 1960s and the early 1970s. School-leavers with the requisite entry qualifications and social background see full-time higher education as a natural step to take. By taking it, they increase their chances of entering desirable employment and enjoying a comfortable life-style. In other words, they subscribe to the selection and socialization functions. What higher education actually does to you is possibly too imponderable a question to address at that age.

Part-time and mature students, as indicated in Chapter 6, generally have a clearer perspective of higher education. Their stated aims on enrolment appear to be mainly instrumental, focusing on the selection and skills development functions. In taking this stance, they share or reflect the attitudes held by most employers. Since most of the students who have been surveyed were studying for qualifications, this orientation is understandable. Mature students who are primarily interested in their personal development, or in studying a particular subject (i.e. scholarship), may opt for less formal kinds of further or adult education.

Conclusions

How, then, does the value of higher education – whether full-time or part-time, as presently or as potentially arranged – compare in a wider context with that of other possible activities or investments? I will attempt to provide some answers to this question by drawing on the complementary analyses of value and purpose just presented.

Figure 2 offers a summary framework within which these answers may be sought. The two main axes represent the characteristics of higher education and the attitudes adopted towards it. A third axis has been suggested by listing the purposes of higher education, as identified above, within these two axes.

Higher education is presented, along the horizontal axis, as a spectrum (or a 'seamless robe'?). Here, the obvious distinction between part-time and full-time provision, with the various gradations between, has been used. Other categorizations could be applied as well: for example, between long and short courses,

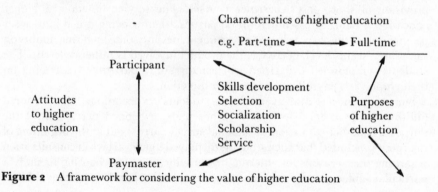

Figure 2   A framework for considering the value of higher education

generalist and specialist subject matter, or initial and continuing forms of provision (cf. Figure 1).

The range of attitudes held by those involved in higher education has been portrayed, down the vertical axis, as varying between those of the participant and the paymaster. This axis is not so much a spectrum as a series of overlapping roles. Thus, the paymaster, though typically the state, might also be the employer or the student; while participants might include employers as well as students. For the paymaster, the alternative investments to higher education, with which its value will be compared, include items such as health care, housing, social security, defence and other forms of education and training: in other words, the headings to be found in any public expenditure White Paper. For the participant, the alternatives cover uses of time as much as money; such as employment, entertainment, social activity, leisure and, again, other forms of education or training.

The relative value of higher education may be thought of within this framework as involving a dynamic balance between different kinds of provision, the different interests concerned and the different purposes considered in the context of possible alternative activities or investments. For the paymaster, a certain minimum level of investment in different kinds of higher education may be viewed as essential in order to service the economy and society, and ensure the production of the desired numbers of people with particular skills. This is, in essence, the manpower planning strategy. The difficulty, of course, lies in judging what the minimum level of investment at any given moment should be; and at what point the available funds and/or time should be directed to other things. Both over-investment and mis-investment – for example, between different kinds of provision – may be as damaging as under-investment. Any disbenefits that arise from such errors will affect both participant and paymaster in the form of diminished returns.

The value of maintaining higher education above the minimum level needed in order to use it as a selection device is doubtful. Less expensive, and possibly more valid, forms of selection are available for most roles (e.g. interview techniques). The case for an expanded system of higher education should probably, therefore, rest at least as much on its value for socialization as for skills development. It matters little to this argument whether socialization is perceived in terms of social control or as social development. But it is in this area that the substitution of alternative activities – for example, employment or leisure-related investment – seems most relevant, and in which the comparative value of higher education is most questionable. Much may then rest on the validity of higher education's most intrinsic purpose, scholarship, and on the persuasive force which potential participants can exercise over potential paymasters.

In an extensive review of the individual and social value of American higher education, Bowen and his colleagues came to the conclusion that:

The monetary returns alone, in the form of enhanced earnings of workers and improved technology, are probably sufficient to offset all the costs. But over and above the monetary returns are the personal development and life enrichment of millions of people, the preservation of the cultural heritage, the advancement of knowledge and of the arts, a major contribution to national prestige and power, and the direct satisfactions derived from college attendance and from living in a society where knowledge and the arts flourish. These nonmonetary benefits surely are far greater than the monetary benefits – so much greater, in fact, that individual and social decisions about the future of higher education should be made primarily on the basis of nonmonetary considerations and only secondarily on the basis of monetary factors . . . In short, the cumulative evidence leaves no doubt that American higher education is well worth what it costs.

(Bowen *et al.* 1978, pp. 447–8; see also Feldman and Newcomb 1969, Hyman *et al.* 1975)

A broadly similar conclusion could be reached regarding the value of higher education in the United Kingdom. *But* such a conclusion does not enable one to say whether a different investment of money and time, between higher education and other activities, would be more or less valuable. However, the conclusion of the first part of this chapter – that there should be a shift of resources within our higher education system, away from full-time and towards part-time provision – is also relevant here. In the case of full-time provision, the decision to participate or not has to be a fairly clear yes or no. Part-time higher education enables us to 'have our cake and eat it', by investing in higher education alongside a portfolio of other activities which are pursued at the same time.

8

Alternative Models

Introduction

In the last chapter, I examined the value and purpose of higher education, contrasting part-time and full-time forms of provision. I concluded that part-time higher education was seriously undervalued at present in the United Kingdom, and that the future expansion of the higher education system should be based mainly on part-time provision. This chapter builds on that analysis, and on the findings reported in earlier chapters, in extending the comparison between full-time and part-time higher education. The focus here is on how higher education could be developed in the future, and on how we could achieve these changes.

The first part of the chapter presents a synopsis of what I have called the dominant model or ideology of British higher education (Tight 1989a) – that is, full-time provision for qualified school-leavers – and indicates why this model has achieved and retained its dominance. Possible alternative models are then reviewed, and their advantages and implications are examined. Finally, the key question of how best to move away from the dominant model, and towards a range of alternatives, is considered.

The dominant model

As I have already indicated (see Chapters 6 and 7), the information available on the expectations of higher education's clients is far from comprehensive. When these expectations are expressed, they are frequently too general or inconsistent to be of practical use. It is not surprising, therefore, that higher education remains essentially supplier-led. Those who work in higher education, particularly at a senior level, largely determine the nature of what it is that they offer to the rest of society. And there is an underlying uniformity in their assumptions and practices which, despite the apparent diversity within the system (Burgess 1977; Halsey 1979), sustains a dominant model of teaching and learning.

This dominant model is strongest in the universities, partly because of the relative priority which they give to research over teaching. It is a model which has become dominant only during the last 40 years (see Chapter 2), though it harks back to the medieval English tradition:

> a university in Britain tends to be evaluated in terms of certain normative criteria. First, it should be ancient: second, it should draw its students, not from a restricted regional locality, but from the nation and internationally: third, its students, whatever their origins, should be carefully selected as likely to fit into and maintain the established life and character of the university: fourth, those who enter should be offered 'education' and not merely 'training'. This end necessitates, fifth, a small-scale residential community affording close contact of teachers with taught in a shared domestic life and, sixth, a high staff–student ratio for individualised teaching . . . A seventh criterion of the traditional ideal is that a university should be politically autonomous which tends to mean richly and independently endowed . . . Eighth and finally the internal affairs of the ideal university should be governed by a democracy of its own academic members . . . The ideal of a university in Britain is accordingly based on a conception, whether accurate or not, of the essential characteristics of Oxford or Cambridge.
>
> (Halsey and Trow 1971, pp. 67, 72)

The dominant model has also been influential in many British polytechnics and colleges, most of whose staff were educated in universities. This influence may have increased in recent years as a consequence of academic drift (Pratt and Burgess 1974); but it is curtailed by the existence of alternative traditions, and by the greater attention paid in the public sector to new developments. Although more than half of British higher education – in terms of the numbers of students enrolled – is now in the public sector, the dominant model holds sway because the universities continue to condition the perceptions of the outside world, and much of academe, regarding the nature of higher education.

The dominant model can best be described by reference to the various characteristics of higher education courses; entry requirements, course length, course location, mode of study, teaching and learning methods, curriculum, timetabling, accreditation, costs and control (cf. Chapter 5). Indeed, the model is based on the notion of the course as the ideal form of teaching provision, just as it is based on the autonomous institution as the ideal provider.

It is interesting that no comprehensive analysis of course characteristics, and the justifications for them, seems to have been attempted in Britain since the time of the Robbins Report (Committee on Higher Education 1963, Appendix 2B; University Grants Committee 1964b). The Leverhulme programme of study produced some interesting work in this area in the early 1980s (Williams and Blackstone 1983), but lacked the facility to either develop its conclusions or put them into practice. This lack of recent analysis is at least partly, and perhaps largely, due to the very success of the Robbins Report. In securing widespread acceptance as a (but *not* the only) blueprint for subsequent development, it effectively removed the need for much discussion:

The Robbins Report helped to justify and chart the great expansion of British higher education in the decade and a half following its publication. But this liberal and expansionist document has also served to limit the growth of British higher education by affirming the values and assumptions that define the English 'idea of a university'. Among these values are: (i) the monopoly by state supported institutions of study leading to degrees; (ii) their commitment to high and common academic standards for the honours degree; (iii) a degree earned through full-time study over three years; and (iv) the costs of student maintenance and instruction being borne wholly (or nearly so) by the state. These values and commitments, accepted by Robbins and the academic world as a whole, are incompatible with the provision of mass higher education to much more than the 15 per cent of the age grade currently enrolled in British higher education. (Trow 1989a, p. 55)

The following characteristics of the dominant model of British higher education may be identified (cf. those identified in the two quotations above):

- an insistence on standard forms of knowlege and certification on entry;
- entry immediately after school;
- a period of study lasting for three or four years full-time, but with long vacations and a considerable amount of spare time during term;
- study away from the (parental) home, but relatively isolated from the surrounding community, and preferably involving residence within the institution;
- study leading to a degree, preferably a specialized honours degree;
- study based on and within 'disciplines', which may have little relevance to the student's prior or subsequent experience;
- the use of expert/novice forms of teaching, exemplified by the lecture and the three-hour unseen written examination, and sustained by the notion of a body of knowledge which has to be mastered;
- the majority of the costs incurred borne by the state and the student's parents.

This characterization is, of course, simplified. There are many examples of provision which vary from it in some way. This is true even within the university sector. Birkbeck College, for example, has long concentrated its efforts on the provision of part-time courses for mature employed students during the evening. Multidisciplinary and modular courses are common in many universities, though there have been indications of a reversion to more traditional patterns in recent years (Hajnal 1972; Squires 1987).

On many courses, students are allowed to exercise some influence over their curricula through project work and dissertations. Sandwich courses, linking periods of study with work placements, are offered by several universities, though they remain essentially confined to institutions which had developed them before they became universities. In Scotland, students typically enter university a year earlier and follow a more general curriculum, although here again there has been a shift towards a more specialized pattern of provision, particularly in the sciences.

Greater variations from the dominant model may be found on the fringes of the university sector. The Open University offers mass access to modular courses, does not have entrance requirements, and teaches its students throughout the country using distance education techniques. And the University of Buckingham, to take another obvious example, is a private institution, receiving little funding from the state. It offers a limited range of intensive courses: first degrees are usually completed within two years, with an extra term in place of the conventional long summer vacation.

Once we move away from the universities and into the public sector, many more examples which differ from the norm that I have described can be identified. At first degree level, the CNAA has overseen the introduction of hundreds of new courses during the last twenty years. There has been a widespread adoption of interdisciplinary and team teaching, modular provision, professional accreditation and other innovations in place of the more restrictive patterns imposed by university degree syllabuses (Lane 1975). Public sector higher education is, of course, not dominated by degree provision in the same way as the university sector. Sub-degree work remains the mainstay in most of the colleges that offer higher education opportunities. A range of block-release, day-release, evening, distance and even open-learning courses may be offered in addition to full-time provision, with the orientation predominantly local and vocational.

These examples could be multiplied with ease, but they all highlight a key point in this argument. Namely, in so far as provision and practice varies from the dominant model, then these variations are perceived by those concerned as acceptable *deviations* from that model. Each deviation has to be carefully justified, and is then effectively limited and controlled, through the range of checks and balances – peer review, external examiners, validation and so on – which exist to maintain standards within the system. These constraints are essentially self-administered. The major driving force behind them is the desire of most polytechnics and colleges of higher education to be thought of as comparable to the universities, and of the universities to be thought of as comparable to Oxbridge, or at least their image of it.

As in society at large, so it is within higher education. Deviations are permitted or tolerated providing that they do not go too far. Change within established institutions is OK so long as it is relatively small-scale and gradual in its impact. In the great majority of cases, therefore, deviations remain confined to particular aspects of provision or to certain courses only.

From this perspective, the significant point about the Open University is not its practice of open access, or its use of distance teaching, but its retention of the honours degree pattern and the three-hour, unseen, written examination (Perry 1976). Similarly, while Birkbeck College may focus on part-time students, its curricula, teaching and assessment methods tend to follow the patterns and practices of full-time provision. Birkbeck's survival as an institution has a lot to do with its location within the federal structure of the University of London. It is significant that no comparable institution has been established elsewhere in the country. Buckingham University, for its part, remains a small and marginal innovation.

In most institutions, multidisciplinary and modular courses are constrained by prerequisite requirements and timetabling clashes; and they normally retain conventional teaching and examination procedures. Project work and dissertations usually make up only a minor part of courses. Continuous assessment seldom counts for as much as the final examination. Non-full-time forms of provision – particularly at first degree and postgraduate levels – are planned and judged in terms of their equivalence to standard full-time courses.

The most significant deviations are mainly to be found at sub-degree and post-experience levels, and in the public sector. Here it is possible, for example, for HNC and HND qualifications to be thought of, at least in principle, as equivalent in standard, even though the part-time HNC route does not cover the subject in as much breadth as the HND. Major deviations at first degree level, such as the independent studies scheme pioneered by the Polytechnic of East London, remain very unusual. Most of those involved in higher education are probably not even aware of such schemes; and, if they are, are likely to be highly suspicious.

The dominant model of teaching and learning that I have described remains the major influence over the provision and practice of higher education in the United Kingdom. This model may well be suited to meeting the needs of particular sorts of clients in particular circumstances. It may, for example, be an excellent means for reproducing the next generation of teachers and scholars to carry on the process of higher education (i.e. the self-perpetuation function referred to in the previous chapter). But it can hardly be thought of as an adequate response to all possible clients in all possible circumstances.

Alternative models

What, then, are the alternatives to the dominant model or ideology which I have just outlined? What would be the advantages and implications of these alternatives for the practice of higher education in the United Kingdom? Some indication of the possibilities has already been given, in passing, in discussing the variations from the norm that are to be found within our present higher education system. There is considerable scope for the adoption and adaptation of these examples by other institutions of higher education. A more extensive appreciation of the possibilities can be had by referring back to the characteristics of the dominant model listed earlier, turning these around and expanding upon them. On this basis, an alternative ideology of higher education would encompass some, most, or all of the following characteristics:

Entry requirements

Entry would not be dependent upon prior knowledge or certification, or on the achievement of some arbitrary standard in examinations. Instead, higher education opportunities and facilities would be available to all those – individuals, groups, organizations – wanting or needing what higher education was capable of providing. Individual entry immediately after school would be atypical: it would still occur, though often after a short break from study. Instead, people would make repeated use of the opportunities offered by higher education at different times during their adult lives.

Study patterns

Study would not normally be thought of in terms of some finite period; and it would not usually be a wholly full-time activity, though it might well involve periods of full-time study. Instead, learning would form one complementary part of adult life, pursued alongside employment, community involvement and social, family and leisure activities. Higher education could then be applied, where desired, to the needs and interests generated by these activities, which would themselves contribute a rich base of experience to the learning process. Institutions would be open for study throughout the day and throughout the year.

Study location

Participation in higher education would not normally necessitate moving away from home, though this would be possible where appropriate. Instead, higher education would be designed so as to minimize disruption in the activity patterns of its participants. Students would make much more use of local provision, whether provided by face-to-face or distance means. Most higher education institutions would function as community service stations within cities or towns, linked to the local economy and community. They would practise outreach, offering courses and facilities off campus as well as on. Interestingly, the outreach approach was pioneered in part by Oxbridge academics in the nineteenth century extension movement (see Chapter 2).

Accreditation

Study might or might not be undertaken with a particular end qualification in view. A range of qualifications would be available, where desired, to accredit different levels and breadths of study. These would allow for credit accumulation and transfer within and between different institutions or schemes of provision. Programmes of study might be specialized or general, long-term or short-term, but would be designed with the needs of the student or client as the priority.

Course content

Study would tend to be based on real problems, activities and interests, rather than on disciplines or subjects. It would be related and applied to students' prior and subsequent experience – at work, at home, in the local community. Skills and knowledge gained by students outside formal education – whether on training courses, through informal study, or by self-directed learning – would be recognized and used. Relevant skills and knowledge could be assessed and credited towards formal qualifications.

Teaching/learning methods

The role of the teacher would become much more that of the facilitator: that is, someone who would help clients to assess what use they could make of the various learning resources available to them, how best to go about their learning, and how to evaluate the results. In such a system, students might be working largely on their own, in one-to-one relationships with particular teachers, or as part of groups of differing sizes. Other students and teachers might be involved in these study groups alongside associates from work or the local community.

Assessment

Students and clients would usually be involved in assessing the progress and results of their studies, and in considering the implications for future study, in partnership with their teachers. A varied range of assessment methods – for example, individual or group project work, supervised job experience, problem solving, pre-disclosed essay questions, portfolios, presentations – would be employed in addition to, or instead of, the three-hour, unseen, written examination (see CNAA 1989). In some cases, assessment would be neither necessary nor sought: the study experience would be sufficient in itself.

Costs

A significant proportion of the costs of engaging in study would typically be borne by the students themselves. This would make the comparative costs and benefits of different kinds of higher education more evident to those most closely involved. Decisions over what to study, and how, when and where to study it, would be taken in the light of this information. Employers, and other organizations which stood to benefit from the study concerned, would normally be expected to contribute to its costs as well. This contribution might take the form of work release, financial assistance, or fully paid educational leave (Wagner 1979; Killeen and Bird 1981). The state would continue to support institutions offering higher education opportunities, though it would no longer be their major funder. It would also financially assist some students, such as the unemployed, who were unable to obtain support from other sources. Since students would usually be *de facto* as well as legal adults, their parents' financial support would be much less common.

The alternative approaches which I have just described could form the basis for a substantially more varied and flexible system of higher education in this country. In such a system, much more emphasis would be placed upon higher education's service function. This does not mean, however, that the other four purposes identified in the previous chapter – skills development, selection, socialization and scholarship – would be ignored. Service shifts the focus away from the institution and towards the client, whether this is an individual, a group, or an organization. Institutions of higher education are then in the business of serving as many clients and as many needs as possible, given the constraints under which they are operating: 'If once we take seriously the idea that the education service is a *service*, and one which seeks to serve everybody, we are committed to fundamental changes' (Burgess 1977, p. 87).

These changes would not, of course, be unproblematic. They would create significantly different work patterns for many of those involved in education. They would also, if seriously implemented, necessitate a general expansion of the system alongside its internal restructuring. This would affect secondary education and non-advanced further education as well as higher education. If higher education is to become more accessible, there is a pressing need to move the emphasis in secondary education away from the preparation of an elite group for full-time degree study (Neave 1985a).

Within the restructured higher education system, much less emphasis would be placed on the conventional university than is currently the case. Indeed, there would probably be proportionately far fewer universities, but there would be many more other institutions offering varied opportunities for engaging in higher learning (Carter 1980; Halsey 1987). Institutional diversity would be positively encouraged, rather than viewed as a weakness (Birnbaum 1983; Trow 1989a).

Such a system would in some ways be more hierarchical than at present, but the hierarchy would be interconnected and open rather than divisive, elitist and closed. Higher education would become part of a broadly conceived and potentially lifelong system of education, drawing in, serving and affecting more people. It would no longer be a brief, once-and-for-all, post-school, but school-like activity. It would be adult rather than adolescent.

Standards would not be neglected in such a system, but they would be approached from a rather different standpoint (Usher 1986). When an academic uses the term 'standards' today, what is being referred to is usually entry standards: that is, keeping potential students out. The hidden agenda here is a wish to ensure that the great majority of entrants successfully exit the system with a standard qualification after completing the standard period of study. This approach effectively minimizes the effort required from teaching staff. If institutions of higher education only admit students with good A-level qualifications, and then give them three years of full-time study, they would really be failing if the great majority of their students did not graduate successfully.

What we ought to be primarily concerned about when we talk about standards is the quality of the service offered, and the effect which it has – that is, the 'value added' – on those making use of it. Exit standards are important, but they should be pitched at a variety of levels and assessed in a variety of ways. Students who do not satisfactorily complete their studies within a given period, whether for educational or non-educational reasons, should not be stigmatized as failures, dropouts, or wastage. They should be helped to achieve their aims and potential by whatever means then seems most appropriate.

Achieving change

The alternative ideology of higher education which I have just put forward is, of course, liable to be dismissed in some quarters as hopelessly utopian or impractical, even if it is considered to be desirable. It should be stressed, therefore, that some changes are already taking place in the directions indicated, albeit rather more slowly than might be wished. Considerable pressures are also being exerted by a range of governmental and non-governmental interests for quicker and more substantive changes.

There are revealing and supportive parallels to this ideology to be found both at home and abroad. In the United Kingdom, adult/continuing education, in both its liberal and vocational forms, embodies many of the alternative characteristics which I have described. Though this sector of provision has long been viewed as marginal, when compared with higher or secondary education (Keddie 1980), it is of growing significance. And it has the potential to form part of an integrated system of post-compulsory education, together with higher and further education (Schuller *et al.* 1988). In an international context, the British higher education system is in many ways atypical (as was shown in Chapter 4). More open access, more flexible curricula and more extensive participation are to be found in North America, Australasia and most Western European countries.

Assuming that the alternative ideological approach which I have outlined is attractive (at least in part) to others than myself, how might we aim to move towards it and away from the present structure? Clearly, it would be foolish to expect to change the current system overnight. The capacity of established institutions for inertia – for ignoring, absorbing and subverting strategies for change – has to be dealt with. Nor can it be realistically expected that changes of this magnitude can be easily imposed from the centre, although central government and its agencies will undoubtedly have a key role to play.

The government's present role as the principal funder of higher education is of particular importance. For example, the current proposals for altering the methods by which students are funded, shifting the balance away from grants and towards loans, will have significant structural consequences (see DES 1988 and Chapter 9). They are likely to produce a gradual blurring of the present distinction between full-time and part-time study. More 'full-time' students will need to spend more of their time working, in order to earn money to support themselves during their studies. If institutions respond to such developments in a positive fashion, by allowing students to vary their study loads, the flexibility of the higher education system will be substantially increased. There is also scope here to use changing patterns of study (and work) to strengthen and expand links between institutions of higher education and employers.

The government's policies regarding the future funding of institutions will obviously be of critical significance as well. It remains to be seen how these policies will be developed and implemented by the newly established Universities Funding Council (UFC) and Polytechnics and Colleges Funding Council (PCFC). What is important in the present context is that part-time forms of provision should be encouraged, and resourced on a more equitable basis than they have been up until now. The performance indicators to be used in assessing institutional productivity should, therefore, focus on the value added by study, rather than on just the output.

The other key element in a realistic strategy for development is attitude change. This will involve altering the attitudes of those who work in higher education, while simultaneously enhancing the expectations of their clients. Providers need to be made more aware of the range of functions which their institutions can usefully serve. Staff development, which is almost non-existent in some institutions at present, will need to be expanded. Staff at all levels will need assistance to gain the skills required to teach in different ways, and to serve alternative clients. New kinds of staff, with more varied backgrounds, experience and skills, will need to be brought in to supplement and extend the abilities of those already in post. The demise of academic tenure – and its replacement by standard contracts of employment, together with necessary incentive schemes – should enable a much greater degree of flexibility to be introduced into staffing as these changes gradually take effect.

Existing and potential clients – individuals, community groups, employers – will need to be reached through publicity and marketing exercises. They will have to be persuaded of the expanded scope for collaboration with their local higher education institutions. They will also need to be persuaded to contribute more resources, both in cash and in kind, to higher education. Much work is already being done along these lines in vocational areas. Further and more expansive developments are now required to shift the burden of higher education funding away from the state.

It is probably advisable at this point to return to the underlying question: why should we attempt to change the ideology of higher education in this way?

Because higher education in the United Kingdom is not currently serving anything like all of its potential clients; and because it is not serving many of those that it does serve as well as it could. All of the rhetoric which we regularly hear about the accelerating pace of change in technology, the economy and society, and the consequent need for more education and training, contains terrible and timely truths. We do need a better educated, more adaptable and more self-reliant population if we are to maintain, far less develop, our position in the world. But we cannot hope to bring more people into higher education, and bring them in more often, if we retain the dominant model of provision and practice that I have described. We will only attract more clients, and be of more use to them, if we introduce less rigid and more client-focused systems of provision much more widely.

9

Prospects and Conclusions

Introduction

In this book I have attempted to provide a distinctive analysis and vision of higher education in the United Kingdom. I have done this by viewing the subject from a part-time perspective, and by comparing the context, characteristics and clients of part-time and full-time forms of provision.

In Chapter 1, a general definition of part-time higher education was given, and its wide and varied scope was indicated. The following three chapters provided the background for the discussion and analysis in the remainder of the book.

Chapter 2 looked at the history of British higher education during the last century and a half. It concluded that part-time forms of provision have always been of considerable significance, and that part-time higher education students have probably outnumbered full-time students throughout this period.

Chapter 3 summarized the current position using the available national statistics. These show that part-time provision remains of great importance, but that it is mainly to be found outside what is perceived as the mainstream of higher education. Part-time provision is concentrated at sub-degree, post-experience and postgraduate levels (i.e. not at first degree level), and outside the conventional universities.

Chapter 4 reviewed the position in other Western developed countries. Part-time forms of provision or attendance account for a substantial and growing proportion of higher education in all of these countries. By contrast with the United Kingdom, this is also true for provision made at first degree level and/or by the universities.

The next two chapters examined the characteristics of British part-time higher education in more detail. Chapter 5 described the providers involved and the provision available at first degree, sub-degree, postgraduate and post-experience levels. The differing lengths, structures, contents, methods, subjects and locations of the courses offered were analysed.

Chapter 6 presented a complementary view of the students and clients who make use of part-time higher education. This illustrated both their heterogeneity and the considerable differences between them and the conventional, full-time, school-leaver student.

Chapters 7 and 8 then used this information and analysis as the basis for a detailed critique of the structure, philosophy and operation of the current British higher education system. Chapter 7 compared the value of part-time and full-time forms of higher education in terms of their stated purposes, and of their relationship to the society of which they are a part. It concluded that part-time higher education was seriously undervalued by comparison with full-time higher education.

Chapter 8 built upon these arguments through an examination of two very different models of higher education. The dominant model of full-time, university-type, residential provision for school-leavers was described first. An alternative model, or models – based much more on part-time provision, and on responding flexibly to the varied needs which higher education is in a position to service – was then put forward. It was argued that we should attempt to move away from the dominant model, and towards the alternative model. The methods by which this might be achieved were then briefly considered.

In this final chapter, I intend to do two things. First, I will look at likely developments in higher education policy in the United Kingdom, stressing the potential role of part-time forms of provision. Second, and finally, I will attempt to reach some general conclusions about where we are now and the way forward.

Policy

In Chapter 2, I referred to a number of major higher education policy reviews which have been carried out by or for the government of the day since the Second World War: most notably, the Anderson Report on student grants, the Robbins Report and its aftermath, and the creation of the binary system. I noted that each of these reviews tended to either pay little attention to part-time forms of provision, or to encourage, whether this was the intention or not, a continuing shift towards full-time higher education. There are, of course, exceptions, the most important being the establishment of the Open University; but, as I argued in Chapter 8, the significant point about these is that they have been *few* in number, and that they remain *exceptions*.

These tendencies have continued virtually right up until the present day; though some recent statements, to be discussed later, appear rather more positive. Ministers and politicians may, occasionally, refer in their rhetoric to the important role which part-time higher education has to play. Yet their policies remain overwhelmingly concerned with full-time higher education, and they typically ignore the knock-on effects of these policies for part-time providers and students.

For example, in its 1985 Green Paper, the government gave part-time higher education – though it did not refer to it as such – a number of relatively favourable mentions. It recognized the case for developing provision to improve access for mature students. It noted the continuing importance of liberal adult education, though under new and more strenuous funding arrangements. And it stressed the need for in-career vocational study, with employers bearing the major responsibility for meeting the costs involved. But, in the same document, it set out – against the evidence – a restrictive view of higher education, seeing no real need for expansion: 'The available evidence suggests that . . . there has continued in practice to be a place somewhere in higher education for all those qualified and seeking to enter' (Secretary of State for Education and Science *et al.* 1985, p. 10).

The glossy White Paper that followed, two years later, heralded a switch in the funding arrangements for institutions of higher education away from block grants, and towards much more specific, performance-related contracts. It stressed the importance of widening access to higher education, without indicating how this would be financed, and reiterated the government's revised version of the Robbins principle: 'Places should be available for all who have the necessary intellectual competence, motivation and maturity to benefit from higher education and who wish to do so' (Secretary of State for Education and Science *et al.* 1987, p. 7). But there was always the proviso that 'the benefit has to be sufficient to justify the cost' (Secretary of State for Education and Science *et al.* 1985, p. 10).

All polytechnics and major colleges in England were removed from the control of the local education authorities by the Education Reform Act of 1988, and placed under the new Polytechnics and Colleges Funding Council (PCFC). This decision split up the planning of part-time higher education, since it left part-time (but not full-time) sub-degree courses as a responsibility of the local authorities.

The 1988 consultative paper which outlined the government's proposals for introducing top-up loans for students was exclusively concerned with full-time students. It did not consider the arguments for introducing a more equitable system, or for making financial support available to part-time students on a similar basis. It did propose the establishment of a number of small access funds, which would be available for institutions to distribute to deserving individuals. But it remains unclear whether these could be used to assist part-time students (DES 1988).

The related 1989 consultative paper on institutional resourcing, which proposed a shift in the balance of the public funding of higher education from grants to fees, similarly skated over the potential effects of such policies for part-time provision. It simply and unconvincingly stated that:

Fees for part-time places are not supported by mandatory awards and a substantial increase in such fees would tend to impair access and adversely affect institutions with a high concentration of part-time students. The Government will therefore not reduce the funds available to the Funding Councils to support part-time places; and it looks to the Councils and other funding bodies to recognise this feature in the grant paid in support of these places. In these circumstances, there is no reason why part-time fees should rise, except as might in any case be appropriate between years, as a result of the proposals in this paper.

(DES 1989b, pp. 5–6)

A similar lack of concern for part-time higher education is apparent in the official projections of student numbers, which are issued periodically by the DES and other government departments. Just over a decade ago, under a previous administration, the DES put forward a series of alternative models for considering the future demand for higher education and its satisfaction. These had been formulated in the light of anticipated fluctuations in the size of the 18-year-old cohort, and they at least recognized the possibility of expanding the audience for higher education beyond traditional groups (DES 1978). The projections which have been produced since then have been less adventurous. They treat part-time students as a very secondary consideration, to be added to the predictions for full-time student numbers in the form of 'full-time equivalents' only when all the other calculations have been carried out.

Thus, the technical report which accompanied the 1984 forecasts made it clear that future part-time student numbers had been extrapolated in an essentially arbitrary fashion (DES 1984a, 1984b). The numbers of Open University students were assumed to remain constant. All other part-time participation was taken to fluctuate in line with changes in the size of the 18–34-year-old age group. This group was identified as the main group involved in part-time higher education, and their participation rate was projected forward from the preceding four-year period.

The 1986 projections showed little methodological development, but were rather more expansive (DES 1986). The most generous projection (projection Q) indicated that part-time student numbers were expected to rise by 12% from 328,000 in 1985 to a peak of 367,000 in 1995, falling back to 341,000 by 2000. Full-time student numbers, by comparison, would rise by only 4% to peak at 602,000 in 1990, drop to 564,000 by 1996, and then rise again to 604,000 by 2000 (ibid, tables A7 and A8). Recent projections for Scotland alone offer a more interesting scenario. Here, the high variant suggests a 50% growth in part-time student numbers, from 46,900 in 1986 to 70,300 in 1997, by which time they would nearly equal the predicted full-time numbers of 79,100 (Scottish Education Department 1988, table 6).

The government's rather restricted view of higher education, and its particular blindness towards part-time provision, has not always been shared by other official bodies. In 1980, for example, the Education, Science and Arts Select Committee of the House of Commons chided the government over the lack of information available on higher education, and its lack of emphasis on the needs of adults. It successfully demanded further information from the DES on part-time and continuing education (Education, Science and Arts Committee 1980, particularly appendix 14).

In 1982, the Chilver Report on the future of higher education in Northern Ireland argued that: 'there is a need to increase the opportunities for access to higher education in areas of Northern Ireland remote from the major institutions, and in particular in regard to part-time studies in vocational subjects' (Department of Education for Northern Ireland 1982, p. 4). Part-time higher education, and its future development, also formed part of the deliberations of the Scottish Tertiary Education Advisory Council in 1985 (Scottish Tertiary Education Advisory Council 1985).

Both the National Advisory Body and the University Grants Committee produced working reports on continuing education in 1984 (NAB 1984a; UGC 1984a). Continuing education was defined to include mature students, part-time degree and diploma courses, extra-mural type provision and post-experience vocational education: in other words, much of what has been considered in this book under the label of part-time higher education. Both bodies, in a joint statement produced later that year – as part of their submissions to the government on the future strategy for higher education – argued that the provision of continuing education should be seen as a fifth objective for higher education, to be added to the four identified by the Robbins Committee twenty years before (NAB 1984b; UGC 1984b).

The financial assumptions made by these bodies, in distributing state resources to institutions of higher education, have become clearer in the last few years. The NAB indicated its support for part-time provision by raising the full-time equivalent (FTE) of part-time students to 0.4. This level was still far from adequate, however, to provide equitable support for many part-time courses, and it was not always translated into increased resources within an institution. The UGC remained less appreciative of the value of part-time study throughout its lifetime, though it latterly adopted a rather more generous FTE of 0.5 for part-time students.

It is reassuring that the successors to the NAB and the UGC, the PCFC and the UFC, appear to have the interests of those involved in part-time provision in mind. Indeed, the UFC, in setting out its twelve aims in 1989, went so far as to express one of them as follows:

4.   Students: A growing range of opportunities for initial and continuing education to be offered to both full-time and part-time students and to both young and mature students. The range of social and educational backgrounds of students to be broadened and the participation of under-represented groups to be increased.

(UFC 1989, p. 2)

We have yet to see how far such aims will be realized in the bodies' funding policies.

Individual commentators on higher education can afford to be much more critical of government policies. In the last few years, an increasing number of people involved in higher education have put forward radical plans for its future development. These have usually involved a considerable expansion of access (see, for example, McIlroy 1987; Ball 1989; Fulton 1989; Smithers and Robinson 1989; Wright 1989; Smith and Saunders 1991). Part-time forms of provision would have a major role to play in achieving such plans. We may be witnessing at least the beginning of the kind of attitude change which I argued for in the previous chapter.

The government, for its part, has recently become much more expansive in its planning for future participation in higher education. Shortly before he left office as Secretary of State for Education, Kenneth Baker was talking in terms of doubling student numbers within 25 years. The practicalities of doing so have not yet been properly addressed.

These changes in policy and attitudes suggest that the prospects for the development of part-time higher education are quite good. It would be naïve, however, to be too optimistic. A great deal of work remains to be done if part-time forms of higher education are to be made as widely available and as relevant as they could be. This work needs to be done both within higher education itself, and, more importantly, within British society as a whole.

Conclusions

We may now be at something of a pivotal point in the history of higher education in the United Kingdom. We have probably already gone about as far as we can in expanding our higher education system using the model established in the 1960s: the dominant, university-based model described in Chapter 8. If participation is to be further increased, and if new kinds of participation are to be encouraged, alternative models of higher education will need to be developed alongside or instead of the dominant model. Of course, as I argued in Chapter 8, this is already happening to some extent, particularly outside the conventional universities.

This state of affairs, and the consequent need for change, has at least been recognized by the present government. Its response has not, inevitably, been what many in higher education would have wished: witness the changes introduced by the Education Reform Act of 1988, and the new approaches which are being developed for student and institutional resourcing. The government has adopted a two-pronged strategy of the kind suggested in the conclusion to Chapter 8. It is both manipulating the funding of higher education and seeking to change attitudes in order to effect desired changes in higher education. And the opposition parties, whatever their present rhetoric, are unlikely to reverse the majority of its policy changes when they eventually return to power.

What is missing in government policy, and in the response to it, is a sufficient and explicit recognition of the central role of part-time higher education in the future development of higher education as a whole.

We should be planning for part-time developments at all levels of provision – sub-degree, first degree, postgraduate and post-experience. Particular attention should be devoted to first degree level (though not necessarily to first degrees), where part-time face-to-face provision is at present very underdeveloped.

We should be planning for more flexible forms of provision. Students should be enabled to mix face-to-face and distance forms of study, and to alternate periods of part-time and full-time study. Modularization and credit transfer arrangements should be further developed. We should be encouraging regular and periodic involvement in continuing higher education throughout life.

We should be planning for higher education based more on individual students' experiences and needs, linked to their work and community responsibilities. We should be offering them more say in the design, delivery and evaluation of their own education.

We should be planning for the introduction of more equitable funding arrangements for higher education. Grants and/or loans should be available to part-time students on the same terms as to full-time students. Part-time provision should receive equivalent support, pro rata, to full-time provision.

Full-time attitudes and misconceptions have dominated and diverted thinking and practice in British higher education for too long. Part-time higher education offers a way forward. Full-time higher education will remain important for certain subjects, students and needs. But it cannot offer a general model for a significantly expanded system of higher education: the sort of system that we need. Only part-time higher education can do that. Only part-time higher education gives a genuinely real-life perspective to higher education, effectively linking it with the society of which it is an integral and crucially important part.

References

Abercrombie, N., Cullen, I., Godson, V., Major, S., Timson, L. and Cowan, P. (1974). *The University in an Urban Environment: a study of activity patterns from a planning viewpoint.* London, Heinemann.

Abner, B. and Tacon, P. (1988). *The Part-time Student in Canada: 1988 survey of Atkinson College.* Toronto, York University.

Abrahamsson, K. (1984). 'Does the adult majority create new patterns of student life? Some experiences of Swedish higher education', *European Journal of Education* 19 (3), 283–98.

Abrahamsson, K. (1986). *Adult Participation in Swedish Higher Education.* Stockholm, Almqvist and Wiksell International.

Academic Advisory Committee on Birkbeck College (1967). *Report.* London, University of London.

Advisory Board for the Research Councils (1982). *Report of the Working Party on Postgraduate Education.* London, HMSO, Cmnd 8537.

Advisory Council for Adult and Continuing Education (1980). 'Comparative statistics on adult students and part-time study for first degrees', in Education, Science and Arts Committee, *The Funding and Organisation of Courses in Higher Education.* London, HMSO, HC 787, pp. 645–50.

Advisory Council for Adult and Continuing Education (1982a). *Continuing Education: from policies to practice.* Leicester, Advisory Council for Adult and Continuing Education.

Advisory Council for Adult and Continuing Education (1982b). *Adults: their educational experience and needs.* Leicester, Advisory Council for Adult and Continuing Education.

Agnello, R. and Hunt, J. (1976). 'The impact of a part-time graduate degree and early-career earnings on late-career earnings', *Journal of Human Resources* 11 (2), 209–18.

Allman, P. (1982). 'New perspectives on the adult: an argument for lifelong education', *International Journal of Lifelong Education*, 1, 41–51.

Allman, P. (1983). 'The nature and process of adult development', in M. Tight (ed.), *Adult Learning and Education.* London, Croom Helm, pp. 107–23.

Anderson, D. and Vervoorn, A. (1983). *Access to Privilege: patterns of participation in Australian post-secondary education.* Canberra, Australian National University Press.

Anderson, R. (1983). *Education and Opportunity in Victorian Scotland: schools and universities.* Oxford, Clarendon Press.

Anisef, P. (1989). 'Studying part-time in Canada's universities: a social change perspective', *Canadian Journal of Higher Education* 19 (1), 11–28.

Anwyl, J. and Powles, M. (1989). 'Priority clienteles for external studies in Australian universities and colleges of advanced education', *Open Learning* 4 (2), 7–15.

Anwyl, J., Powles, M. and Patrick, K. (1987). *Who Uses External Studies? Who Should?* Melbourne, University of Melbourne Centre for the Study of Higher Education.

Argles, M. (1964). *South Kensington to Robbins: an account of English technical and scientific education since 1851.* London, Longman.

Armytage, W. (1955). *Civic Universities: aspects of a British tradition.* London, Benn.

Ashman, S. and George, A. (1980). *Part-time Evening Study for a Degree: a study of some educational implications of a new evening degree scheme at the Polytechnic of North London.* London, Polytechnic of North London.

Association of Polytechnic Teachers (1985). *The Distribution and Funding of Sub-degree Courses in Public Sector Higher Education.* London, APT.

Australian Government Publishing Service (1988). *Higher education: a policy statement.* Canberra, AGPS.

Ball, C. (1989). *Aim Higher: widening access to higher education.* London, Royal Society for the Encouragement of Arts, Manufactures and Commerce.

Banfield, J. (1990). 'Unit course development: a part-time degree for adults', *Adults Learning*, 1 (5), 143–4.

Barnett, R. (1985). 'Higher education: legitimation crisis', *Studies in Higher Education*, 10 (3), 241–55.

Barnett, R. (1987). 'Part-time degree courses: institutional provision in the United Kingdom', *Higher Education Review*, 19 (3), 7–25.

Barnett, R. (1988). 'Does higher education have aims?', *Journal of the Philosophy of Education*, 22 (2), 239–50.

Bates, A. and Pugh, A. (1975). 'Designing multi-media courses for individualised study: the Open University model and its relevance to conventional universities', *British Journal of Educational Technology*, 3 (6), 46–56.

Beaglehole, J. (1937). *The University of New Zealand: an historical study.* Wellington, Council for Educational Research.

Belanger, R., Lynd, D. and Mouelhi, M. (1982). *Part-time Degree Students: tomorrow's majority?* Ottawa, Minister of Supply and Services.

Bell, R. (1973). 'The growth of the modern university', in R. Bell and A. Youngson (eds), *Present and Future in Higher Education.* London, Tavistock, pp. 13–28.

Bell, R. and Tight, M. (forthcoming). *The History of Distance Education in the British Isles.* Milton Keynes, Open University Press.

Bellot, H. (1929). *University College 1826–1926.* London, University of London Press.

Berger, G., Catz, T. and Coulon, A. (1985). 'Paris VIII-Vincennes: a university of the contemporary world', *Higher Education in Europe*, 10 (1), 51–7.

Bertrand, M.-A. (1982). 'To whom is postsecondary education available?', in Council of Ministers of Education, *Postsecondary Education Issues in the 1980s.* Toronto, CMEC, pp. 59–91.

Beswick, D. (1987). *The Role of Government in Higher Education in Australia.* Melbourne, University of Melbourne Centre for the Study of Higher Education.

Bettenson, E. (1971). *The University of Newcastle upon Tyne: a historical introduction 1834–1971.* Newcastle, University of Newcastle upon Tyne.

Bewley, D. (1982). 'Correspondence as the core: the Centre for University Extramural Studies, Massey University', in D. Teather (ed.), *Towards the Community University.* London, Kogan Page, pp. 89–101.

Birkbeck College (1989). *Calendar 1989-90*. London, Birkbeck College.

Birnbaum, R. (1983). *Maintaining Diversity in Higher Education*. San Francisco, Jossey-Bass.

Bishop, R. (1989). 'Part-time higher education in Northern Ireland', *Open Learning*, 4 (2), 21-5.

Blackburn, R., Stewart, A. and Proudy, K. (1980). 'Part-time education and the alternative route', *Sociology*, 14, 603-14.

Boucher, L. (1982). *Tradition and Change in Swedish Education*. Oxford, Pergamon Press.

Bourdieu, P. and Passeron, J.-C. (1977). *Reproduction in Education, Society and Culture*. London, Sage.

Bourdieu, P. and Passeron, J.-C. (1979). *The Inheritors: French students and their relation to culture*. Chicago, University of Chicago Press.

Bourner, T. (1979). 'The "cost" of completing a part-time degree by full-time study', *Higher Education Review*, 12 (1), 55-68.

Bourner, T. (1983). 'Part-time first degree courses of the Council for National Academic Awards', *Educational Studies*, 9, 17-30.

Bourner, T. and Hamed, M. (1987). 'Degree awards in the public sector of higher education: comparative results for A-level entrants and non-A-level entrants', *Journal of Access Studies*, 2 (1), 25-41.

Bourner, T., Hamed, M., Barnett, R. and Reynolds, A. (1988). *Students on CNAA's Part-time First Degree Courses*. London, CNAA.

Bourner, T., Reynolds, A., Hamed, M. and Barnett, R. (1991). *Part-time Students and their Experience of Higher Education*. Milton Keynes, Open University Press.

Bowen, H., Clecak, P., Doud, J. and Douglass, G. (1978). *Investment in Learning: the individual and social value of American higher education*. San Francisco, Jossey-Bass.

Boyer, E. (1987). *College: the undergraduate experience in America*. New York, Harper and Row.

Braithwaite, B. and Batt, K. (1975). 'Open learning: the Australian contribution', in N. MacKenzie, R. Postgate, J. Scupham, *et al.* (eds), *Open Learning: systems and problems in post-secondary education*. Paris, UNESCO Press, pp. 95-120.

Brandes, U. and Raters, E. (1981). 'Demographic trends as a stimulus to extended post-secondary education in the Federal Republic of Germany', *European Journal of Education*, 16 (3-4), 393-401.

Brook, C. (1984). 'Something strange in our regions', *Teaching at a Distance*, 25, 77-83.

Brothers, J. and Hatch, S. (1971). *Residence and Student Life: a sociological inquiry into residence in higher education*. London, Tavistock.

Bruce, A., Cooper, A. and Doherty, G. (1989). *The DipHE Experience: longitudinal study (1983-87) of the 1983 cohort of students registered on CNAA's Diploma of Higher Education courses*. London, CNAA.

Burgess, T. (1977). *Education after School*. London, Gollancz.

Burgess, T. and Pratt, J. (1970). *Policy and Practice: the Colleges of Advanced Technology*. London, Allen Lane, The Penguin Press.

Burns, C. (1924). *A Short History of Birkbeck College*. London, University of London Press.

Burrows, J. (1976). *University Adult Education in London: a century of achievement*. London, University of London.

Bynner, J. (1985). 'Collaborative schemes and the ethos of distance education: a study of Australian and New Zealand universities', *Higher Education*, 14 (5), 513-33.

Byrd, P. and Schuller, T. (1988). 'Parlaying change in education: part-time degrees at the University of Warwick', *Studies in Continuing Education*, 10 (2), 125-36.

Canadian Organization of Part-time University Students (1987). *Part-time University*

Students in Canada: an analysis of the 1974–75 and 1983–84 postsecondary student surveys. Toronto, COPUS.

Cant, R. (1946). *The University of St. Andrews: a short history.* Edinburgh, Oliver and Boyd.

Cantor, L. and Roberts, I. (1969). *Further Education Today: a critical reivew.* London, Routledge and Kegan Paul.

Cantor, L. and Roberts, I. (1986). *Further Education Today: a critical review.* London, Routledge and Kegan Paul (3rd edition).

Careers Research and Advisory Council (1988). *The Directory of Further Education and Many Higher Education Courses in the United Kingdom.* Cambridge, Hobsons Press.

Carswell, J. (1988). 'What Robbins took for granted', *Oxford Review of Education*, 14 (1), 21–32.

Carter, C. (1980). 'Not enough higher education and too many universities?', in N. Evans (ed.), *Education beyond School.* London, Grant McIntyre, pp. 29–45.

Carter, C. (1983). 'Human and material resources', in R. Bourne (ed.), *Part-time First Degrees in Universities.* London, Goldsmiths' College, pp. 42–7.

Caulcott, E. (1983). *Adult Students in the 1970s: a profile of Goldsmiths' College adult evening students in 1970 and 1977.* London, Goldsmiths' College.

Center for Education Statistics (1987). *Digest of Education Statistics 1987.* Washington DC, Government Printing Office.

Central Statistical Office (1989). *Social Trends 19.* London, HMSO.

Cerych, L. (1983). 'International comparisons', in G. Williams and T. Blackstone, *Response to Adversity: higher education in a harsh climate.* Guildford, Society for Research into Higher Education, pp. 133–46.

Cerych, L. and Sabatier, P. (1986). *Great Expectations and Mixed Performance: the implementation of higher education reforms in Europe.* Stoke-on-Trent, Trentham Books.

Charlton, H. (1951). *Portrait of a University 1851–1951.* Manchester, Manchester University Press.

Chickering, A. (1974). *Commuting versus Resident Students: overcoming the educational inequities of living off campus.* San Francisco, Jossey-Bass.

Ciucci, R. (1984). 'Students in 1984: a part-time activity along with other jobs? Illustrations from Italy', *European Journal of Education*, 19 (3), 299–308.

Committee of Vice-Chancellors and Principals (1988). *British Universities' Guide to Graduate Study.* London, Association of Commonwealth Universities.

Committee on Higher Education (1963). *Report.* London, HMSO, Cmnd 2154.

Committee on Higher Education Funding (1988). *Report.* Canberra, Australian Government Publishing Service.

Commonwealth Tertiary Education Commission (1987). *Selected Higher Education Statistics.* Canberra, CTEC.

Connor, S. and Wylie, J. (1985). 'Post-experience vocational education: an investigation of its role in linking colleges, universities and business', *Scottish Journal of Adult Education*, 7 (2), 14–22.

Cotgrove, S. (1958). *Technical Education and Social Change.* London, George Allen and Unwin.

Cottle, B. and Sherborne, J. (1959). *The Life of a University.* Bristol, University of Bristol.

Council for National Academic Awards (1987). *Credit Accumulation and Transfer Scheme: background papers.* London, CNAA.

Council for National Academic Awards (1988a). *Annual Report 1986–87.* London, CNAA.

Council for National Academic Awards (1988b). *Directory of First Degree and Diploma of Higher Education Courses.* London, CNAA.

Council for National Academic Awards (1988c). *Directory of Postgraduate and Post-experience Courses*. London, CNAA.

Council for National Academic Awards (1989). *How Shall We Assess Them?* London, CNAA.

Cross, K. (1981). *Adults as Learners: increasing participation and facilitating learning*. San Francisco, Jossey-Bass.

Cross, K. (1987). 'The changing role of higher education in the United States', *Higher Education Research and Development*, 6 (2), 99–108.

Culshaw, J. (1987). 'Evaluating the sandwich degree', in P. Linklater (ed.), *Education and the World of Work: positive partnerships*. Milton Keynes, Society for Research into Higher Education and Open University Press, pp. 65–81.

Cunningham, I. (1981). 'Self-managed learning in independent study', in T. Boydell and M. Pedler (eds), *Management Self-development: concepts and practices*. London, Gower, pp. 188–204.

Dahllof, U. (1977). *Reforming Higher Education and External Studies in Sweden and Australia*. Stockholm, Almqvist and Wiksell.

Dahllof, U., Willen, B. and Kim, L. (1978). 'Strategies for broader enrolment in Swedish higher education: two case studies', in International Council for Educational Development, *Innovation in Access to Higher Education*. New York, ICED, pp. 247–327.

Davie, G. (1961). *The Democratic Intellect: Scotland and her universities in the nineteenth century*. Edinburgh, Edinburgh University Press.

Dent, H. (1949). *Part-time Education in Great Britain: an historical outline*. London, Turnstile Press.

Dent, H. (1977). *The Training of Teachers in England and Wales 1800–1975*. London, Hodder and Stoughton.

Department of Education and Science (1978). *Higher Education into the 1990s*. London, HMSO.

Department of Education and Science (1984a). *Demand for Higher Education in Great Britain 1984–2000*. London, DES, Report on Education no. 100.

Department of Education and Science (1984b). *Technical Report to DES Report on Education Number 100*. London, DES.

Department of Education and Science (1985a). *An Assessment of the Costs and Benefits of Sandwich Education: a report by a committee on research into sandwich education*. London, DES.

Department of Education and Science (1985b). *Selected National Education Systems: a description of six countries as an aid to international comparisons – France, Italy, United States of America, Japan, Federal Republic of Germany, Netherlands*. London, DES.

Department of Education and Science (1985c). *Part-time Advanced Further Education: an HMI survey of vocational courses*. London, HMSO.

Department of Education and Science (1985d). *Statistics of Further Education, November 1984*. Darlington, DES.

Department of Education and Science (1986). *Projections of Demand for Higher Education in Great Britain 1986–2000*. London, HMSO.

Department of Education and Science (1987a). *Statistics of Further Education, November 1986*. Darlington, DES.

Department of Education and Science (1987b). *International Statistical Comparisons in Higher Education*. London, DES, Statistical Bulletin 4/87.

Department of Education and Science (1988). *Top-up Loans for Students*. London, HMSO, Cmnd 520.

Department of Education and Science (1989a). *Universities in the Training Market: an evaluation of the University Grants Committee PICKUP Selective Funding Scheme*. London, DES.

Department of Education and Science (1989b). *Shifting the Balance of Public Funding of Higher Education to Fees*. London, DES.

Department of Education and Science *et al.* (1988). *Education Statistics for the United Kingdom*. London, HMSO.

Department of Education for Northern Ireland (1982). *The Future of Higher Education in Northern Ireland*. Belfast, HMSO.

Department of Education, New Zealand (1988). *Education Statistics of New Zealand 1987*. Wellington, Department of Education.

Devlin, L. (1989). 'Part-time students: a closer look', *Canadian Journal of University Continuing Education*, 15 (1), 29–38.

Duke, C. (1967). *The London External Degree and the English Part-time Degree Student*. Leeds, Leeds University Press.

Duke, C. and Marriott, S. (1973). *Paper Awards in Liberal Adult Education*. London, Michael Joseph.

Education, Science and Arts Committee (1980). *The Funding and Organisation of Courses in Higher Education*. London, HMSO, HC 787.

Educational Counselling and Credit Transfer Information Service (1989a). *Educational Credit Transfer: ECCTIS Handbook 1989*. Milton Keynes, ECCTIS.

Educational Counselling and Credit Transfer Information Service (1989b). *Access to Higher Education Courses Directory*. Milton Keynes, ECCTIS.

Elliott, S. (1973). *Tuition by Correspondence: a study of growth in Britain, principally during the period 1870 to 1914*. Leicester, University of Leicester M.Ed. thesis.

Elliott, S. (1978). 'Tuition by post: an historical perspective', *Teaching at a Distance*, 11, 12–16.

Elliott, S. (1989). *University First Degrees by Part-time Evening Study in England and Wales: an examination of opportunity and attitudes during two centuries*. University of Birmingham Ph.D. thesis.

van Enckevort, G. and Leibbrandt, G. (1988). 'The Open University of the Netherlands', *Open Learning*, 3 (1), 18–22.

Entwistle, N. (1983). 'Learning and teaching in universities: the challenge of the part-time student', in R. Bourne (ed.), *Part-time First Degrees in Universities*. London, Goldsmiths' College, pp. 20–41.

Evans, F. (1969). *Borough Polytechnic 1892–1969*. London, Borough Polytechnic.

Evans, N. (1983). *Curriculum Opportunity: a map of experiential learning in entry requirements to higher and further education award bearing courses*. London, Further Education Unit.

Evans, N. (1984). *Access to Higher Education: non-standard entry to CNAA first degree and DipHE courses*. London, CNAA.

Evans, N. (1988). *The Assessment of Prior Experiential Learning*. London, Council for National Academic Awards.

Faherty, J. (1976). *From Technical College to University: a case study of Brunel College*. Brunel University M.Phil. thesis.

Farrant, J. (1981). 'Trends in admissions', in O. Fulton (ed.), *Access to Higher Education*. Guildford, Society for Research into Higher Education, pp. 42–88.

Faure, E. *et al.* (1972). *Learning To Be: the world of education today and tomorrow*. Paris, UNESCO.

Feldman, K. and Newcomb, T. (1969). *The Impact of College on Students*. San Francisco, Jossey-Bass.

Fiddes, E. (1937). *Chapters in the History of Owens College and of Manchester University 1851–1914*. Manchester, Manchester University Press.

Foden, F. (1951). 'The national certificate', *The Vocational Aspect of Secondary and Further Education*, 3 (6), 38–46.

de Francesco, C. (1984). 'Italy: a part-time higher education system?', *European Journal of Education*, 19 (2), 173–82.

de Francesco, C. (1986). 'How enrolment data may miss the point', *European Journal of Education*, 21 (4), 385–96.

Fulton, O. (ed.) (1989). *Access and Institutional Change*. Milton Keynes, Open University Press.

Gallacher, J., Leahy, J., Sharp, N. and Young, A. (1989). *Part-time Degree Provision in Scotland: courses and students (1987/88)*. Glasgow, Glasgow College.

Glatter, R., Wedell, E., Harris, W. and Subramanian, S. (1971). *Study by Correspondence: an enquiry into correspondence study for examinations for degrees and other advanced qualifications*. London, Longman.

Gleeson, J. (1980). 'Part-time tertiary education in Australian colleges of advanced education: cheap or expensive?', *Journal of Educational Administration*, 18, 148–57.

Godwin, G. (1939). *Queen Mary College: an adventure in education*. London, Queen Mary College.

de Goede, M. and Hoksbergen, R. (1978). 'Part-time education at tertiary level in the Netherlands', *Higher Education*, 7, 443–55.

Gordon, A. (1983). 'Attitudes of employers to the recruitment of graduates', *Educational Studies*, 9 (1), 45–64.

Gosden, P. and Taylor, A. (eds) (1975). *Studies in the History of a University 1874–1974*. Leeds, E. J. Arnold.

Graham, B. (1989). *Older Graduates and Employment*. London, Careers Services Trust.

Green, D., O'Shea, J. and Thomas, K. (1989). *Evaluating Satisfaction with Educational Experience among Part-time Students: a report to the CNAA*. Birmingham, Birmingham Polytechnic.

Hajnal, J. (1972). *The Student Trap: a critique of university and sixth form curricula*. Harmondsworth, Penguin.

Halsey, A. (1979). 'Are the British universities capable of change?', *New Universities Quarterly*, 33 (4), 402–16.

Halsey, A. (1987). 'Who owns the curriculum of higher education?', *Journal of Educational Policy*, 2 (4), 341–5.

Halsey, A., Heath, A. and Ridge, J. (1980). *Origins and Destinations: family, class and education in modern Britain*. Oxford, Clarendon Press.

Halsey, A. and Trow, M. (1971). *The British Academics*. London, Faber.

Hargreaves, J. and Searle, C. (1981). 'Investigating a part-time MSc course', in R. Oxtoby, (ed.), *Higher Education at the Crossroads*. Guildford, Society for Research into Higher Education, pp. 89–99.

Harris, W. (1972). *Home Study Students*. Manchester, University of Manchester Department of Adult Education.

Harte, N. (1986). *The University of London 1836–1986*. London, Athlone Press.

Hearnshaw, F. (1929). *The Centenary History of King's College London 1828–1928*. London, Harrap.

Higgins, T. and Keen, C. (1988). *Knowledge of Higher Education in the Sixth Form*. Banbury, Higher Education Information Services Trust.

Higher Education in Europe (1986). 'Sweden', *Higher Education in Europe*, 11 (2), 82–3.

Hinchcliffe, K. (1971). 'Teachers, the Open University and the rate of return', *Higher Education Review*, 3 (3), 49–56.

Holt, J. (1977). *The University of Reading: the first fifty years*. Reading, Reading University Press.

Hopper, E. and Osborn, M. (1975). *Adult Students: education, selection and social control.* London, Frances Pinter.

Hordley, I. and Lee, D. (1970). 'The "alternative route": social change and opportunity in technical education', *Sociology*, 4, 23–50.

Horner, D. (1986). 'The experience of non-traditional higher education', *Adult Education*, 59 (2), 153–7.

Huber, L. (1987). 'Changes in the student role', *Studies in Higher Education*, 12 (2), 157–68.

Hubert, G. (1989). 'Mixed mode study: has it got a future?', *Studies in Higher Education*, 14 (2), 219–29.

Hufner, K. (1987). 'Differentiation and competition in higher education: recent trends in the Federal Republic of Germany', *European Journal of Education*, 22 (2), 133–44.

Hussain, A. (1976). 'The economy and the educational system in capitalistic societies', *Economy and Society*, 5, 413–34.

Hutchinson, E. and Hutchinson, E. (1978). *Learning Later: fresh horizons in English adult education.* London, Routledge.

Hyman, H., Wright, C. and Reed, J. (1975). *The Enduring Effects of Education.* Chicago, University of Chicago Press.

James, A. (1982). 'The Universidad Nacional de Educación a Distancia, Spain', in G. Rumble and K. Harry (eds), *The Distance Teaching Universities.* London, Croom Helm, pp. 147–66.

Jansson, H. (1986). 'Formal versus factual competencies: traditional and non-traditional methods in the Swedish scheme of university access', *Higher Education in Europe*, 11 (2), 39–47.

Jarvis, P. (1983a). *Professional Education.* London, Croom Helm.

Jarvis, P. (1983b). *Adult and Continuing Education: theory and practice.* London, Croom Helm.

Jobling, R. (1970). 'The location and siting of a new university', *Universities Quarterly*, 24, 123–36.

Johnson, S. and Hall, R. (1985). *A Hard Day's Night: a study of evening degree students at the Polytechnic of North London.* London, Polytechnic of North London.

Johnston, R. and Bailey, R. (1984). *Mature Students: perceptions and experiences of full-time and part-time higher education.* Sheffield, Sheffield City Polytechnic Department of Applied Social Studies.

Jones, B. (1985). *Adults on the Campus: recurrent education and widened admission to higher education in Sweden.* Manchester, Manchester University Centre for Adult and Higher Education.

Jones, H. and Williams, K. (1979). *Adult Students and Higher Education.* Leicester, Advisory Council for Adult and Continuing Education.

Jones, L. and Wylie, A. (1979). 'Routes for part-time study: student wastage and comparative costs', *Education and Training*, 18, 77–9, 82.

Kato, H. and Postgate, R. (1975). 'Open Learning in Japan', in N. MacKenzie, R. Postgate and J. Scupham (eds), *Open Learning: systems and problems in post-secondary education.* Paris, UNESCO Press, pp. 231–51.

Keddie, N. (1980). 'Adult education: an ideology of individualism', in J. Thompson (ed.), *Adult Education for a Change.* London, Hutchinson, pp. 45–64.

Keegan, D. (1982). 'The Fernuniversität, Federal Republic of Germany', in G. Rumble and K. Harry (eds), *The Distance Teaching Universities.* London, Croom Helm, pp. 88–106.

Kellermann, P. and Sagmeister, G. (1988). 'Study orientations of Austrian students: recent trends', *Higher Education in Europe*, 13 (1–2), 146–51.

Killeen, J. and Bird, M. (1981). *Education and Work: a study of paid educational leave in England and Wales*. Leicester, National Institute of Adult Education.

Kyvik, S. and Skoie, H. (1982). 'Recent trends in Norwegian higher education', *European Journal of Education*, 17 (2), 183–92.

Laidlaw, B. and Layard, R. (1974). 'Traditional versus Open University teaching methods: a cost comparison', *Higher Education*, 3, 439–68.

Lane, M. (1975). *Design for Degrees: new degree courses under the CNAA 1964–1974*. London, Macmillan.

Lavin, D. and Alba, R. (1983). 'Assessment of the open admissions policy of the City University of New York', in H. Hermans, U. Teichler and H. Wasser (eds), *The Compleat University: break from tradition in Germany, Sweden and the USA*. Cambridge, Mass., Shenkman, pp. 77–99.

Laws, S. (1946). *Northampton Polytechnic, London EC1, 1896–1946*. London, Northampton Polytechnic.

Lawson, J. (1975). 'Higher education before Robbins', *Aspects of Education*, 18, 7–25.

Layard, R., Sargan, J., Ager, M. and Jones, D. (1971). *Qualified Manpower and Economic Performance: an inter-plant study in the electrical engineering industry*. London, Allen Lane.

Lee, B. and Bibby, J. (1986). *The Feasibility of Adapting Open University Materials for use in Polytechnics and Similar Institutions*. London, CNAA.

Lee, C., Stevens, B. and Rudd, E. (1979). *Surveys of Part-time and Short Full-time Postgraduate Courses and of Part-time Graduate Students in Science and Technology*. Colchester, University of Essex.

Legge, D. (1982). *The Education of Adults in Britain*. Milton Keynes, Open University Press.

Leslie, L. and Brinkman, P. (1988). *The Economic Value of Higher Education*. New York, Macmillan.

Lewis, B. (1971). 'Course production at the Open University', *British Journal of Educational Technology*, 2, 4–13, 111–23, 189–204; 3, 108–28.

Locke, M. (1978). *Traditions and Controls in the Making of a Polytechnic: Woolwich Polytechnic 1890–1970*. Woolwich, Thames Polytechnic.

Lowe, R. (1983). 'The expansion of higher education in England', in K. Jarausch (ed.), *The Transformation of Higher Learning*. Chicago, University of Chicago Press, pp. 37–56.

Lowe, R. (1988). *Education in the Post-war Years: a social history*. London, Routledge.

Lucas, S. and Ward, P. (eds) (1985). *A Survey of 'Access' Courses in England*. Lancaster, University of Lancaster School of Education.

Luzzatto, G. (1988). 'The debate on the university reform proposals in Italy and its results', *European Journal of Education*, 23 (3), 237–48.

Lynton, E. and Elman, S. (1987). *New Priorities for the University: meeting society's needs for applied knowledge and competent individuals*. San Francisco, Jossey-Bass.

McDowell, L. (1981). 'Regional inequality and higher education in England and Wales', *Higher Education Review*, 13 (3), 17–26.

McDowell, R. and Webb, D. (1982). *Trinity College Dublin 1592–1952: an academic history*. Cambridge, Cambridge University Press.

McIlroy, J. (1987). 'Continuing education and the universities in Britain: the political context', *International Journal of Lifelong Education*, 6 (1), 27–59.

McIntosh, N. (1974). 'The OU student', in J. Tunstall (ed.), *The Open University Opens*. London, Routledge and Kegan Paul, pp. 54–65.

McIntosh, N., Calder, J. and Swift, B. (1976). *A Degree of Difference: a study of the first year's intake of students to the Open University of the United Kingdom*. Guildford, Society for Research into Higher Education.

McIntosh, N., Woodley, A. and Morrison, V. (1980). 'Student demand and progress at the Open University', *Distance Education*, 1 (1), 37–60.

MacKenzie, N., Postgate, R., Scupham, J. (eds) (1975). *Open Learning: systems and problems in postsecondary education*. Paris, UNESCO Press.

Manpower Services Commission (1987). *Enterprise in Higher Education*. Sheffield, MSC.

Marriott, S. (1981). *A Backstairs to a Degree: demands for an Open University in late Victorian England*. Leeds, University of Leeds Department of Adult and Continuing Education.

Marriott, S. (1984). *Extramural Empires: service and self-interest in English university adult education, 1873–1983*. Nottingham, University of Nottingham Department of Adult Education.

Marris, P. (1964). *The Experience of Higher Education*. London, Routledge and Kegan Paul.

Marris, P. (1977). 'The Open University as a forum for the implementation of new approaches to learning', in M. Howe (ed.), *Adult Learning: psychological research and applications*. Chichester, Wiley, pp. 267–82.

Marris, R. (1983). *The Economics of the Degree Industry*. London, Birkbeck College.

Michaels, R. (1979). 'A custom built degree for mature students', *Studies in Higher Education*, 4 (1), 103–11.

Ministère de l'Education Nationale (1987). *Repères et Références Statistiques sur les Enseignements et la Formation*. Paris, Ministère de l'Education Nationale.

Ministry of Education (1951). *Education 1900–1950*. London, HMSO, Cmnd 8244.

Ministry of Education (1956). *Technical Education*. London, HMSO, Cmnd 9703.

Ministry of Education, Scottish Education Department (1960). *Grants to Students*. London, HMSO, Cmnd 1051.

Ministry of Education and Science of The Netherlands (1985). *Higher Education in The Netherlands*. Paris, UNESCO.

Ministry of Education, Science and Culture, Japan (1987). *Outline of Education in Japan*. Tokyo, Ministry of Education, Science and Culture.

Moody, T. and Beckett, J. (1959). *Queen's, Belfast 1845–1949: the history of a university*. London, Faber and Faber.

Morgan, D. and McDowell, L. (1979). *Patterns of Residence: costs and options in student housing*. Guildford, Society for Research into Higher Education.

Moscati, R. (1985). 'Reflections on higher education and the polity in Italy', *European Journal of Education*, 20 (2–3), 127–39.

Mugridge, I. and Kaufman, D. (eds) (1986). *Distance Education in Canada*. London, Croom Helm.

Munn, P. and MacDonald, C. (1987). *Adult Participation in Education and Training*. Edinburgh, Scottish Council for Research in Education.

Muta, H. (1985). 'The economics of the University of the Air of Japan', *Higher Education*, 14, 269–96.

Nakayama, S. (1989). 'Independence and choice: western impacts on Japanese higher education', *Higher Education*, 18, 31–48.

National Advisory Body (1984a). *Report of the Continuing Education Group*. London, NAB.

National Advisory Body (1984b). *A Strategy for Higher Education in the late 1980s and Beyond*. London, NAB.

National Institute of Adult Continuing Education (1989). *Adults in Higher Education: a policy discussion paper*. Leicester, NIACE.

National Institute of Adult Education (1970). *Adult Education: adequacy of provision*. Leicester, NIAE.

Neave, G. (1984). 'On the road to Silicon Valley? The changing relationship between higher education and government in Western Europe', *European Journal of Education*, 19 (2), 111–29.

Neave, G. (1985a). 'Elite and mass higher education in Great Britain: a regressive model?', *Comparative Education Review*, 29 (3), 347–61.

Neave, G. (1985b). 'Higher education in a period of consolidation: 1975–1985', *European Journal of Education*, 20 (2–3), 109–24.

Neave, G. (1988). 'The reform of French higher education, or the ox and the toad: a fabulous tale', *Higher Education Quarterly*, 42 (4), 353–69.

Newman, J. (1852). *The Idea of a University*. 1976 edition with introduction and notes by I. Ker. Oxford, Clarendon Press.

Noble, K. (1989). 'What a marketing survey of part-time university students reveals about barriers to learning', *Open Learning*, 4 (2), 16–20.

Nolan, D. (1977). 'Open assessment in higher education: the New York Regents external degree', *International Review of Education*, 23, 231–48.

Office of Population Censuses and Surveys (1984). *Key Statistics for Local Authorities: Great Britain*. London, HMSO.

Open University (1982). *First Year Student Handbook*. Milton Keynes, Open University (revised annually).

Open University (1986). *The Role of the Open University in the National Provision of Part-time Higher Education*. Milton Keynes, Open University.

Open University (1989). *Open University Statistics 1987: students, staff and finance*. Milton Keynes, Open University.

Organization for Economic Co-operation and Development (1971). *Development of Higher Education 1950–1967: analytical report*. Paris, OECD.

Organization for Economic Co-operation and Development (1981). *Educational Statistics in OECD Countries*. Paris, OECD.

Organization for Economic Co-operation and Development (1983). *Policies for Higher Education in the 1980s*. Paris, OECD.

Overell, A. (1984). 'The Open University and the others', *Teaching at a Distance*, 25, 17–20.

Paquet, P. (1987). 'Adults in higher education: the situation in Canada', in H. Schutze (ed.), *Adults in Higher Education: policies and practice in Great Britain and North America*. Stockholm, Almqvist and Wiksell International, pp. 121–81.

Parton, H. (1979). *The University of New Zealand*. Auckland, Auckland University Press.

Patterson, A. (1962). *The University of Southampton: a centenary history 1862–1962*. Southampton, University of Southampton.

Payne, P. (ed.) (1983). *The Part-time Student in the Library*. London, City of London Polytechnic.

Pedro, F. (1988). 'Higher education in Spain: setting the conditions for an evaluative state', *European Journal of Education*, 23 (1–2), 125–39.

Peisert, H. (1985). 'Students in the Federal Republic of Germany: diversity in motives and prospects', *Higher Education in Europe*, 10 (1), 18–29.

Penhallurick, P. (1988). *The Contribution Made to Career Development by Qualifications Obtained through Part-time Degree Study at the University of Ulster*. University of Ulster M.Sc. dissertation.

Percy, K. (1988). 'Opening access to a modern university', in H. Eggins (ed.), *Restructuring Higher Education*. Milton Keynes, Open University Press, pp. 108–20.

Percy, K., Ramsden, P. and Lewin, J. (1980). *Independent Study: two examples from English higher education*. Guildford, Society for Research into Higher Education.

Perry, W. (1976). *Open University: a personal account by the first vice-chancellor*. Milton Keynes, Open University Press.

Pike, R. and Creet, M. (1978). 'Part-time undergraduate studies in Ontario', in International Council for Educational Development, *Innovation in Access to Higher Education*. New York, ICED, pp. 3–146.

Pratt, J. and Burgess, T. (1974). *Polytechnics: a report*. London, Pitman.

Psacharopoulos, G. (1981). 'Returns to education: an updated international comparison'. *Comparative Education*, 17, 321–41.

Raffe, D. (1979). 'The "alternative route" reconsidered: part-time further education and social mobility in England and Wales', *Sociology*, 13, 47–73.

Ram, G. (1989). *Going Modular*. London, Council for National Academic Awards.

Redpath, B. and Harvey, B. (1987). *Young People's Intentions to Enter Higher Education*. London, HMSO.

Reports from Universities and Colleges in Receipt of Grant. London, HMSO (annual). Series starts in 1908–9, though earlier reports are published for individual institutions. The title varies slightly from year to year, with most reports published as command papers.

Richardson, J. (1981). 'Geographical bias', in D. Piper (ed.), *Is Higher Education Fair?* Guildford, Society for Research into Higher Education, pp. 40–56.

Richter, I. (1988). 'Selection and reform in higher education in Western Europe', *Comparative Education*, 24 (1), 53–60.

Rickman, H. (1981). 'University education: full or part-time?', *Higher Education Review*, 14 (1), 71–3.

Ritter, I. (1986). 'Part-time students: rule or exception?', in *Proceedings of the Twelfth International Conference on Improving University Teaching*. Heidelberg, pp. 114–22.

Roberts, R. (1906). 'The inwardness of the university extension movement', *University Review*, 2, 54–67.

Robinson, E. (1968). *The New Polytechnics*. London, Cornmarket.

Roderick, G., Bell, J., Dickinson, R., Turner, R. and Wellings, A. (1981). *Mature Students: a study in Sheffield*. Sheffield, University of Sheffield.

Roderick, G., Bell, J. and Hamilton, S. (1982). 'Unqualified mature students in British universities'. *Studies in Adult Education*, 14, 59–68.

Roizen, J. and Jepson, M. (1985). *Degrees for Jobs: employer expectations of higher education*. Guildford, Society for Research into Higher Education and NFER-Nelson.

Rontopoulou, J. and Lamoure, J. (1988). 'French university education: a brief overview 1984–1987', *European Journal of Education*, 23 (1–2), 37–46.

Rothblatt, S. (1983). 'The diversification of higher education in England', in K. Jarausch (ed.), *The Transformation of Higher Learning*. Chicago, University of Chicago Press, pp. 131–48.

Roweth, B. (1987). 'Continuing education in science and technology: a survey of part-time postgraduate students and their employers', *Studies in Higher Education*, 12 (1), 65–85.

Rudd, E. (1980). 'Halls of residence for students: a cautionary tale of decision-making', *Political Quarterly*, 51, 164–74.

Rudd, E. (1985). *A New Look at Postgraduate Failure*. Guildford, Society for Research into Higher Education and NFER-Nelson.

Rudd, E. and Simpson, R. (1975). *The Highest Education: a study of graduate education in Britain*. London, Routledge and Kegan Paul.

Rumble, G. (1982). *The Open University of the United Kingdom: an evaluation of an innovative experience in the democratisation of higher education*. Milton Keynes, Open University Distance Education Research Group.

Rumble, G. and Harry, K. (eds) (1982). *The Distance Teaching Universities*. London, Croom Helm.

Sanderson, M. (1972). *The Universities and British Industry 1850–1970*. London, Routledge and Kegan Paul.

Scales, D. (ed.) (1981). *Fifty Years of Adult Studies at Goldsmiths'*. London, Goldsmiths' College.

Schuller, T., Tight, M. and Weil, S. (1988). 'Continuing education and the redrawing of boundaries', *Higher Education Quarterly*, 42 (4), 335–52.

Scottish Education Department (1988). *Higher Education Projections for Scotland*. Edinburgh, Scottish Education Department, Statistical Bulletin no. 7.

Scottish Tertiary Education Advisory Council (1985). *Future Strategy for Higher Education in Scotland*. Edinburgh, HMSO, Cmnd 9676.

Scupham, J. (1975). 'The Open University of the United Kingdom', in N. MacKenzie, R. Postgate and J. Scupham (eds), *Open Learning: systems and problems in postsecondary education*. Paris, UNESCO Press, pp. 320–64.

Secretary of State for Education and Science *et al.* (1985). *The Development of Higher Education into the 1990s*. London, HMSO, Cmnd 9524.

Secretary of State for Education and Science *et al.* (1987). *Higher Education: meeting the challenge*. London, HMSO, Cmnd 114.

Selby Smith, C. (1970). *The Costs of Further Education: a British analysis*. Oxford, Pergamon Press.

Selby Smith, C. (1975). *The Costs of Post-secondary Education: an Australian study*. Basingstoke, Macmillan.

Silber, J. (1987). 'The paradox of democratic education: the American experience', *Higher Education in Europe*, 12 (4), 38–42.

Silver, H. and Silver, P. (1981). *Expectations of Higher Education: some historical pointers*. Uxbridge, Brunel University.

Silver, H. and Teague, S. (eds) (1977). *Chelsea College: a history*. London, Chelsea College.

Slowey, M. (1988). 'Adult students: the new mission for higher education?', *Higher Education Quarterly*, 42 (4), 301–15.

Smith, A. (1989). 'Part-time vocational degrees: a student-centred approach', *Journal of Further and Higher Education*, 13 (2), 70–77.

Smith, B. (1983). 'Learning difficulties of part-time mature students', *Journal of Further and Higher Education*, 7 (3), 81–5.

Smith, D. (1987). *Costing Part-time Higher Education: some models and their consequences*. London, Middlesex Polytechnic.

Smith, D. and Saunders, M. (1988). 'Part-time higher education prospects and practices', *Higher Education Review*, 20 (3), 7–26.

Smith, D. and Saunders, M. (1989). 'Costing part-time provision', *Open Learning*, 4 (3), 28–34.

Smith, D. and Saunders, M. (1991). *Other Routes: part-time higher education policy*. Buckingham, Open University Press.

Smithers, A. and Griffin, A. (1986a). 'Mature students at university: entry, experience and outcomes', *Studies in Higher Education*, 11, 257–68.

Smithers, A. and Griffin, A. (1986b). *The Progress of Mature Students*. Manchester, Joint Matriculation Board.

Smithers, A. and Robinson, P. (1989). *Increasing Participation in Higher Education*. London, BP Educational Service.

Squires, G. (1981). 'Mature entry', in O. Fulton (ed.), *Access to Higher Education*. Guildford, Society for Research into Higher Education, pp. 148–77.

Squires, G. (1986). *Modularisation*. Manchester, Consortium for Advanced Continuing Education and Training.

Squires, G. (1987). *The Curriculum beyond School*. London, Hodder and Stoughton.

Statistics Canada (1988). *Education in Canada: a statistical review for 1986–87*. Ottawa, Minister of Supply and Services.

Statistics of Education: further education. London, HMSO (annual).

Statistisches Bundesamt (1988). *Statistisches Jahrbuch 1988 fur die Bundesrepublik Deustchland*. Wiesbaden, Statistisches Bundesamt.

Stephenson, J. (1980). 'Higher education: school for independent study', in T. Burgess and E. Adams (eds), *Outcomes of Education*. London, Macmillan, pp. 132–49.

Teichler, U. (1989). 'Research on higher education and work in Europe', *European Journal of Education*, 24 (3), 223–47.

Thompson, J. (ed.) (1980). *Adult Education for a Change*. London, Hutchinson.

Tight, M. (1982). *Part-time Degree Level Study in the United Kingdom*. Leicester, Advisory Council for Adult and Continuing Education.

Tight, M. (1986). 'The provision of part-time first degree courses in the United Kingdom', *Studies in Higher Education*, 11 (2), 173–88.

Tight, M. (1987a). 'Mixing distance and face-to-face higher education', *Open Learning*, 2 (1), 14–18.

Tight, M. (1987b). 'Access and part-time undergraduate study', *Journal of Access Studies*, 2 (1), 12–24.

Tight, M. (1987c). 'London University external developments', *Open Learning*, 2 (2), 49–51.

Tight, M. (1987d). 'The value of higher education: full-time or part-time?', *Studies in Higher Education*, 12 (2), 169–85.

Tight, M. (1987e). 'The location of higher education', *Higher Education Quarterly*, 41 (2), 162–83.

Tight, M. (1989a). 'The ideology of higher education', in O. Fulton (ed.), *Access and Institutional Change*. Milton Keynes, Open University Press, pp. 85–98.

Tight, M. (1989b). *Part-time Degrees, Diplomas and Certificates*. Cambridge, Hobsons Press (3rd edition).

Toyne, P. (1979). *Educational Credit Transfer: feasibility study*. London, DES, 2 volumes.

Trotman-Dickenson, D. (1987). 'Employers demand for and the provision of part-time higher education for employees', *Studies in Higher Education*, 12 (2), 187–99.

Trotman-Dickenson, D. (1988). 'Learning and teaching problems in part-time higher education', *Higher Education Review*, 20 (2), 47–59.

Trow, M. (1969). 'Elite and popular functions in American higher education', in W. Niblett (ed.), *Higher Education: demand and response*. London, Tavistock, pp. 171–201.

Trow, M. (1989a). 'The Robbins trap: British attitudes and the limits of expansion', *Higher Education Quarterly*, 43 (1), 55–75.

Trow, M. (1989b). 'American higher education: past, present and future', *Studies in Higher Education*, 14 (1), 5–22.

United Nations Educational, Scientific and Culture Organization (1983). *Education Statistics: latest year available*. Paris, UNESCO Press.

United Nations Education, Scientific and Cultural Organization (1987). *UNESCO Statistical Digest*. Paris, UNESCO Press.

Universities Council for Adult and Continuing Education (1989). *Annual Report 1987–88*. Leicester, UCACE.

Universities Council for Adult and Continuing Education (1990). *Report of the Working Party on Part-time Degrees*. Leicester, UCACE.

Universities Funding Council (1989). *The Aims of the Universities Funding Council*. London, UFC.

Universities Statistical Record (1986). *University Statistics 1984–1985. Volume 1: Students and Staff.* Cheltenham, USR.

Universities Statistical Record (1987). *University Statistics 1986–1987. Volume 1: Students and Staff.* Cheltenham, USR.

Universities Statistical Record (1988a). *University Statistics 1987–1988. Volume 1: Students and Staff.* Cheltenham, USR.

Universities Statistical Record (1988b). *University Statistics 1987–1988. Volume 3: Finance.* Cheltenham, USR.

University Grants Committee (1957). *Report of the Sub-Committee on Halls of Residence.* London, HMSO.

University Grants Committee (1964a). *University Development 1957–1962.* London, HMSO, Cmnd 2267.

University Grants Committee (1964b). *Report of the Committee on University Teaching Methods.* London, HMSO.

University Grants Committee (1984a). *Report of the Continuing Education Working Party.* London, UGC.

University Grants Committee (1984b). *A Strategy for Higher Education into the 1990s.* London, HMSO.

University of London Committee for External Students (1988). *Annual Report 1987–88.* London, University of London.

University Review (1905). 'University news and notes'.

University Review (1907). 'University news and notes'.

Usher, R. (1986). 'Reflection and prior work experience: some problematic issues in relation to adult students in university studies', *Studies in Higher Education*, 11 (3), 245–56.

Venables, E. (1967). *The Young Worker at College: a study of a local tech.* London, Faber and Faber.

Venables, E. (1972). 'The human costs of part-time day release', *Higher Education*, 1, 267–85.

Venables, E. (1975). 'The local tech: an agent of social mobility?', in W. van der Eyken and S. Barry (eds), *Learning and Earning: aspects of day release in further education.* Slough, NFER, pp. 14–25.

Venables, P. (1978). *Higher Education Developments: the technological universities 1956–1976.* London, Faber.

Vincent, E. and Hinton, P. (1947). *The University of Birmingham: its history and significance.* Birmingham, Cornish Brothers.

Vinegrad, M. (1979). 'A part-time psychology degree course for mature students: an empirical study', *Psychology Teaching*, 7 (2), 163–9.

Vinegrad, M. (1980). 'A profile of part-time adult degree students', *Studies in Adult Education*, 12, 147–54.

Wagner, A. (1987). 'Adults in higher education: the situation in the United States', in H. Schutze (ed.), *Adults in Higher Education: policies and practice in Great Britain and North America.* Stockholm, Almqvist and Wiksell International, pp. 75–120.

Wagner, L. (1972). 'The economics of the Open University', *Higher Education*, 1, 159–83.

Wagner, L. (1977). 'The economics of the Open University revisited', *Higher Education*, 6, 359–81.

Wagner, L. (1979). 'Planning for part-time higher education in the 1980s', *Educational Policy Bulletin*, 7, 67–79.

Wagner, L. and Watts, A. (1976). 'The penalties of part-time study for 18-year olds', *Times Higher Education Supplement*, 12 November, p. 13.

Waniewicz, I. (1976). *Demand for Part-time Learning in Ontario*. Toronto, Ontario Institute for Studies in Education.

Watson, D., Brooks, J. Coghill, C., Lindsay, R. and Scurry, D. (1989). *Managing the Modular Course: perspectives from Oxford Polytechnic*. Milton Keynes, Open University Press.

Webb, S. (1904). *London Education*. London, Longmans Green.

Wedemeyer, C. (1981). *Learning at the Back Door: reflections on non-traditional learning in the lifespan*. Madison, University of Wisconsin Press.

Weil, S. and McGill, I. (eds) (1989). *Making Sense of Experiential Learning: Diversity in theory and practice*. Milton Keynes, Open University Press.

Whalley, A. (1982). *Postgraduate Education in Universities and Polytechnics*. London, Policy Studies Institute.

Whitburn, J., Mealing, M. and Cox, C. (1976). *People in Polytechnics: a survey of polytechnic staff and students 1972/3*. Guildford, Society for Research into Higher Education.

Whiting, C. (1932). *The University of Durham 1832–1932*. London, Sheldon Press.

Williams, G. and Blackstone, T. (1983). *Response to Adversity: higher education in a harsh climate*. Guildford, Society for Research into Higher Education.

Williams, G., Woodhall, M. and March, L. (1977). 'Independent further education', *Higher Education Bulletin*, 6 (1), 45–84.

de Winter Hebron, C. (1983a). 'Some problems of teaching part-timers', *Bulletin of Educational Development and Research*, 25, 18–24.

de Winter Hebron, C. (1983b). 'Part-time management students: have we got it right?', *Evaluation Newsletter*, 7 (1), 16–24.

Wood, A. (1953). *A History of the University College Nottingham 1881–1948*. Oxford, Blackwell.

Woodley, A. (1978). *Applicants Who Decline the Offer of a Place at the Open University: a preliminary report*. Milton Keynes, Open University Institute of Educational Technology.

Woodley, A. (1981). 'Age bias', in D. Piper (ed.), *Is Higher Education Fair?* Guildford, Society for Research into Higher Education, pp. 80–103.

Woodley, A. and Parlett, M. (1983). 'Student dropout', *Teaching at a Distance*, 24, 2–23.

Woodley, A., Wagner, L., Slowey, M., Hamilton, M. and Fulton, O. (1987). *Choosing to Learn: adults in education*. Milton Keynes, Society for Research into Higher Education and the Open University Press.

Woodrow, M. (1988). 'The access route to higher education', *Higher Education Quarterly*, 42 (4), 316–34.

Woodward, R., McGinn, P. and Kennan, A. (1985). *Part-time Students' Perception of University Provision*. Belfast, University of Ulster.

Wright, P. (1989). 'Access or exclusion? Some comments on the history and future prospects of continuing education in England', *Studies in Higher Education*, 14 (1), 23–40.

Wyatt, J. (1977a). '"Collegiality" during a period of rapid change in higher education: an examination of a distinctive feature claimed by a group of colleges of education during the 1960s and 1970s', *Oxford Review of Education*, 3, 147–55.

Wyatt, J. (1977b). 'The idea of "community" in institutions of higher education', *Studies in Higher Education*, 2 (2), 125–35.

York University (1987). *Report of the Committee to Review Education for Mature and Part-time Students*. Toronto, York University.

Zetterblom, G. (1986). 'Postgraduate education in Sweden: reforms and results', *European Journal of Education*, 21 (3), 261–74.

Index

design *see* art and design
diplomas, 10, 13, 62–4, 70, 75, 103, 142
  in Higher Education, 64
  higher national (HNDs), 20, 24, 62,
    69–74, 84, 94, 131
  in Management Studies (DMSs), 81,
    83
  ordinary national (ONDs), 73, 94, 105
  postgraduate, 80–81
  in Professional Studies, 83
distance education, 3, 19, 24, 31, 33, 36,
    44, 51–2, 55, 66–7, 87–8, 96, 101,
    103, 111, 113, 118–19, 130
  mixed with face-to-face study, 3, 58,
    96, 103, 143
Doncaster Metropolitan Institute of
    Higher Education, 56
drama, 26–8
Dundee Institute of Technology, 56
Durham University, 9, 16

Ealing College of Higher Education, 56
East Anglia, 67–8, 74, 81, 101–2
East (formerly North East) London
    Polytechnic, 4, 65, 131
economic change, 111, 137
economics, 7, 19, 43, 59–61, 79
Edge Hill College of Higher Education,
    56
Edinburgh University, 7, 12, 14–15, 21,
    83, 114
education (as a subject of study), 26–9,
    32, 38, 43, 51, 58–9, 61–2, 64,
    79–80, 83, 89–90, 94
Educational Counselling and Credit
    Transfer Information Service
    (ECCTIS), 53–4
Education Reform Act 1988, 140, 143
electrical engineering, 59, 61, 72–3, 79, 90
employers
  attitudes of, 99, 117, 122–5, 136
  as educational providers, 23, 82
  recruitment policies of, 122–3
employment
  categories of, 91–3, 96–9
  changes in, 40, 92, 111
engineering, 7, 13, 16, 19–20, 26–9, 38,
    43, 51, 58–64, 72, 75, 79–80, 89–91,
    94, 107, 113
England (regions of), 67–8, 74, 81,
    100–101
English (as a subject of study), 59, 61,
    79, 90

Enterprise in Higher Education, 121
estate management, 57
Europe, Western, 31, 39–46, 51, 135
  studies of, 59, 61, 79
European Community, 39, 40, 44
evening study, 3, 8–9, 11, 13–16, 20–21,
    25, 38–9, 41, 43–4, 55–8, 60–61,
    63–4, 67, 71–2, 74, 78, 88, 90, 94,
    100, 104, 113, 119, 129–30, 133
examinations, 4, 8, 10–11, 19–20, 35, 42,
    56–7, 60–61, 104–5, 130–31
  City and Guilds, 9, 105
  civil service, 10, 14
Expectations of Higher Education
    project, 122
experiential learning, 4, 66–7, 118, 133
extension, university, 10, 14
external study, 4, 8–11, 14, 16–19, 22,
    24, 26, 28–9, 35–6, 38, 42, 56–8, 60,
    88, 110
extra-mural studies, 10–11, 14–15,
    18–19, 21–2, 24, 26–7, 29, 70, 74–7,
    82–4, 142

face-to-face study, 3, 26, 36–7, 39, 51,
    55–6, 67–8, 74, 81, 87, 95–6,
    99–102, 118–19
  mixed with distance study, 3, 58, 96,
    103, 143
Faure Report (*Learning to Be*), 111
Fernuniversitat (West Germany), 45
Florida, 36
France, 40–42, 48–50
Francesco, Corrado de, 42
full-time equivalent, 44, 141–2
full-time higher education
  costs of, 116–18
  definition of, 2, 3, 30, 34, 40, 42, 64–5,
    112, 136
  mixed with part-time study, 3, 30, 54,
    56, 58, 65, 69, 73, 78, 81, 102–3,
    118–19, 144
  purposes of, 108–26
further education, 6, 11, 15, 18–21, 56,
    62, 69, 71, 87, 91–2, 94, 98–9, 134
  advanced, 87, 98–9
  alternative route through, 91–2, 94

Gallacher, Jim, 87, 90, 92, 95, 97
geography, 59, 61, 79
Georgia State University (United
    States), 34
Germany, West, 40, 44–6, 48–51

The Society for Research into Higher Education

The Society exists both to encourage and co-ordinate research and development into all aspects of higher education, including academic, organizational and policy issues; and also to provide a forum for debate – verbal and printed.

The Society's income derives from subscriptions, book sales, conference fees, and grants. It receives no subsidies and is wholly independent. Its corporate members are institutions of higher education, research institutions and professional, industrial, and governmental bodies. Its individual members include teachers and researchers, administrators and students. Members are found in all parts of the world and the Society regards its international work as amongst its most important activities.

The society is opposed to discrimination in higher education on grounds of belief, race etc. The Society discusses and comments on policy, organizes conferences, and encourages research. Under the imprint SRHE & OPEN UNIVERSITY PRESS, it is a specialist publisher of research, having some 40 titles in print. It also publishes *Studies in Higher Education* (three times a year) which is mainly concerned with academic issues; *Higher Education Quarterly* (formerly *Universities Quarterly*) mainly concerned with policy issues; *Abstracts* (three times a year); an *International Newsletter* (twice a year) and *SRHE News* (four times a year).

The Society's committees, study groups and branches are run by members (with help from a small secretariat at Guildford). The groups at present include a Teacher Education Study Group, a Staff Development Group, a Continuing Education Group and a Women in Higher Education Group. The groups may have their own organization, subscriptions, or publications (e.g. the *Staff Development Newsletter*). A further Questions of Quality Group has organized a series of Anglo-American seminars in the USA and the UK.

The Society's annual conferences are held jointly: 'Access and Institutional Change' (1989, with the Polytechnic of North London). In 1990, the topic will be 'Industry and Higher Education' (with the University of Surrey). In 1991, the topic will be 'Research and Higher Education', with the University of Leicester; in 1992 it will be 'Learning and Teaching' (with Nottingham Polytechnic). Other conferences have considered 'HE After the Election' (1987) and 'After the Reform Act' (July 1988).

The Editorial Board of the Society's imprint seeks authoritative research or study in the field. It offers competitive royalties, a highly recognizable format in both hardback and paperback and the world-wide reputation of the Open University Press.

Members receive free of charge the Society's *Abstracts*, annual conference Proceedings (or *Precedings*), *SRHE News* and *International Newsletter*. They may buy SRHE & Open University Press books at discount, and *Higher Education Quarterly* on special terms. Corporate members also receive the Society's journal *Studies in Higher Education* free (individuals on special terms). Members may also obtain certain other journals at a discount, including the NFER *Register of Educational Research*. There is a substantial discount to members, and to staff of corporate members, on annual and some other conference fees.

Further Information: SRHE at the University, Guildford, GU2 5XH UK (0483) 39003